THE PREACHER

as storyteller

THE PREACHER

as storyteller

AUSTIN B. TUCKER

the power of narrative in the pulpit

Nashville, Tennessee

Published by B&H Publishing Group
Nashville, Tennessee

Dewey Decimal Classification: 251
Subject Heading: PREACHING\CLERGY—BIOGRAPHY\
STORYTELLING

1 2 3 4 5 6 7 8 9 10 11 12 • 16 15 14 13 12 11 10 09 08
VP

To Beverly,
David, Christie, and Jeff,
and to
Chase, Erin, and Allison
and

To all who are telling the story of Jesus
and want to do a better job of
connecting with all who hear

CONTENTS

Foreword by Michael Duduit   ix
Preface   xiii
Introduction   1

Part 1. The Basics of Storytelling

Chapter 1   The Great Appeal of Narrative   10
Chapter 2   The Essential Elements of Narrative   22
Chapter 3   The Seven Basic Plot Plans   35
Chapter 4   Telling Your Own Story   45
Chapter 5   The Persuasive Power of Testimony   58

Part 2. Getting the Story Straight

Chapter 6   Step-by-Step to the Narrative Sermon   74
Chapter 7   Telling the Bible Story   90
Chapter 8   Remembering the Children   104
Chapter 9   Ten Ways to Sharpen Storytelling Skills   117
Chapter 10   An Endless Supply of Stories   127
Chapter 11   It's All in How You Tell It   140

Part 3. Learning from the Masters of Storytelling

Chapter 12   Gotham in the Golden Age   150
Chapter 13   London Luminaries in the Age of Spurgeon   164
Chapter 14   Bible Biography Preachers   177
Chapter 15   The Story for America's Lost Generation   189

Suggested Reading   209
Name Index   215
Subject Index   216
Scripture Index   218

FOREWORD

ONCE UPON A TIME . . . there is something about those four words that stirs an emotional response in all of us. From the earliest days when we can understand language, we are drawn to stories. They entertain us, teach us, engage our emotions. At their best, stories can transform our lives.

Stories are all around us. We live in a culture of story. Stories come to us in the form of books and songs. We are amused by stories on television—from situation comedies to dramas to reality programming. (Who will be voted off the island this week? Which contestant will overcome the obstacles and succeed this time?) Even the commercials we watch are mini-stories of joy and sorrow, failure and success.

At the heart of our Christian faith is a story—the story of God's creation, man's fall, and Christ's redemptive act. The pages of Scripture overflow with stories—the story of a Creator God crafting the universe, then shaping men and women to fellowship with Him; the story of Noah obeying God despite the jeers of the crowd and ultimately preserving humanity; the story of Abraham, who left home to go to a place he did not know because God told him to do so; the story of Joseph, who experienced pain and abuse in so many ways, yet eventually receiving amazing authority that enabled him to save his own family; the story of David, who emerged from the obscurity of the sheepfold to become the king of Israel; and on it goes. Cut the stories from the Bible and there would be so little left.

No one understood the power of a well-told story better than Jesus. He came proclaiming the kingdom of God, and He primarily did that through telling stories. He knew that the kingdom is too important for rational explanation alone; some things can only be understood through stories.

He told us about a Samaritan who helped a man who would not have given him the time of day, and we learned that we are to serve our neighbor—even when that neighbor isn't the one we might choose. He told us about a lost coin, a lost sheep and a lost son, and we understood that God seeks us out no matter what. He told us about a treasure hidden right under our noses. He told us about builders whose wisdom (or lack thereof) could be determined by the foundation on which they built. Virtually every time people gathered around Him, Jesus told them a story.

No wonder, then, that good preachers know the value of story. Stories help us grab the imaginations of listeners as they identify and recreate those stories in their own thoughts. Stories help us recognize and understand truth in new ways.

In recent years, preaching has rediscovered and reemphasized the place of story. Narrative as a rhetorical tool has become a widely discussed topic in homiletical literature. Yet the use of story in preaching is nothing new.

In *The Preacher as Storyteller,* Austin Tucker has done his preaching colleagues a valuable service by providing a toolbox for using story in our proclamation. In this useful book, he demonstrates the power of story and helps us better understand what makes a good story work. He helps us see how to craft and share stories that make a difference. The book is filled with valuable resources to help preachers become more strategic storytellers.

The section that portrays those great preachers who have modeled the art of storytelling would alone make the book worth the price! Tucker allows us to walk alongside pulpit giants like Beecher and Talmage, Spurgeon and Boreham, Meyer and Moody. In the process we gain valuable insights on how to use stories to shape lives.

Good preaching and storytelling go together. This excellent book will help me do a better job of using story to communicate biblical truth in the days ahead. I hope it does the same for you.

Michael Duduit
Editor, *Preaching* magazine (www.preaching.com)

PREFACE

IN MY CHILDHOOD, BEFORE TELEVISION came to every house in the community, we used our imaginations to entertain ourselves and one another. We told one another ghost tales and other stories, and we heard parents and grandparents tell stories from their own experience. In church, stories informed our understanding, shaped our values, and stirred our wills to commitment to Christ. Indeed, except for hymns we used in worship and the rote learning of Scripture memory assignments, the stories are most of what stuck in memory over the years.

My interest in storytelling grew as I became a pastor and sometimes a teacher of preachers. That interest spiked when I was privileged to be a guest professor one year in Wake Forest, North Carolina, and the next year in New Orleans, Louisiana. In both seminaries my assignment was to teach, among other courses, electives in narrative preaching. My interest has grown ever since. It is my strong conviction, and the thesis of this book, that you can greatly improve your preaching by sharpening your storytelling skills.

Any book worth reading, though it may have one named author, is the sum of many minds. In addition to the many who are quoted and acknowledged in the notes, thanks is due to the friends who read chapters and offered suggestions.

Tyler Durham, Casey Holland, Joe McKeever, and Skip Rainbolt are preachers who read chapters. So did my son David Tucker and my son-in-law, Jeff Deyo. Thanks, fellows. My wife Beverly read most chapters more than once and often caught errors the computer programs miss. I am grateful for all this help, though I did not always accept every suggestion. They made the work a better book, but I accept responsibility for all shortcomings.

John Landers deserves special thanks for guiding the proposal through the editorial committee before he retired from B&H Publishing Group. Then he agreed to continue as my editor on contract with his former employer. Thanks, Brother John. It has been a joy working with you.

There are many examples of narrative in these pages. How could anyone talk about illustrations without illustrating? Some of these narratives are my own compositions, and some were previously published. I thank the newspapers, magazines, and other publishers who first considered them worth printing for permission to reproduce them here. Many other examples are selected from the writings of others. Both in the footnotes and in the context, I have labored diligently to acknowledge those I owe. If I missed giving anyone due credit, please forgive me; it was certainly not intentional.

May God bless these pages to the sharpening of the storytelling skills of many servants of the Word. May this bring greater glory to Christ our Savior and greater joy to those who proclaim that greatest of all stories. May souls be saved and the church built up in the most holy faith.

INTRODUCTION

IN OUR THURSDAY MORNING MEN'S prayer breakfast, a friend asked me what writing project I was working on. I told him I was writing a book for preachers on storytelling. Since men in our close-knit group have been comfortably candid with one another for many years, it was no surprise that two of them expressed strong and negative opinions about the whole concept of storytelling in the pulpit. They did not consider it preaching the Bible. It happens that both men are members of the same church. Their pastor uses a lot of anecdotes and other stories in preaching—too many, they feel, with not enough Bible exposition. At least one of them began to rethink the issue when I pointed out that the one thing that stood out above all others in the teaching and preaching of Jesus was His use of parables. Jesus was the quintessential storyteller. We will say more about that later, but first, there is some confusion of terminology among preachers that we need to clarify.

Narrative Preaching or Story Preaching?

In this book we are talking mainly about storytelling in preaching and not much about what is called *narrative preaching*. Just what is *narrative preaching*? It's almost as bad as the Cheshire Cat in *Wonderland:* a word means whatever the user wants it to mean. Some mean the text is narrative or at least biographical. It may be a sermon on the life of Joseph or on a single episode in that life, such as Joseph in Pharaoh's prison.

Others mean long narrative illustrations within a sermon structured in a more traditional rhetorical fashion. The late C. Roy Angell (1889–1971), for example, was famous for this style. All five volumes of his sermons were very popular: *Iron Shoes*, *Shields of Brass*, *The Price Tags of Life*, *God's Gold Mines*, and *Rejoicing in Great Days*. He usually opened with a story and introduced his poetic title. This might be taken from a brief Scripture text or some other literature and more or less tied to a text. Then he would develop the theme in as many as five sermon divisions. After a clear statement of each point, the sermon development was almost exclusively narrative illustrations. This is what some mean by *narrative preaching*. Although a really good storyteller will never want for a hearing, this style has been criticized, and with reason, as "just a string of stories."

Still others use the term *narrative preaching* to mean fashioning the sermon as a contemporary parable. The sermon is entirely narrative in form, or nearly so. The story may have an implied point, or it may not. Outstanding homilitician H. Grady Davis listed the story as one of five organic forms a sermon may take. So does the premier teacher of preaching in our day, Haddon W. Robinson. The story may or may not have the application clearly stated. Davis advocated that the preacher let the listener "draw his own conclusions and make his own application to himself" or miss the point of the story altogether. He said, "If a preacher cannot trust his hearers to do this, he should not use the story form."[1]

Eugene Lowry is a preacher and teacher of preachers who, at least as early as his 1988 paper presented to the Academy of Homiletics meeting at Princeton, distinguished *narrative preaching* from *story preaching*. A story as a literary genre may be a parable, a fairy tale, a historical vignette, an anecdote or some other narrative. When Lowry speaks of *narrative preaching* or a *narra-*

---

[1] H. Grady Davis, *Design for Preaching* (Philadelphia: Fortress, 1958), 161; Haddon W. Robinson, *Biblical Preaching* (Grand Rapids: Baker, 2001), 129–31. Fred Craddock, likewise, taught a generation of preachers to tell stories to stimulate reflection. Later everyone may make his or her own application or none at all. See four audiocassettes by Fred Craddock, "Preaching as Story-Telling," 1980 Furman Pastors' School (Atlanta: GA: PRTCV Audio Cassettes, 1980). See also Craddock's trend-setting volume *As One without Authority* (Nashville: Abingdon, 1979).

tive sermon, he describes a sermon that may or may not be based on a narrative text. Furthermore, the sermon may or may not be in a story form. A *narrative sermon*, as Lowry uses the term, will be structured so as to begin or move early on into some kind of tension, conflict, or disequilibrium. This will escalate (just as the plot of a story does) into complications that continue until a sudden reversal brings it into a final resolution. Whether the sermon is a narrative and regardless of the literary genre of the text, if the sermon follows this "homiletical plot," Lowry calls it a *narrative sermon*. The justification for the label is in the sermon organization. The preacher presents the listener with an opening conflict or "bind" that calls for resolution. Then after struggling with this conflict or discrepancy or mystery, the tension is relieved, and the complication dissolves into a final resolution. Lowry's distinction has not been universally accepted or even broadly understood.[2]

Lowry speaks of the first stage of a sermon as "opening disequilibrium" gaining complication toward the second stage of "escalated ambiguity." The final stage provides some sort of resolution. Emotionally we like stories that have a happy-ever-after ending. Sometimes life is not that way. The great conflict in the story of Job resolves happily in the end, even though Job never knows what has been going on behind the curtain as God deals with our adversary.

The parable of the prodigal son in Luke 15 ends with the unresolved question of whether the older brother ever came in to the homecoming party. But after all, perhaps that is the main message of the trilogy of parables in that chapter. The tax collectors and other outcasts of society gladly embraced God's grace in Christ. The fellows on the fringe of the crowd, Pharisees and the teachers of the Law, were there to grumble and find fault. Would they come in to the party too? The Father in heaven searches for every last

[2] Lowry said, "By *narrative sermon* I mean an event-in-time which moves from opening disequilibrium (or conflict) through escalation (complication) to surprising reversal (*peripetia*) into closing denouement. . . . A narrative sermon may include a story or stories. Then again, it may not." Eugene L. Lowry, "The Difference between Story Preaching and Narrative Preaching," Papers of the Annual Meeting of the Academy of Homiletics (Madison, NJ: Academy of Homiletics, 1988), 141. Compare Jerry Vines and Jim Shaddix, *Power in the Pulpit: How to Prepare and Deliver Expository Sermons.* (Chicago: Moody, 2001). This widely used homiletical textbook, for example, incorrectly defines Lowry's method strictly in terms of the literary genre of the sermon's text! A narrative sermon is *not* necessarily based on a narrative text in Lowry's method.

one as a shepherd with one hundred sheep goes out for the one last stray. He looks and looks until He finds it. A woman with ten coins loses one. She is not content with having the other nine. She lights a lamp and cleans house until that last coin turns up. In each case there is a great celebration when the lost sheep or the lost coin is found. There surely ought to be a celebration when the lost son comes home. But the question remains, will the other prodigal come in and join the party or stay outside and grumble?

Andy Stanley uses the hook from Scripture's tensions and disequilibrium to open his sermons. Preaching on the temptations of Christ, he began with a two-verse Scripture reading which tells us that Jesus was led by the Holy Spirit into the wilderness to be tempted. That's odd, the preacher pointed out, especially in light of the teaching of Jesus in the model prayer asking the Father to "lead us not into temptation." Then Stanley talked about his own struggle with temptation; Andy likes to talk personally before he moves to engage the listener with his or her personal need in the light of the text.[3]

The book before you will talk more about storytelling than *narrative preaching*. When I do use the term *narrative preaching*, I am thinking of that preaching that magnifies the story features of the sermon, whether the sermon has a narrative text or narrative development of a text of another genre. *Narrative preaching* is shaping the message in story form as Jesus often did in parables.

Jesus the Storyteller

Jesus used a variety of rhetorical shapes for His teaching and preaching, but the parable was His staple. In the Sermon on the Mount, He used beatitudes, metaphors, and similes. He used comparison and contrast to distinguish His kingdom teaching from the prevailing religious instruction. He gave a pattern for prayer in the

---

[3] Andy Stanley and Lane Jones, *Communicating for a Change* (Sisters, OR: Multnomah, 2006), 138. Andy Stanley advocates a structure for sermons that does not divide a topic or thesis into so many points. Instead he likes to organize a sermon into five sections he calls "Me-We-God-You-We." He starts the *Me*-section with a personal issue his congregation should be able to identify with. The *We*-section brings the congregation along as he shows them that this is their problem too. Then the *God*-section sheds the light of a Scripture text on this problem. It is explained as required and then applied in the *You*-section and brought full circle in the final *We*-section.

template we call the Lord's Prayer. That sermon or teaching ends with a pair of parables. On other occasions Jesus admonished, reproved, rebuked, and warned. Sometimes He spoke encouragement and blessing, but mostly He told stories.

For centuries interpreters tended to treat the parables of Jesus as allegories. The Reformation began to reform that too, but Martin Luther was one Reformer who was sometimes slow to break with traditional patterns of hermeneutics. In his interpretation of the parable of the good Samaritan, we are the wounded traveler. The robbers represent the Devil who wounded us and robbed us. Jesus is the good Samaritan. The priest and the Levite in the story represent the Old Testament patriarchs and their priesthood. The donkey also represents the Lord Jesus. The inn represents the church with the innkeeper as preacher. At least in theory, Luther as well as Calvin and other reformers broke from this centuries-old allegorical treatment of the parables that dated back to Origen and Augustine. Aristotle's *Rhetoric* argued for the parable as a rhetorical device. Much of New Testament scholarship today remains under the sway of German scholar Adolph Julicher, who in 1888 insisted that instead of a multitude of meanings, each parable makes only one point. Not until the mid-twentieth century did we begin to break away from our obsession with "points" and decide to let the parables be stories. We insist on knowing the *point* of the story. We don't like for someone to tell us that the story *is* the point.

Preachers still have a hard time letting the parables speak for themselves. We need to listen again to Jesus as the master storyteller. Try to forget about getting the point and focus on getting the *story*. What if the story really *is* the point? It might help us to be better interpreters of Jesus and better preachers of His parables and all the Word of God if we could keep a few matters in mind. For one thing, the stories of Jesus are extremely earthy, tangible, and human. Of course they may lift us to thoughts heavenly, spiritual, and divine, but we ought not to let that get in the way of hearing the story on the level of daily living.

Second, it is the nature of any story to have movement. A story is not a snapshot but a film clip. There is an inevitable tension in this what-comes-next nature of a story. Tension tends to distress us. We want things to be on a level plane and firmly fixed on a foundation, not tilted as if they would topple. But life is not always rooted like a great oak. The winds come along and upset things. Towers fall down. The stories of Jesus speak to the ambiguity and stress of life as it is. If we can see that there is a goal or destination in all this shaking and scattering, we can tolerate the tension.

Third, there is sometimes a twist in the characters who play their roles in the parables of Jesus. Not everyone in the real world is clearly a hero or a villain. We may be surprised that the plantation owner in the parable praises the shrewd manager's forward thinking, even though he is a thief. He is cooking the books before he is terminated, and he is ingratiating himself with his employer's clients. Our world is in living color too; things are not always black and white. Can you identify with that?

Fourth, we like stories to end on the happy-ever-after in a neat package, no loose ends. But sometimes there is more value in a parable that leaves us with unanswered questions. We ask, "Who is my neighbor?" And Jesus tells us a story that turns the question upside down: "To whom will you be a neighbor today?" Then we must answer the same question today and tomorrow and the day after. And finally, we should expect Bible stories to surprise us—including the parables of Jesus. Somehow we must shake off that familiarity that breeds something bordering on contempt. We should pray that God will speak a fresh word to us, even if we can never find in it a sermon we can take into the pulpit on Sunday. The best way to do this is to climb into the story instead of standing off and viewing it as one would scan canvasses on a museum wall, a few minutes here and a few seconds there. If that sounds like work, so be it, but for someone really called of God and committed to speak for Him, it is the most glorious labor ever to occupy a life. Thrilling agony! Who could ask for anything more?[4]

The Pages Ahead

The chapters that follow are grouped into three parts. Part 1, "The Basics of Storytelling," begins with a look at the great appeal

---

[4] I do not wish to credit all of this too-brief treatment of the parables of Jesus to the influence of Patrick J. Willson's article "Entertaining Stories," *Journal for Preachers* 12, no. 2:5–13; he might not recognize his influence at all, but I commend his article's well-expressed insights and gladly confess to reaping where he has sown.

of narrative. What makes everyone love a story? Then we get acquainted with the five essential elements of any story: the setting, the characters, plot, point of view, and unifying significance. We need a closer look at the matter of plot, and we get that in a chapter on the seven basic plot plans. All the stories of all human history, including Bible stories, seem to fit at least one of these five plans. One chapter explores three personal stories that every preacher must master, and another considers the power and peril of persuasion by personal testimony.

Part 2, "Getting the Story Straight," begins with a step-by-step plan for building sermons with stories and then turns attention to telling the Bible story and the special skills needed for ministry to children. After a chapter on ten ways to sharpen your narrative skills and another on the secret to an endless supply of stories, this section ends with some guidance for preachers on telling stories effectively.

Part 3 is all about learning storytelling skills from the pulpit masters of the past. Four chapters introduce us to preachers who excelled in the use of stories in sermons. How did they do it? What can we learn from them?

At the end of each chapter, there are two or three suggested exercises. You will profit most from your stewardship of this study if you pause at the end of each chapter to complete at least one of the learning exercises. Before you turn this page, will you pause and join me in this prayer?

Dear Father, I want to learn to preach and teach like Jesus. I know that unless the Spirit of Christ opens my eyes, I will continue to stumble in the dark. Unless the Spirit kindles a fire within me, I will never warm the heart of anyone else. Create in me the heart of a true disciple of the Master lest all my preaching be in vain. Gracious Father, make me more like Jesus every time I preach. In the name of the Lord Jesus. Amen.

part one

THE BASICS OF
STORYTELLING

Chapter 1

THE GREAT APPEAL OF NARRATIVE

LISA LAX, NBC-TV'S SENIOR SPORTS producer needed to know how to keep viewers watching the Atlanta Olympics. The network paid $456 million for the broadcast rights and budgeted $3.5 billion for Olympics coverage through the year 2008. They simply could not afford for you and me to tune out as so many did the Seoul Olympics. In the six years leading up to Atlanta, the network interviewed ten thousand viewers. What do people like, and what do they dislike about sports on TV? The big finding of all that research came down to one fact: *Tell them stories, and they will watch.* The result was more than 135 two-to-three minute narratives the network produced and scattered throughout the successful Atlanta Olympics coverage.[1]

Many preachers today could have saved the network all that expense. We know that stories, even brief ones, lift the attention level of our listeners. This opening chapter lists six reasons for the great appeal of narrative in preaching. Then it candidly admits that storytelling in the pulpit still meets with a few vocal critics. We will let them have their say. But now, what is the great appeal of narrative? We have already suggested the first value of the story in preaching.

---

[1] Jim Impco, "NBC Goes for Women Viewers and Platinum Ratings," *U.S. News & World Report* (July 15–22, 1996): 36.

A Story Grabs Our Attention and Holds It

Every preacher has seen it. You are doing your best to explain the text and apply it to the lives of those who sit before you. Glazed eyes gaze back at you or stare right through you. You know you are not connecting. Then you say, "Let me tell you a story," or some other equivalent of "once upon a time." Suddenly eyes blink into focus. Children stop doodling and look up. The teenagers on the back row pause in their whispering and note passing. The lady making her grocery list and the businessman mentally planning his week all lend you their ears—at least for this. That is the first and most important thing about storytelling that gives it such appeal for preaching: there is high *attention value* in stories. Henry Ward Beecher said, "He who would hold the ear of the people must either tell stories or paint pictures."

Stories Stick in the Memory

Jesus made the truth portable in parables. It is narrative that gives this *portability value* to preaching or teaching. Chip Heath teaches at Stanford University. For the past few years, he has been teaching a class for MBA students called "Making Ideas Stick." He runs a demonstration exercise to show how much the average business presentation falls short of sticking in the mind of the listener. He gives his students detailed numbers on U.S. property crime rates and asks them to make impromptu, 60-second speeches for or against tougher crime laws. Not surprisingly, the students resort to the statistics. They typically use two or three statistics in a one-minute talk. Only one in ten tells a story.

Chip then distracts the class for ten minutes by showing a clip from a *Monty Python* movie. When this diversion is over, he asks them what they remember about the presentations. A nervous laughter goes around the room. Only one out of every 20 people in the class is able to recall any statistic from any of the presentations they heard. When a speaker told a story about a personal experience with property crime, on the other hand, two out of three students remembered it. Stories may not fit neatly into a spreadsheet or a PowerPoint presentation, but narratives stick with us when the charts and graphs are gone.[2]

What do you remember from the last sermon you heard? Chances are, if you remember anything, you remember a narrative. Perhaps the text was a narrative; about three-fifths of the Bible is narrative. My childhood pastor was an excellent preacher, T. C. Pennell Sr. of Shreveport, Louisiana. Yet I do not recall a single sermon title or outline from those years. I do recall, after half a century, many of his narrative illustrations. I recall that he often preached on Bible characters in the Sunday evening service. Biographical sermons tend to have more narrative. The precept illumined by the narrative is probably clearer now than it was to me as a child. If so, it is because the story stayed with me long enough to bring the spiritual truth along with it. Stories have staying power.

Stories Have Persuasive Power

A third explanation for the great appeal of narrative is the *persuasive value* of story. A story finds an open-door welcome where facts and logic are barred by closed minds. When President Abraham Lincoln first met Harriet Beecher Stowe, author of *Uncle Tom's Cabin*, he remarked: "So you're the little lady who started this war." It was not just flattery. Her novel, first published in 1851 or 1852, attracted millions of readers. Her characters still live; Uncle Tom, Simon Legree, and Little Eva St. Clare have become stereotypes. Harriet was the daughter of a famous pastor, Lyman Beecher, and she had four preacher brothers. One of them, Henry Ward Beecher (1803–1895), was widely considered the greatest preacher of his day. Yet arguably this one story told by their sister had more impact on American history than all of their sermons together.

Part of the persuasive power of a story is the indirect approach it affords. Pluralism is the prevailing philosophy of our culture. Few preachers dare to say, "Thus saith the Lord!" The prophet is banished from the modern church. The resentful voices of Miriam and Aaron blend with their modern counterparts in the chorus of democratic sentiment. "Has the LORD spoken only through

---

[2] Justin Ewers, "Making It Stick," *U.S. News & World Report* (January 29–February 5, 2007): 8.

Moses? . . . Hasn't he also spoken through us?" (Num 12:2 NIV). Their faces flushed with resentment against their younger brother Moses. Any minister who thinks he is anointed to be a spokesman for God must find a way to proclaim the Word in our culture of ecclesiastical egalitarianism. While this is not a new problem, it is more acute in this twenty-first century. Jesus faced the opposition of the religious establishment in His day; they considered Him a blasphemer. Christ coped with the opposition and continued His preaching and teaching, often tucking theological truth into earthy stories or parables. We must learn to do the same.

Is the preacher today "one without authority," as Fred Craddock insisted?[3] You may hear a loud chorus of *amens* in the affirmative. Certainly increasing secularism leads to more and more rejection of sacred authority, and egalitarianism eliminates all claims to authority. Yet those who disregard the officer with badge and pistol do not cancel his or her authority. Preachers need not buy the whole communication theory to benefit from the insights of those who believe the minister, in fact, has no authority. Admonition is like sailing into the wind; it can be done, but it is slow and difficult. Narrative is like the more oblique progress of a to-and-fro tact of the sailboat. The story more quickly gains the harbor of human will.

This also is not new. How did Nathan the prophet confront King David? David was notoriously guilty of wife stealing and adultery. He compounded his offense by ordering the assassination of Uriah, her husband. The prophet might have gone into the king's presence with the thunders of Sinai. Instead he told the king a story of a rich and powerful man who forcibly took the only little lamb, a family pet, from his poor neighbor. The rich man slaughtered it to entertain a guest. Predictable indignation flared in the face of the shepherd king. "Who is this man? He will surely pay!"

Then the prophet got personal: "You are the man!" (2 Sam 12:7 NIV). The story captivated the attention of King David and stirred his righteous anger. By the time he realized that he was indeed that man, what else could he do but turn his heart to God in humble repentance? A simple story stirred his conscience and bent his will.

The pastor of an all-white congregation in a Louisiana plantation community found his people reluctant to face the race issue with

---

[3] Fred Craddock, *As One Without Authority* (Nashville: Abingdon, 1971).

anything but deep-rooted prejudice. They certainly did not want to hear about that issue at church on Sunday unless, of course, it was perhaps a racist joke that reinforced their intolerance. Over time, stories from literature and from life slowly brought the issue into focus. One such story was from Sir Thomas Mallory's King Arthur and his *Knights of the Round Table*. Riding a black horse with all black livery and black silks, the Black Knight on the forest road one day met the White Knight riding a white horse with all white regalia. They lowered their visors and leveled their lances. Time and again they charged each other until finally they both lay bleeding and dying. Only then did they lift their visors to discover that they were brothers.

Max Lucado likened the use of stories in preaching to a Trojan Horse. "Truth can arrive a bit incognito within the story."[4] In another chapter we will delve deeper into the ethics of persuasion. Here we note that some object to any persuasive power in preaching beyond the cold logic of a syllogism. Frederick Buechner, a notable preacher as well as a great storyteller, says that he "leans over backwards not to preach or propagandize" in his fiction. He is "simply trying to conjure up stories in which people are touched with what may or may not be the presence of God in their lives." He further argues about fiction: "If you're preaching or otherwise grinding an ax, you let happen, of course, only the things you want to happen; but insofar as fiction, like faith, is a journey not only forward in space and time, but a journey inward, it is full of surprises."[5]

Yes, it is, but we should not be surprised that stories shape our worldview and our vision of what the world could be. One of my young seminary students said, "Movies are our modern-day philosophers." Galileo was convinced that the sun was the center of our solar system. The sun did not orbit the earth, but in fact the earth orbited the sun. The rotation of the earth made it appear that the sun came up and went down. Galileo went to Rome to answer for his heresy. Cardinal Bellarmine, and behind him the Office of the Inquisition, ordered the astronomer not to hold or defend these ideas of the earth and the sun. In 1623, a friend and admirer of Galileo, Cardinal Barberini was elected Pope Urban

---

[4] "Preaching and Story: An Interview with Max Lucado," *Preaching* (March-April 2006): 7–12.
[5] Frederick Buechner, *The Clown in the Belfrey: Writings on Faith and Fiction* (San Francisco: Harper, 1992). See chap. 11, "The Truth of Stories," 129ff and 17–18.

VIII. Soon Galileo wrote a story. He created three characters. One took Galileo's view in the discussion; another took the unscientific view common in that day, and the third moved the story along. The writer got permission from the church to publish his book, *Dialogue Concerning the Two Chief World Systems.* By the time the Inquisition felt the barb of the hook in the author's tale, it was too late. A story can't be untold. Too many people had read the book to consider banning it.[6]

The preacher's task is not only to convey truth but also to move the will. In this we may learn from artists of all kinds, especially literary artists. We tend to lean on logic as we proclaim propositions. The artist can show us how to stir the imagination and prompt the listener to become involved in the preaching event. Norman N. Holland some years ago explored the mental process of the human response to literature. What is going on in the brain when people become absorbed in a well-told tale? He developed a complex model to explain literature as transformation. Two of his concepts are particularly helpful to the preacher. One is the listener's willingness to suspend disbelief while enjoying a story he or she knows to be fiction. The other is the human tendency to identify with a character in the story.

This is what brings tears to our eyes when we read in a book or see in a movie the death of a character we have come to know and love. We know it's only a story played by an actor. The imaginary character may never have lived and certainly did not really die. Neither did the actor portraying that character. Knowing this, we are still moved. Why? Because we have chosen to suspend disbelief for a while, and we have chosen at least subconsciously to identify with some character in the story. The characters are real to us because we decide to visit their world. Doing so meets some need in us. It is a choice, but it may not be deliberate or an altogether conscious choice. The story has persuaded us.

As preachers we try to prompt people to think certain thoughts and accept certain truths. What if we could incite them to do more? What if we could stir them to participate in a story emotionally? What if, instead of telling them what they are supposed to believe,

---

[6] Thanks to Joe McKeever for bringing this bit of history to my attention. A version of it was published in his article, "How to Handle a Hot Potato," *Preaching* (March-April 2007): 19.

we could bring them into a narrative where they personally discover truth? What if, instead of telling them about Jesus of Nazareth, we could introduce them to Him in person? What if, instead of exhorting them to love one another, we could involve them in a love story that stirred them to be more loving? Jesus Himself did that masterfully. Just think of His story of the good Samaritan.[7]

Stories Clarify the Truth

The essential function of any sermon illustration is to shed light on the subject. Narrative illustrations seem to have a special power to make the truth plain. This *explanation value* of stories shines in the parables of Jesus. Let's go back to the parable of the good Samaritan. Jesus was teaching about love for our neighbors when someone asked, "And who is my neighbor?" (Luke 10:29). The Master Teacher told a story that made the answer clear such as no definition of "neighbor" ever could. The parables of Jesus, of course, are more than sermon illustrations. They do make the truth attractive and memorable, but mainly they make the Master's meaning clear. And the parables of Jesus did more than reveal truth. As strange as it seems, they sometimes also intentionally concealed truth—at least temporarily. His parables have been compared to the shell of a nut that keeps the meat *for* the diligent but *from* the careless. It was a mercy of the Lord that He disclosed spiritual truth to those ready to receive it but hid it from those who would reject it. To reject it would bring greater judgment on the hearer.

Consider again the trilogy of parables in Luke 15: the lost sheep, the lost coin, and the lost son. The third one, which we traditionally call the prodigal son, is the best-known of the three and perhaps most beloved of all parables. The parable (or *story*, as some would prefer) of the rich man and Lazarus is another dramatic narrative. Centuries fail to dim its brilliance.

For hundreds of years, teachers of preaching have drilled their students in how to convert the sacred story into sermon propositions and points. They want us to structure sermons in the fashion of scholasticism's rigid framework. But what if the transfer dis-

---

[7] Norman N. Holland, "The Willing Suspension of Disbelief," in *The Dynamics of Literary Response* (New York: Oxford University Press, 1968), cited in Steven Shuster, *The Journal of Communication and Religion* (March 1989): 22–27.

torts the story? What if the message is all wrapped up in the story? Novelist Flannery O'Conner said: "When you can state the theme of a story, when you can separate it from the story itself, then you can be sure the story is not a very good one. The meaning of a story has to be embodied in it, has to be made concrete in it. A story is a way to say something that can't be said any other way, and it takes every word in the story to say what the meaning is."[8]

Narrative Adds Aesthetic Value to a Sermon

A fifth reason for the great appeal of narrative in the pulpit is its *aesthetic value*. Everyone loves a good story. Is there anywhere a preacher whose explanation of Scripture and applications to life are so uniformly excellent that they cannot be made more appealing? Sometimes a preacher needs to present a truth that is unattractive. A story in a sermon can be like a woman's judicious use of cosmetics. Makeup can never make an ugly woman beautiful, but it might highlight the beauty that is there. The message more easily gains a hearing adorned in story as the following old Jewish teaching story puts it.

Long, long ago *Truth* walked down the street as naked as the day she was born. People ran from her. They ran into their houses and closed her out. She was turned away from every door in the village until *Parable* found her huddled in a corner, shivering and hungry. Taking pity on her, *Parable* gathered her up and took her home. There she dressed *Truth* in some of her own fine clothes, warmed her, fed her, and sent her out again. Clothed in story, *Truth* knocked again at the villagers' doors and found a ready welcome into every home. They invited her to eat at their table and warm herself by their fire. Since that time, *Truth* and *Parable* have been closest friends.[9]

Ian Macpherson's book on *The Art of Illustrating Sermons* was influential to my generation of seminary students. Macpherson asked whether an illustration might legitimately function as adornment in a sermon. This issue is still good for a lively discussion

---

[8] Quoted by storytelling master Steven James, *Story: Recapture the Mystery* (Grand Rapids: Fleming H. Revell, 2005).
[9] This story often appears in storytelling literature. See Annette Simmons, *The Story Factor: Inspiration, Influence, and Persuasion through the Art of Storytelling* (Cambridge, MA: Perseus, 2001), 27, and a similar version in James A. Feehan, *Preaching in Stories* (Dublin: Mercier Press, 1989), 19.

among preachers. That distinguished Welch preacher and educator made a convincing case to me for the ornamental use, at least collaterally. He cited some notable pulpit masters who used illustrations to add beauty to their presentations of the message. He noted John Henry Jowett's contrast of a decorative table lamp drawing all eyes to itself and a streetlamp all unseen but shedding light on the road. "Yet even streetlamps need not be without a charm of their own, combining beauty with utility, adorning while they enlighten." Henry Ward Beecher said, "An illustration is never a mere ornament, although its being ornamental is no objection to it."[10]

The gospel preacher is no entertainer. No one should attempt to rival the pitiable prophet whose speech had a pleasing sound and a lovely voice but no power in his proclamation. "My people come to you, as they usually do, and sit before you to listen to your words, but they do not put them into practice. . . . To them you are nothing more than one who sings love songs with a beautiful voice and plays an instrument well, for they hear your words but do not put them into practice" (Ezek 33:31–32). Even so, the sermons of Jesus managed to present eternal truth in metaphors and parables that are unsurpassed for sheer beauty of expression as well as the unmatched message in them.

We See Ourselves in Stories

A sixth and final value we will mention for sermonic narrative is what we may call the *listener-identity value*. In a well-told tale we who listen see our friends, our enemies, and ourselves. We also see our problems and the possibility of solutions in the characters and action of the story.

Skip knew he had a problem when he first stood before the shareholders: he was thirty-five years old and still looked thirteen. He was already third-generation wealthy when he bought controlling interest in the publicly traded company. Would he be able to convince them he could run this company without running it into the ground? He decided to tell them a personal story.

"My first job was drawing the electrical engineering plans for a boat building company," he began. "The drawings had to be per-

---

[10] Ian Macpherson, *The Art of Illustrating Sermons* (Nashville: Abingdon, 1964), 21.

fect because if the wires were not accurately placed before the fiberglass form was poured, a mistake might cost a million dollars, easy. At twenty-five I already had two masters' degrees. I had been on boats all my life; and, frankly, I found drawing these plans a bit mindless! One morning I got a call at home—a six-dollar-an-hour worker asking me, 'Are you sure this is right?'"

Of course he was *sure*. With a bit of salty language, he insisted they "just pour the thing!" The supervisor called an hour later, woke him up *again*, and asked, "Are you sure this is right?" Now he had even less patience, "I said I was sure an hour ago, and I'm still sure." A third phone call came from the president of the company. This finally got him out of bed and down to the site. If he had to hold those guys by the hand, so be it. He started with the worker who called him first. He was still looking at the plans with his head cocked to one side. With exaggerated patience Skip began to explain the drawing. After a few words his voice got weaker, and *his* head began to cock to one side. It seemed he had transposed starboard and port so that the drawing was an exact mirror image of what it should have been. He tried a lame excuse about being left-handed, but thank God this six-dollar-an-hour worker had caught his mistake before it was too late.

The next day Skip found a shoebox on his desk. The crew wanted him to have a "remedial" pair of tennis shoes for future reference. Holding up the shoes, he showed the shareholders one green left shoe for the starboard side and one red right shoe for the port side. He confessed, "Those shoes don't just help me remember port and starboard; they help me remember to listen when I think I know what's going on."

There were many smiles and some chuckles among the stockholders and maybe a few smirks. Most of those present decided maybe this youngster had learned a thing or two already. At least he had learned to admit his humanity. Probably he had learned a few things about working with people. His personal story convinced them he was one of them. He could be trusted.[11]

Surely a part of the success of Alcoholics Anonymous is members' sharing their personal stories. In addition to the therapeutic value to the one confessing, there is great bonding value for the

---

[11] Simmons, *The Story Factor*.

whole group. Members soon feel "I am not alone; we are in this together." Megachurches discover that there is something missing if there is no small group where members may tell a bit of their own stories to one another, come to know one another, and be known as real persons.

Objections to Storytelling in Sermons

In spite of these advantages, we admit candidly that some preachers and some who listen to sermons object to storytelling. One of the best-known evangelical preachers today is John MacArthur. In answer to a question about where storytelling might fit into expository preaching, he answered: "I am not into storytelling. I fail to see the value of multiple, long, drawn-out illustrations. . . . Stories tend to shut down the level of intensity that I prefer people to maintain." But in the same book MacArthur quoted a four-page narrative about a natural history student learning to develop his powers of observation in the laboratory by meticulous study of a smelly fish specimen. Somehow MacArthur finds stories OK in a book about preaching but not in a sermon.[12]

When I was a seminary student, I wrote to D. Martyn Lloyd-Jones of Westminster Chapel, London, to ask his opinion on the use of sermon illustrations. He responded graciously with a note about his "strong views on this subject." He reminded me that he had always been a critic of a man like W. E. Sangster, who used to carry a little notebook in his pocket to take down any stories he heard and who had a "card-index of illustrations appropriate to various subjects." Lloyd-Jones said, "I always described that as the prostitution of preaching!"[13]

In spite of my great admiration of John MacArthur, Martyn Lloyd-Jones, and other faithful expositors of God's Word who have little use for storytelling, the conviction of this writer is that sermon illustration is a skill that every preacher should cultivate and that storytelling is the essence of sermon illustration.

---

[12] John MacArthur Jr. and the Master's Seminary Faculty, *Rediscovering Expository Preaching: Balancing the Science and Art of Biblical Exposition* (Dallas: Word, 1992), 342–43.
[13] Note to the author from D. Martyn Lloyd-Jones, 1965.

Laymen who listen to sermons have criticized preachers who make too much use of stories. Let us agree that stringing a series of anecdotes together will never be a substitute for solid exposition. Illustration must always be the servant of explaining and applying the text. Interesting table decorations may make the food more appealing, but they must never substitute for the pure milk and nourishing meat of the Word of God. Those who scorn stories and other sermon illustration, however, must take note of the homiletical method of Jesus. The most striking feature of His style was His use of parables. Jesus preached in stories most of all.

Others object that the modern sermon is too brief for stories. Ian MacPherson answered them, "If a sermon is too short to be illustrated, it is too short to be preached."[14] Still others think that storytelling insults the intelligence of any adult congregation. Ronald A. Ward, for example, says, "Take a few pretty stories, mix well with some moral platitudes, place in the refrigerator, and serve cold."[15] Admittedly some preachers do a poor job of storytelling and of preaching in general. This is not a good enough reason for abandoning either preaching or storytelling. Most of the objections arise from the misuse of stories. This we certainly want to avoid. In the following chapters we will give ourselves to learning how to tell stories and how to do it well. Let's start with mastering the basics in a chapter on the essential elements of any story. But first, take time for at least one of the following learning exercises. If you will do so at the end of each chapter, it will be better than a review in reinforcing your learning.

Exercise 1. In this first chapter you found six reasons for the great appeal of narrative as one tool in the minister's toolbox in building for eternity. How many of those six values of narrative can you recall? Here is a hint: the word APPEAL is an acronym for them all. Review them now with that in mind.

Exercise 2. Can you recall a story or two from years ago that made a difference in your life? Review the narrative in your mind. Can you tell why it stuck in memory? And what eternal truth did the narrative convey to you?

---

[14] MacPherson, *The Art of Illustrating Sermons*, 34.
[15] Ibid.

Chapter 2

THE ESSENTIAL ELEMENTS
OF NARRATIVE

THERE IS A LOT TO storytelling, and much of it is easier caught than taught. The essential elements of a story, however, are not hard to master. In this chapter and the next, you will learn to use a Narration Worksheet (p. 25) and a Plot Movements Worksheet (p. 33). These simple tools will help you master the elements of narrative for preaching. The first worksheet introduces the preacher to the five crucial elements of any story. These are plot, character, setting, point of view, and unity. The second worksheet surveys the five stages of a well-ordered plot.

To have a story, you must have *characters*, or at least one character, a *plot*, and a *setting*. These must be held together by some *unifying significance*. The setting tells us where we are in time and space; character tells us who is involved, and the plot or action as it is sometimes called, tells us what is happening. So there are four questions to answer about a story:

- Where are we?
- Who is involved?
- What is happening?
- Why is it happening?

Let's begin by sketching the overview of these elements of narrative before giving more detailed attention to plot.

22

Overview of Narrative

Plot is the plan of the story. It is the chain of events in the narrative. In the plot something is at stake. There is a conflict to be resolved, a source of tension to be relieved, or a mystery to be solved. In mystery stories the term *denouement* is used to describe the unraveling of the tangle of the conflict. The conflict may be between two characters or between a character and his environment. It may be an inner conflict such as David confessed in Psalm 51. In Scripture the basic conflict is between a rebellious person (or people) and God. This is probably the place where preachers most need help as they tell stories in the sermon.

Character is the second essential. Usually there is more than one character in a story. I recall a short story by Jack London entitled "To Build a Fire." There was only one character in the story, and he is identified only as "the man." The conflict is not between a hero and a villain but between "the man" and his environment. All alone the mortal was trekking from one camp to another along the Yukon trail. It is 75 degrees below zero. He has to stop and build a fire to keep himself from freezing to death. Can he do it in time?

In storytelling the characters usually deal with some constriction or tension between them. It may be a life-threatening physical peril or great conflict in personal relationships threatening contentment and well-being. Perhaps some event triggers marital discord or sibling rivalry or tension between neighbors. It may be a conflict in the life of one character or man against his environment as in Jack London's story above. More often it is a complex of conflicts; a conflicted person rarely resolves his or her problem without making waves for others. When we deal in detail with plot, we will note that the characters move from some bondage toward liberty, from danger toward safety, from some problem to a solution. A story may have one or two characters or a cast of thousands. In preaching we do well to keep it simple. Even if we had no time constraints, people have a hard time keeping up with more than two characters at a time.

In a well-told tale, as we have seen, our listeners tend to identify with one character or another. At least they sympathize with one. The preacher needs to help the listener see himself or herself in one character or another. Sometimes the preacher may describe the heart of a character overtly as R. G. Lee did in the introduction to "Payday Someday": "I introduce you to Ahab, the vile human toad who squatted upon the throne of his nation."

At other times it is better to let the narrative and the dialogue unveil that heart. In a helpful workshop on Preaching as Storytelling, Fred Craddock recommended the preacher avoid introducing a story with something like, "Let me tell you about one of the finest, most noble and generous of laymen who ever warmed a pastor's heart and blessed a church with unselfish service." Already we are instructed how we should regard this person. Craddock also discouraged summary application such as, "Now aren't we all sometimes like that older brother?"[1]

One might object that a sermon illustration does not afford time to develop a full character sketch. Of course there are time restraints, but recent research supports the theory that our first impressions and snap judgments tend to be accurate.[2] Let the story include enough data for a first impression of a character. And remember that this may come in dialogue and action as well as in description.

Stories to enjoy personally or to entertain others need not be true stories as long as they are true to life. In sermons, however, a preacher must make clear that an illustration is a work of fiction if that is what it is. A pastor once described in some detail a pitiful case of poverty in the community. A layman in the church was moved with compassion and wanted to help that family. He asked the pastor for the name and address and was disgusted to learn that the family was a creation of the preacher's imagination. The pastor confessed that it was not a real family at all but the kind of needs that might be readily found in the community if anyone cared to look.

You may certainly create characters for sermon illustrations as long as you make clear that you are doing so. There is a case to be made for favoring characters you create over real people. The advantage is that you may create vivid, compelling characters through exaggeration of certain traits that you need in your

---

[1] Craddock, audiotapes, 1971.

[2] Malcolm Gladwell, *Blink: The Power of Thinking without Thinking* (New York: Little, Brown, 2005).

NARRATION WORKSHEET

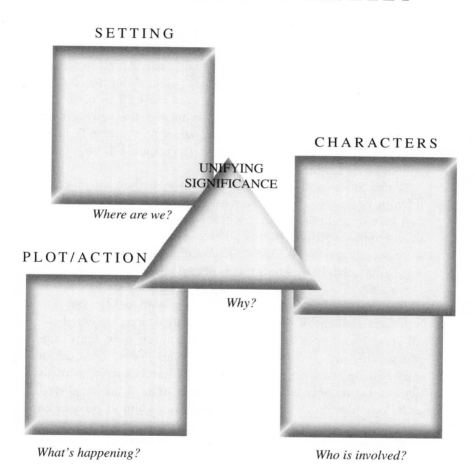

SETTING

Where are we?

CHARACTERS

UNIFYING
SIGNIFICANCE

PLOT/ACTION

Why?

What's happening?

Who is involved?

story. If you create characters, they must be more than cardboard. Make them believable. The characters must care about something or someone. Whatever they do in the story must also be plausible. And it helps the reader if each character has some identifying personality trait. You may or may not describe them physically, but they do need to be fleshed out enough to make them real. What motivates your character? What does it take to make her happy? What ticks him off? These are things that the best writers tell us in the action and dialogue rather than a narrator's revelation. "Everything George did was for money." Yuk! Point the characters in your story toward the one thing that most drives them and keeps them moving in that direction. In their dealings with other people, most people are motivated by one of four human desires: the need for security, for recognition, for response from others, and for some adventure.[3]

Setting provides the boundaries of the story in time and space. Is it reality or fantasy? Is it in the past or present or even the future? Is it here or there or just somewhere? This need not take a lot of time. Suppose the story begins, "Three teenage girls from our city were speeding down I-35 last Sunday night in a BMW convertible." Immediately we know this is not set in ancient Jerusalem or Damascus.

Point of view may be considered along with setting, but it is a distinct element of the storyteller's craft. It may be either the all-knowing narrator or a more realistic point of view. For example, the first-person storyteller in Edgar Allen Poe's "The Cask of Amontillado" tells his own thoughts and motives as well as his actions, but he only tells the words and actions of his hated rival as he gets him drunk and brick-by-brick seals him up alive in an alcove of the wine cellar.

Whatever point of view you select, be consistent and stick with it from beginning to end. It is annoying for the point of view to shift during the story. Franz Kafka was a much-read author in the late twentieth century. One of his most famous short stories is "Metamorphosis." It is a surreal sci-fi story of a man named Gregor Samsa who wakes up one morning to discover that he is

---

[3] W. I. Thomas, sociologist of another day, cited by Dwight V. Swaine, *Creating Characters: How to Build Story People* (Cincinnati, OH: Writer's Digest Books, 1990).

undergoing some strange transformation. It turns out that he is changing into a giant insect like a cockroach. The story is told by a third-person narrator. But it unfolds from the point of view of Gregor, the principle character. We have his thoughts as well as words until he has no more speech than the chirp of an insect. The storyteller gives the words and deeds but not the thoughts of other characters. And these we have only in so far as they are seen or heard by Gregor. He can listen at the door to others talk about him and argue about what to do about him. But what do you do when the point-of-view character dies? Kafka jumped to a different character, so the conclusion is in the words of the housekeeper. The shift in point of view is just one thing that is disconcerting about the story.

A storyteller has three basic choices on point of view. You may tell the story from the perspective of the third-person narrator who knows the thoughts and motives of each actor as well as his or her own. Or you may use a third person who is more objective and not omniscient. Historians tend to use the third person, though, of course, they are not omniscient. Only the fiction writer who creates the characters and knows the mind of each can be truly omniscient. New Testament historical books normally use the third-person pronouns. In Acts, for example, Luke the historian reports the deeds of Peter and Stephen and Paul and Silas and Barnabas, as well as of many minor characters. On the missionary journeys he tells us *they* went here and there; *he* said this and that. But several sections in the Acts are called the *"we* sections," leading us to believe that Luke joined the team on these episodes and reports as a full participant.

Old Testament history also tends to be third person even in the five books of Moses, where Moses is assumed to be the author except perhaps for such matters as Exodus 34, which records his death and burial. And of course, verse 10 evaluates his life from some later perspective: "Since then no prophet has risen in Israel like Moses." Some suppose Joshua likewise authored the book that bears his name except, of course, for the account of his death. Ezra and Nehemiah are historical records, but they include autobiographical passages. Ezra is mostly a chronicle with heavy documentation, but it includes first-person testimony from the narrator. So we hear him speak of God's "favor to me . . . [and] the hand of the Lord my God was on me" (Ezra 7:28). In like manner Nehemiah speaks in first person singular and plural: "So built we the wall. . . . I looked . . ." (Neh 4:6,14).

A storyteller may narrate as a third-person observer. This person sees and hears what people say and do but does not know their hearts and minds except as words and actions may reveal them. Newspaper reporters usually adopt this fly-on-the-wall perspective. They try to be objective or at least want the reader to think they are.

The important thing for the preacher as storyteller is to be consistent in the point of view in any story. If you start out telling the story from the point of view of the protagonist in a story, such as Gulliver in one of *Gulliver's Travels*, be careful not to drop back to the role of a third-person reporter or narrator.

Unity is another important element in any story. A chronological frame of reference gives unity even if the so-called "epic formula" (flashback technique) is used. Unity in storytelling requires integrity of detail; we include only what advances the story and exclude all else. The setting tells *where* we are; the plot tells *what's happening*, and character tells *who* is involved. The question of *why* provides the unifying significance that pulls the other elements together in a coherent whole. The rule of rhetoric is the "test of removability." Submit every character, every scene, and every incident in the story to this test: can the climax occur without this? If the answer is yes, then cut that detail.[4]

Here the preacher must make a decision. How should a preacher apply the point of a narrative? Craddock taught a generation of preachers to tell stories to stimulate reflection. Later everyone may make his or her own application or none at all. This is consistent with the estimate of the person in the pulpit "as one without authority."[5] Grady Davis also, writing earlier about the "story sermon" as one of five organic forms a sermon may take, said, "The listener must draw his own conclusions and make his own application to himself, or he will miss the point of the story. If a

---

[4] Richard E. Hughes and P. Albert Dunamel, *Rhetoric: Principles and Usage* (Englewood Cliffs, NJ: Prentis-Hall,1962), 67.
[5] Fred Craddock, *As One without Authority* (Nashville: Abingdon, 1971).

preacher cannot trust his hearers to do this, he should not use the story form."[6]

The rhetoricians Hughes and Dunamel caution against leaving too much room for individual creativity on the part of those who hear the story: "[In persuasive speech] the point of the story must stand out clearly. . . . Every part of the story must make its contribution. The writer who includes details for the sake of variety runs the risk of distracting the audience and even suggesting another interpretation of the sequence of events."[7]

So there is something to be said for stating the significance blatantly as in the thesis of a sermon or the explication of one of the sermon points. And there is a case to be made for trusting the narrative to do its magic and make the point. The following story about an object lesson might be helpful in deciding. Or not! As the story goes, a teacher took four glass beakers to Bible school and an assortment of earthworms. Two or three worms were placed in each of the beakers of soil. The soil in one of the beakers was saturated with alcohol, one was mixed with chocolate, one with tobacco, and the other remained ordinary dirt. The next day all the worms in the adulterated soil of whatever kind were now dead. The teacher asked if anyone might say what we learn from this. The first answer was: "If you drink and smoke and eat lots of chocolate, you will never have worms!" Be sure *your* story makes *your* point.

Calvin Miller is right to insist that "the preacher must spell out the relationship of every sermon's story to the sermon's text, and the two must make the very same point." "May they not ask for two different morals—if both are noble—to be accepted?" Miller answers firmly, "No, they may not."[8]

What about the parables of Jesus? Were these stories designed mainly to stimulate reflection and to make the truth portable? Or were they like the ideal sermon in homilitician Grady Davis's analogy of the orange tree bearing fruit and flower at the same time? Isn't there in them something of food for "present nourishment" and something also "for the harvest of a distant day"?[9]

---

[6] H. Grady Davis, *Design for Preaching* (Philadelphia: Muhlenberg, 1958), 161.

[7] Hughes and Dunamel, *Rhetoric*, 67.

[8] Calvin Miller, *Preaching: The Art of Narrative Exposition* (Grand Rapids: Baker, 2006), 163.

[9] Davis, ibid., 15–16.

Jesus quoted Isaiah to explain his use of parables. The parables of Jesus, like the ministry of that prophet, reached the hearts of those ready to receive it and veiled the truth from those of hard heart and ready to reject it. To the insiders the secrets were given, but to the outsiders everything was said in parables. Therefore rebellious people "will be ever hearing but never understanding; . . . ever seeing but never perceiving. For this people's heart has become calloused. . . . Otherwise they might see with their eyes, hear with their ears, understand with their hearts and turn, and I would heal them" (Matt 13:14–15, quoting Isa 6:9–10).

A well-crafted story, like a parable of Jesus, can convey spiritual truth to those open to it and yet be just a story to those whose hearts are not ready to let God's truth enter. Therein is its splendor, and there is its risk. To really hear God's message and reject it is to invite judgment. That is risky for the preacher and risky for the congregation.

The Plot as the Essence of Story

All five elements of a story are essential. There must be plot or action. There must be characters or at least a character. And every story has a setting, a point of view, and some sense of unity. Preachers, however, seem to need most help with getting the plot in place. The following is an illustration from a seminary student's sermon. It is a good example of how *not* to tell a story.

> Let me tell you about a particular situation in my own life which left me disoriented and confused for a while. In December of 1982 my wife, my children, and I saw a man jump into the icy waters of a canal to take his own life. The incident has replayed itself in my mind many times, like a slow-motion video. I saw the look of terror on the man's face as he gasped his last breath and then let out a terrifying scream that sent chills to the very depth of my soul. I felt a great loss, even though I didn't know the man. The incident has served to give me an imperative to help people realize that there is hope and that help is available to them . . . through Jesus Christ.

We are moved to sympathy for the seminary family and pity for the suicide victim, but the narrative leaves much to be desired. Like a newspaper account, it gives the whole story in the first two sentences. The rest of the paragraph expands on the lingering shock to the life of the seminarian. A narrative needs a plot that starts with a *situation*, moves right away to something of *stress*, then on to *searching* until we arrive at a *solution* and perhaps a *new situation*. In the student preacher's story, we would like a little more about the setting. What canal? The seminary was in New Orleans near the Intercoastal Waterway for oceangoing vessels. Or perhaps we should think of one of the smaller canals such as connect Lake Pontchartrain with the central city. Was the man on a bridge? We don't even know if it happened in New Orleans, since it happened twelve years before the student wrote this sermon.

"Icy water" suggests wintertime. It might help if the story started with bundling up the children in their cold-weather coats and caps. Where are we going? Out for a walk? Emotionally, we need more setting of the scene. Was this seminarian already a ministerial student when this happened, or does he mean to suggest by his last sentence that this shock was crucial in shaping his sense of vocation? Step 1 in the story is missing; we do not know the starting *situation*. The whole paragraph is step 2, *stress*. Step 3, *search*, is also wanting. We wonder if the student is stalled in step 3, waiting for his own internal stress to play itself out. Certainly the story does not move to a *solution* or a *new situation*. He introduced his wife and children in the beginning, but he did not mention them again. How did this trauma impact them? In this testimony we are left with too many unanswered questions.

Perhaps the student could start the story by describing himself as less caring. Then he could move through the dramatic narrative that expanded his vision. At first he cared for himself and his little family; at the end he answered God's call to compassion for a world filled with desperate souls.[10] We need a plot! The plot is what gives a story a beginning, a middle, and an end. The

---

[10] As it turns out, the incident happened in Mississippi. The family was passing by in an automobile. The children might have been excluded from the story altogether since they were too young to know what was happening except as the reaction of the parents may have impacted the children. The controlling purpose of the story as originally stated in the student sermon was an incident that changed the preacher.

beginning starts everything—the action and sometimes a little of what motivates it. We meet the characters or at least one of them. We discover the setting in time and space. The *middle* of the story is the unfolding of the tension or stress in the story. Characters make choices and do things that have consequences. The *ending* is the resolution of those consequences for better or for worse.

Let's take an example of a narrative with a better plot. Use the Plot Movements Worksheet to mark the progress in the following bit of early history. Move from (1) *situation* to (2) *stress*, to (3) *search*, to (4) *solution* and (5) *the new situation*.

Toward the end of the fourth century in a monastic community lived a monk named Telemachus. He was happy in his peaceful vocation of prayer and Bible study. He also tended a vegetable garden for the cloister.

In time he came to the conviction that God was calling him to the distant city of Rome. It did not seem to make sense for a modest and humble monk to go all the way across Asia to the greatest city in the world. Why would God send him away from his quiet and contented community? Why should he leave his devout companions to go to that pagan center of business and government? The poor monk did not understand God's call, but neither did he doubt it. God was sending him to Rome. So he packed his meager belongings in one knapsack and went to Rome.

He was right about Rome: he didn't fit there. People were preoccupied with pleasure and political power, with violence and amusement. One day he found himself swept along with the crowd into the great Coliseum. He was startled to see one gladiator after another stand before the emperor and say, "We who are about to die salute you!" He could not bear to watch as they battled each other to the death with swords and shields, with trident spears and nets.

He could not stand it! But what could he do? The humble little man in a monk's robe ran and jumped up on top of the perimeter wall and cried, "In the name of Christ stop this! Stop this now!" No one in the vast stadium listened. The fighting and killing went on. Finally he jumped down into the arena and began to go to the combatants. "In the name of Christ, stop this! Stop it!" One gladiator and another pushed him aside with his shield or the heel of his sword. The crowd was not amused. Someone shouted, "Run him

PLOT MOVEMENTS WORKSHEET

1. Situation

2. Stress

5. New Situation

4. Solution

3. Search

through! Kill him!" And with a flash of his blade, a gladiator opened the monk's stomach in one stroke. The little monk sank to his knees and gasped once more, "In the name of Christ . . . stop this!"

Then a strange thing happened. Warriors and watchers alike turned to watch the monk die, his blood turning the sand crimson. This death was different. There was no roar for the victor. Instead the tens of thousands of spectators stood in silence. Then someone in the top tier began to walk down the stone steps to an exit. Then another and another followed. All over the arena spectators began to stream out until the Coliseum was deserted. That was the last time men ever killed each other for entertainment in the Roman arena.[11]

Exercise 1. Scan now the five paragraphs of that story again and label the plot movements in order: *Situation, Stress, Search, Solution,* and *New Situation.* Notice that in this case, the search occupies two long paragraphs, but the new situation is capsuled in a single sentence.

Exercise 2. Describe someone you know well in a one-page sketch. You may include physical appearance, but stretch yourself to write a character sketch. Avoid making summary judgments such as, "She could have been the poster child for the beatitude of Christ, 'Blessed are the pure in heart.'" Try to portray inner character using narrative and dialogue alone.

Exercise 3. Select a parable of Jesus from the Gospel of Luke. Use the Narration Worksheet to analyze the constituent elements of the story: setting, characters, plot, and unifying significance. Can you also name the storyteller's point of view?

---

[11] The Telemachus story is told with some variation in details at least since Foxe's *Book of Martyrs* in the sixteenth century. My version shows the influence of the telling by Chuck Colson and retelling by Chuck Swindoll. Charles W. Colson, *Loving God* (Grand Rapids: Zondervan, 1983), 241–43, cited with revisions in Charles R. Swindoll, *Living on the Ragged Edge: Coming to Terms with Reality* (Waco: Word, 1985), 109–10.

Chapter 3

THE SEVEN BASIC PLOT PLANS

WHAT IF A PREACHER COULD master seven basic templates for storytelling and have in them the pattern for virtually every story that has ever been told? Is it possible that storytellers of countless cultures on every continent and in every era of human history have all told stories in the same basic patterns? Christopher Booker, a British writer and editor, recently completed the magnum opus that he considers his life's work. His hefty tome treats one vital element of storytelling, the plot. It is a remarkable analysis of the plots of hundreds of stories. There are Bible stories as well as Greek myths, fairy tales and Shakespeare, from Beowulf to James Bond, and all in between. Booker believes that every story can be classified into one of seven basic plot plans, each in five stages, which, incidentally, echo nicely the five already diagrammed in my graphic. Booker's seven basic plots are (1) Overcoming the Monster, (2) Rags to Riches, (3) the Quest, (4) Voyage and Return, (5) Comedy, (6) Tragedy, and (7) Rebirth.[1]

---

[1] Christopher Booker, *The Seven Basic Plots: Why We Tell Stories* (London: Continuum, 2004). Others before Booker have noticed the remarkable similarity of plots throughout human history. Samuel Johnson once projected a work he apparently never wrote "to show how small a quantity of real fiction there is in the world." He planned to point out that the same images with very little variation "have served all the authors who have ever written." James Boswell's *Life of Johnson* cited by Booker, 1.

Overcoming the Monster

The story of David and Goliath is in the pattern of an overcoming-the-monster plot. The Philistines threaten to enslave God's people Israel. Their army has a giant of a warrior named Goliath who intimidates all King Saul's troops. Then the little shepherd boy David comes on the scene. With his slingshot and five smooth stones in his pouch, he confronts the monster in the name of the Lord God of hosts, and he prevails.

The earliest recorded story so far discovered is *The Epic of Gilgamesh*. In 1872 a brilliant young worker at the British Museum deciphered the ancient Sumerian cuneiform riddle to let the world hear the story. The kingdom of Uruk is overshadowed by a great and mysterious evil. The monstrous figure is Humbaba in a deep cavern far, far away. The hero, Gilgamesh, will make the perilous journey and confront the monster. His two weapons are a great bow and a mighty axe. He cannot conceivably conquer the mighty monster, yet with supernatural power he does. He saves the kingdom and returns a hero.

The same plot shapes the stories of *Beowulf* and many fairy tales such as Hansel and Gretel and Jack and the Beanstalk. Why do these same patterns pop up in stories all over the world throughout human history? According to one theory, first put forward by Adolf Bastian (1826–1905), the human mind works in certain forms and grooves and around certain basic images. Bastian thought all humans have certain elemental ideas in common. Sigmund Freud in the 1890s, and Carl Jung following him, suggested that psychologically we are all constructed essentially the same.[2] We who are acquainted with the Creator should find this no mystery. Might all these tales be parables of the cosmic struggle of human history? We have an adversary or enemy: "The devil prowls around like a roaring lion" (1 Pet 5:8). We are obliged to resist him, standing firm in the faith. We know that ultimately and eternally we shall prevail but only by the power of Christ.

Although Christopher Booker has made a major contribution to the study of plot in storytelling, there are simpler explications of plot. One attributed to Elmer Rice reduces drama to its simplest

---

[2] Ibid., 10.

form in three acts. Act 1: Get man up tree. Act 2: Throw stones at him. Act 3: Get him down.[3]

In literature "the monster" tends to be not only a "Predator" but what Booker calls a "Holdfast," typically keeping the princess character in his clutches. And he is the "Avenger" ready to retaliate against anyone who challenges. In Jack and the Beanstalk the giant is all three of these. But there is always one limiting weakness or vulnerability. This Achilles' heel is handy for the great reversal in the resolution stage of the story.

The standard ending in monster stories is the thrilling escape from death, "the last enemy to be destroyed" (1 Cor 15:26). This is the goal toward which melodramas drive. So do war stories. World War II stories follow this plot whether they are told as history or as fiction. The movie *The Guns of Navarone*, for example, does not record a historical battle, but it is true to the time and comes across as true to life.

Hollywood westerns use the monster motif over and over with little variation in plot. *High Noon* is a classic example. Gary Cooper's character is about to marry. On the morning of the wedding day, the couple learns that a villain is out of prison and arriving on the noon train to kill him. Several of the killer's companions are already in town waiting to help. The bride makes plans to leave on the same train since she is a devout Quaker who cannot condone violence. Everyone else in town goes into hiding. In the end the bride appears in the street with a rifle and helps her groom defeat the monster gang.

You will find the same five-stage pattern in every James Bond story. First the hero is summoned to headquarters and assigned the case of some new threat to the empire or even the whole world. In this "anticipation stage" he visits the armory to be fitted with the latest secret weapons. There is some initial success on the mission. Booker calls this the "dream stage." Third, there is a confrontation with the enemy in a "frustration stage." The monster reveals his evil plans, usually after Bond is his captive. There is usually a "beautiful princess" type also for Bond to rescue from captivity. The plot escalates to the fourth or "nightmare stage" in a

---

[3] Hallie and Whit Burnett, *Fiction Writer's Handbook* (New York: Harper & Row, 1975), 128.

gauntlet of great danger. Finally, there is the "miraculous escape" and, typically, the death of the monster. If the characters and setting were not changed from story to story, there would only be one James Bond adventure.

Science fiction tends to follow the same five-stage plot of overcoming the monster. The story will begin with arousal of curiosity in the first stage. Then in the "frustration stage" we discover the monster's true deadly nature. This leads to the "nightmare stage" and to a fourth stage when catastrophe seems inevitable. Finally, something or someone appears to provide our escape. The Martians invading Earth in H. G. Wells's *War of the Worlds* were destroyed by bacteria on Earth to which they had no natural resistance. The common cold caught them just in time to save the Earth. George Lucas's *Star Wars* follows this classic plot. Anyone who has read the Bible must see the kinship in the story line. Like Lucifer, Darth Vader led his rebel empire against the Republic's Jedi knights. Darth Vader was himself once a Jedi but rebelled to become the monstrous Black Knight.

All the monster stories have the thrilling escape from death or disaster. It usually comes at the moment of greatest threat. Cartoons often lampoon this fixed formula. Tom and Jerry blow each other up over and over, iron each other flat, or tie each other on a railroad track. Wiley Coyote has an endless supply of mail-order traps for Roadrunner but ends up going over the cliff himself over and over and over again.

Rags to Riches

The Cinderella story is found in literature all over the world and has been for centuries. The plot appears in countless other stories. Horatio Alger Jr. (1832–1899), for example, wrote 135 dime novels and rivaled the storytelling fame of his contemporary Mark Twain. Many of the Alger stories featured down-and-out boys who by hard work and determination pressed on to win the American dream. Often luck and virtue brought the lad to the attention of some wealthy gentleman who, like Cinderella's fairy godmother, could help him achieve his dream.

One thinks of the Bible story of Joseph, rejected by his brothers and sold into Egypt. There he faces many trials including false accusation and prison. But God does not forget Joseph, even though others do. In time Joseph's integrity wins his release and elevation to the position of vice-regent of all Egypt. When his brothers are forced by famine to come to Egypt seeking grain, Joseph is there to be their deliverer.

In popular literature the rags-to-riches plot controls tales like "The Ugly Duckling" and plays like *Pygmalion* (*My Fair Lady*). This is also the formula for *David Copperfield* and for *Superman*. In the days of silent movies, it was the plan for the 1925 Charlie Chaplin movie *The Gold Rush*, which still replays on TV. The ancient Arabic tale of Aladdin and the Lamp is a rags-to-riches plot.

The Quest

Homer's *Odyssey*, Virgil's *Aeneid*, and Dante's *Divine Comedy* are ancient tales built around a great quest. It is a plot that certainly appears in the Bible and classical Christian literature. The exodus is a quest. So is *Pilgrim's Progress*, which unfortunately our generation hardly knows. In John Bunyan's classic, Christian sets out to journey from the City of Destruction to the Celestial City. He has many trials and adventures along the way. He must traverse the Slough of Despond and do battle with Apollyon and Giant Despair before he reaches that final river to cross. Typical of quest stories, he has one or more companions on the journey from time to time. One named Hopeful is there to offer reassurance while Christian is held captive in the dungeon of Doubting Castle. Another is named Faithful and is there with Christian as he crosses that final river.

Sometimes in quest stories the companion figure has complementary traits such as brawn to match the brains of the hero or vice versa. And sometimes the companion is more an alter ego. On the exodus quest, Aaron sometimes plays this subtle role. He is not always the faithful and loyal companion to Moses. While the hero Moses is on the mountain hearing God's voice, Aaron is facilitating the defection of the nation in the worship of the golden calf.[4]

Some see a subtle Christian allegory in Herman Melville's *Moby Dick* (1851). This tale of Captain Ahab and his mad quest to track and kill the great white whale is at least a morality tale. In quest-type plots the hero and companions go through a series of life-threatening ordeals. There are sometimes periods of respite to regain strength and return to the test.

Voyage and Return

Voyage and return is a plot similar to quest. When Booker was doing his monumental "quest" of classifying all stories into basic plots, he found himself with "one intractable pile of stories which did not seem to fit any patterns." They seemed too diverse: *Peter Rabbit* and *Peter Pan*, *Alice in Wonderland*, *Robinson Crusoe*, and the *Wizard of Oz*. "Then the penny dropped," he said, "that all these stories were in fact shaped by the same plot," which he named "voyage and return."[5] He placed in the same category H. G. Wells's *The Time Machine* and Margaret Mitchell's *Gone with the Wind*.

Jesus used this plot outline in some of his most enduring parables. Think of the prodigal son as just one example. Typical of this genre, the hero is changed by his journey and homecoming. It should not be a stretch to think of the whole story of Christ in this pattern. The incarnation, the cross, resurrection, and ascension employ this pattern as well as in the quest pattern just mentioned. Believers live in hope today between the ascension and the second coming as our Lord's voyage and promised return.

In literature typically the five stages of voyage and return follow one plan. First, there is an "anticipation stage." The central figures, hero or heroine or both, find themselves suddenly removed out of their comfortable life into some strange new world. Next is what Booker calls a "dream stage." They explore their new and strange environment with fascination. The "frustration stage" comes third as the adventure turns oppressive and rapidly becomes alarming.

---

[4] Booker, *Seven Basic Plots*, 83.
[5] Ibid., 5.

The "nightmare stage" is next, when they wonder if they can possibly survive, and we wonder with them. Finally, when the threat seems to have no way out comes the "escape stage," which ends in the return home. This plot often has a bit of epilogue, while we decide if they were really changed by their adventure. Maybe it was all just a dream. To have a happy ending, we want them to grow and resolve problems by the voyage and return. It is satisfying if the ordeal makes them more loving—at least toward each other.

In many stories what Booker calls the "nightmare stage" is not clearly distinct from the earlier "frustration stage." One writing instructor recommends a simple two-step plot. Step 1: put your characters in hot water. Step 2: turn up the heat. In any case, the storyteller creates stress or conflict in the story which tends to escalate before it finds resolution.[6]

Comedy and Tragedy

Comedy and tragedy are two separate types of plot that we may treat briefly since they are more important to a study of Shakespeare than to preaching. Indeed, one theory of the development of Romeo and Juliet is that the bard started out to write a comedy but that it ended up a tragedy since his main characters were never successful in their plan to be married. Instead of ending with a wedding, they both ended up dead. Of course, comedy may be serious also. The novels of Jane Austin seem to echo her own troubled life. On the other hand, comedy may be little more than slapstick, as in Laurel and Hardy movies. Tragedy as a love story is basically the same as comedy except that the story does not end as happy-ever-after. It ends with someone dead.

In the five stages of a tragedy plot, the main character finds a focus in the "anticipation stage." It will be something or someone that will bring satisfaction. In the "dream stage" he makes his pact with the devil—or whatever development makes it seem as though his goal is just around the corner. The third stage, or "frus-

---

[6] Jane McBride Choate, "Conflict: The Secret to Great Children's Fiction," *The Writer* (April 2006): 26–27.

tration" stage, may come on gradually. Perhaps he slowly realizes that there are teeth in that contract with the devil; he may never get out. The "nightmare stage" is all downhill. Things rapidly escalate out of control. His doom seems sealed. Finally, the tragedy ends in death or destruction of some kind. *Macbeth* is the classic tragedy.

Sometimes history tells stories in this pattern. Bonnie and Clyde were real characters. They played out their tragedy not far from where I pen these lines, and their story follows the plot outline exactly. I don't know if I have ever used them as a sermon illustration, but anyone who does would do well to sketch their story in the fivefold plot of the classic tragedy.

In the earlier plot plans we have considered, the hero or heroine receives a "call" in the first stage, and we know he or she should accept it. In a tragedy we know they should *not* accept the call. It is a temptation that if entertained can lead only to ruin. When Faustus ends his inner struggle by making his pact with the devil, we know the story can end only in tragedy no matter how much struggle may ensue.

Samson is a Bible story that is written in this ancient pattern. With so much promise in the beginning, he makes wrong choices. Physical strength, even supernatural strength, does not make up for moral weakness. When he falls in love with a prostitute, it seems he might get away with it, but she proves to be his downfall. The Philistines seize him and soon blind him and treat him like a big ox forced to roll the millstone to grind their grain. The story ends with Samson in their arena for their cruel sport. In a final act of mass murder against his enemies and his own suicide, Samson pulls down the supporting columns and turns the coliseum into rubble (see Judg 13–16).[7]

Rebirth

Booker's final basic plot of the seven is certainly one every preacher should study carefully. We encounter the rebirth story in fairy tales like Sleeping Beauty and Snow White. These two have similar story lines in the same rebirth plot. Each of these heroines

---

[7] Cf. Booker, *Seven Basic Plots*, 186–87.

is born a princess, but each soon has a dark shadow threaten her well-being. After a web of waiting and foreboding, each falls prey to the dreaded curse and seems to die. But finally a hero comes by and awakens the beautiful princess, who falls in love with her hero and marries him.

Other fairy tales in the rebirth pattern include the Frog Prince and Beauty and the Beast. They resonate with us because they say something about the redeeming power of love. A true classic is Charles Dickens's *A Christmas Carol*. Morley is dead, and Scrooge is as good as dead when the story opens. There is not a graying ember of human kindness in him even at Christmastime. But on Christmas Eve Scrooge has a visit from three apparitions in order—the Ghost of Christmas Past, the Ghost of Christmas Present, and the Ghost of Christmas Future. In the last nightmare he realizes that he himself is dead and appropriately unmourned. He awakens to discover that these three visitors have all come in the same nightmare, and it is now Christmas Day. It is not too late for him to repent of his money-grubbing self-absorption. He is soon off to visit his clerk Bob Cratchit and family including Tiny Tim, their crippled son. Scrooge brings the biggest Christmas turkey in town and a radically changed disposition. He announces a long-overdue raise for his clerk. The storyteller assures us this transformation continued for the rest of his natural life.

Stories of rebirth are so akin to the heart of the gospel story, and they abound throughout literature. *Silas Marner, Crime and Punishment*, and others begin with a young hero falling under the shadow of some dark power. At first he seems to suffer no great harm. Then the power takes him down, down, down toward destruction. In the third stage our hero is in total darkness and alone. The next stage is the climax of the crisis that sets the stage for the great reversal. Finally, the hero finds rebirth. The storytellers do not often make this rebirth explicitly Christian salvation, though Dostoyevsky does in *Crime and Punishment*. Raskolnikov committed cold-blooded murder just to see if he could do such a thing and to see if he could get away with it. It sounds like some of the depravity we read about in the newspapers daily. But in the end of the story Raskolnikov discovers love for Sonia, who followed him to Siberia. Then he reads the story of Lazarus in her New Testament. The novelist ends the story with the convict, wondering if it is possible that Jesus might raise him to new life also.[8] Rebirth stories provide narrative illustrations of the gospel story. They picture Christ in His death, burial, and resurrection. And like Christian baptism, they also picture the death to sin of a Christian, putting away the old life and rising to new life in Christ.

In this chapter we have noted that the plan of action or plot for any story will move through five stages in order. We may call these situation, stress, searching, solution, and new situation. Others, including Christopher Booker, have noted a quite limited number of variations on this plan. Booker's *Seven Basic Plots* appear over and over through the ages and across diverse cultures.

Exercise 1. Select a narrative from any storybook except the Bible. It may be a children's bedtime story or one from a collection of short stories. It may be a full novel you have already read. With the help of the Plot Movements Worksheet, sketch the moves from the opening situation through the five stages to the solution and new situation.

Exercise 2. Do the same thing with a Bible story of your choice. It may be an Old Testament narrative or one of the major parables of Jesus or some other story in Scripture. How well does it fit the pattern?

Exercise 3. Look at a narrative or two in one of your recent sermons. Can you label the five stages of the plot? Did you skip any stages or get any of them out of order? The novice tends to give a "headline" introduction to the story that gives away the ending. "Did you hear about the woman who was so mad at her husband she parked his BMW in their swimming pool?" Oops! I think we just heard the whole story; spare us the details of the narrative.

---

[8] See ibid., 200–1.

Chapter 4

TELLING YOUR OWN STORY

A PREACHER NEEDS TO BE ready to tell three personal stories. The pulpit is not the only place a pastor will need to tell them, but these three will be an important part of your pulpit ministry. First, you need to be able to tell your own conversion experience. Second, you need also to be able to bear witness to God's daily dealing with you. Such stories from your pilgrimage might include communicating your understanding of vocation, confessing your struggles, your victories, and your defeats as you grow in grace. And third, a pastor needs to be able to convey to his church what is commonly called the vision story.

Your Personal Testimony

People to whom you preach want to know who you are. They *need* to know you. Besides, as we discuss elsewhere, there is probably nothing as persuasive as personal testimony. Madison Avenue learned many years ago the power of testimony in marketing. The "overheard" testimonial for a product has more impact than the direct sales pitch, but even "the talking head" has some persuasive power if it is framed as a testimonial. If this ever ceases to be the case, you will know it by the absence of such ads on television; corporate decision makers will quit spending megabucks on such ads.

I grew up the middle child of three children. When our father was away in the Navy, an uncle made it his duty to come and get the three of us every Sunday morning and take us to church. He was searching for a suitable church in those years, so he took us with him for a while to a Church of God, then to a Christian church, finally to a Baptist church.

Along the way I received such Bible instruction as was afforded a child in the church and Sunday school and not much at home beyond morals and manners. By the time I was 10 or 11 years old, I understood enough of the gospel to know that I was a sinner in need of Christ the Savior. And about as soon as I really understood that, I placed my trust in Christ alone. If my salvation were dependant on my ability to date the moment of my new birth, as some traveling evangelists insist, I would be hopelessly lost. It was real in my life, nonetheless.

I do remember the Sunday I went home from church and asked permission to join the church and be baptized. My mother, who was not yet a believer, tried to impress me with the seriousness of this decision but gave her permission. My older brother heard the conversation and came into the room to say he wanted to do likewise. So the next Sunday morning while the congregation sang an invitation hymn, we both walked to the altar where the pastor stood to receive us.

I do not recall the pastor's words on that occasion, nor mine, but a few weeks later we were notified there would be a Sunday evening baptismal service. My baptism is still vivid in my memory. We dressed in white baptismal robes and waited our turn with several others. When it was my turn to be immersed, I remember standing in the water as the pastor recited my name in his baptismal formula: "Austin Tucker, upon your profession of faith in the Lord Jesus Christ as your personal Savior, I baptize you in the name of the Father and of the Son and of the Holy Ghost. Amen. 'We are buried, therefore, by baptism into death and raised to walk in newness of life.'"

My older brother was standing at the top of the baptistery steps waiting his turn. With a puzzled expression he asked me, "Austin, why are you crying?" I did not answer, of course, and could not have put into words then the sentiment of my heart. Deep inside I knew that for me this was more than just a religious ritual. I understood that the water was not washing my heart new and clean; Christ had already done that. Still, I counted this as a turning point in my life. It was a public dedication of my whole life to Jesus my Savior. Certainly I had a lot to learn about what that meant, but I was glad for everyone to know that I belonged to Jesus now. That is my personal testimony of conversion. Your own story may resonate on certain notes in that story and be very different at other places.

In another chapter we will talk about the power of story to persuade. In this context let us note why personal testimony has particular persuasive power. Part of the reason is that personal testimony, honestly told, makes a person more human and more believable. Without personal stories, traits of personality remain invisible; and the preacher, therefore, remains a stranger. Your story reveals who you are.

In most evangelical traditions, before you may be ordained, the church or a council will ask you to relate your call to Christ and your call to preach. Then also any church that considers inviting you to be their pastor will likely ask the same. Actually, the call to preach is not a story often told except in these two settings. It seems the apostle Paul often told his Damascus Road experience and the sequel to that in his call to be an apostle. But he was often under attack by those who doubted his commission to apostleship.[1]

A personal story does more than demonstrate who you are. Perhaps nothing is more convincing than a personal testimony. Any believer should be able to tell his or her testimony of salvation. If you are not sure you can do so, pause now to take a clean sheet of paper and make a few notes under each of these four headings: first, what my life was like before I met Christ; second, how I came to know that I needed a Savior; third, how I came to trust Christ; and finally, what my life has been like since then.

Stories from Your Pilgrimage

Your testimony does not end with your conversion experience. That is really the beginning. The story of the apostle Paul's conversion is told three times in the Acts of the Apostles (Acts 9:1–19; 22:1–22; 26:4–23). First, Luke narrates the history. Then Luke

[1] Some evangelical traditions consider the vocational decision to be a matter of personal preference more than divine call. The Christian Church, Disciples of Christ, some Presbyterian traditions, and others may take this approach.

records the testimony Paul delivered from the steps of Fortress Antonio in Jerusalem adjacent to the temple area. On this occasion a riot interrupted him when he uttered the word *Gentiles*. The third time is when Paul gave witness in court before Agrippa and Bernice. He took the opportunity to give them his testimony of conversion to Christ. In addition, testimonies of God's ongoing grace abound in Paul's letters. For example, the apostle spoke of finding God's promised grace sufficient for whatever "thorn" in his flesh tormented him (2 Cor 12:1–10). And in his letter to the Galatians, Paul gave considerable detail of his Christian pilgrimage in defending his apostolic authority.

Many preachers are uncomfortable talking about themselves. Some of us probably need to do more of it. But might a preacher talk too much about himself or herself? Yes, of course. A preacher might talk so much of himself that he would come across as a little too self-absorbed. If the story holds the speaker up as an example too often, some will think the preacher a little too pious. On the other hand, a preacher can overdo the "true confessions" theme. I recall an incidental comment in a sermon from Luke 15 that I made once. I mentioned that I had a hard time loving hypocrites. It did not seem to me to be a deep dark confession since the point of that chapter was that Jesus even loved the hypocrites. One dear and devout brother missed that main point completely in his distress that his pastor had a hard time loving hypocrites. When self-revelation might be too much a barrier to communication, telling the story of others may meet the need.

The preacher may prefer to retell his story in third-person pronouns instead of the normal first-person shape of a true testimony. Occasionally it is effective to tell the story in the words of the principal person. In this case two precautions need attention. Do not switch back and forth from "I" to "he." And be sure to make clear to those listening that this is not *your* story but one you are telling in the words of the one who told it. You might need to do that at the beginning and again at the end of the testimony for those who are not giving full attention. You might introduce it by saying something like this: Let me tell you about a spiritual crisis in the life of James McConkey, one of my favorite Bible teachers and writers of a hundred years ago. It began as a financial crisis when he was a young businessman. Let me tell it in his own words. McConkey said:

> In my early life I entered into a partnership with a friend in a wholesale ice business. Both of us were young men and had invested all we had, and considerably more, in the business. As time passed we met with disappointments. For two seasons in succession our ice was swept away by winter thaws. Things had come to a serious pass. It seemed very necessary that we should have ice in the winter of which I now speak. The weather became very cold. The ice formed and grew thicker and thicker, until it was ready to gather. I remember the joy that came into our hearts one afternoon when an order came for thousands of tons of ice which would lift us entirely out from our financial distress.
>
> Not long before, God had shown me the truth of committal. He had impressed me that I was to commit my business to Him and absolutely trust Him with it. And I did, as best I knew how. I never dreamed that such testing would come. And so I lay down that Saturday night in quietness. But, at midnight there came an ominous sound—rain! By morning it was pouring in torrents. I looked at the river from my home on the hillside. Yellow streaks of water were creeping over the ice. I knew what it meant. The water was at flood stage. The same condition had twice swept our ice away before. By noon the storm was raging in all its violence, and by afternoon I was facing a great spiritual crisis.
>
> It may seem strange that a spiritual crisis would come over something seemingly trivial. But I have learned that a matter, though seemingly trivial, may have a profound and far-reaching impact on one's life. And so it was with me. By mid-afternoon I had come face to face with the fact that deep in my heart was a spirit of rebellion against God. That rebelliousness seemed to develop through a suggestion to my heart like this: *You gave everything to God. You say you are*

going to trust God with your business. Is this the way He rewards you? Your business will be swept away, and tomorrow you will come into a place of desperate financial distress. And I found my heart growing bitter at the prospect of God taking away my business when I only wanted it for legitimate purposes. Then another voice whispered: *My child, did you mean it when you said you would trust me? Can you trust me in the dark as well as in the light? Would I do anything, or suffer anything to come into your life which would not work out for your good?* Then came the other voice: *But it is hard. Why shouldn't God spare your ice? Why should He take your business when it is clean and honest and you want to use it in the right way?* It was a very plausible sort of voice, and for the moment I did not detect the serpent hiss in the word *why*.

Back and forth, with ever increasing intensity waged one of the greatest spiritual battles of my life. At the end of two hours, I was able to cry out by the grace of God, *Take the business; take the ice; take everything; only give me the supreme blessing of a fully submitted will.* Then came peace.

The storm was still raging and flooding my ice. But it did not seem to matter whether it continued raining or not. Then and there I discovered that the secret of anxious care was not in surroundings but in the failure of allowing life and will to not be wholly given to Him regardless of circumstances or surroundings.

That night I slept in perfect peace. The rain continued to pour down on my ice, and it seemed my business would lie ruined in the morning. But it did not. At midnight there came another sound, the sound of the wind. By morning the worst blizzard of the year was upon us. By evening the mercury had fallen to zero. And in a few days we were harvesting the finest ice.

God did not want my ice. But He did want my yielded will and absolute trust in Him. When the matter of yielding my will had been settled, He gave back the ice. Not only that, but He blessed the business, and led me on, and out, until He finally guided me from it entirely and into the place He had chosen for me from the beginning: a teacher of His word. If you give your life to God, will God ruin it? No! As you trust in Jesus Christ, God will restore, enrich and glorify your life as never before.[2]

That is an unusually long story for a sermon illustration. If the preacher wants to use it in a shorter version, it might be better to retell it from the less-personal stance of a third party. "In his early life before he became a Bible teacher, James McConkey went into the wholesale ice business. In those days before refrigeration, ice was harvested in the dead of winter and transported many miles to be kept in ice cellars for use throughout the summer. One winter . . ." and so on.

There are other advantages to recasting the story into third person, but it forfeits much of its value as a testimony. You may omit unnecessary detail such as the friend in the partnership. He plays no role at all in the spiritual struggle that the story is all about. You may also add helpful detail such as the explanation of how ice business was possible before the invention of refrigeration. If you recast the story, preserve dialogue and detail enough to make the story real. You should never have to say, "This is a true story."

A story of self-disclosure may be a powerful influencer. If I trust you enough to be open about my flaws, maybe you will trust me with yours. The New Testament tells us to confess our sins to each other and to pray for each other as a way to healing (see Jas 5:13–16). There is power in openness to make broken persons whole. There is a limit, however, to how much a preacher should "unzip the viscera," as Calvin Miller calls such confessional preaching. One needs to beware of the "sin-as-entertainment syndrome."[3]

Your testimony does more than tell others who you are; it may also tell them why you are here. Those you seek to influence naturally question your motives. If the preacher tries to hide legitimate

---

[2] James H. McConkey, *The Surrendered Life* (Pittsburgh, PA: Silver, 1923).
[3] "The strongest kind of preaching is confessional," says Miller, but he cautions against letting sin "take center stage instead of the grace of God." George Henson, *Baptist Standard* (TX), quoted in *Western Recorder* (KY), January 11, 2005.

self-interest, the congregation is not deceived. Everyone has some self-interest. That is acceptable if we are candid and honest.

Imagine the CEO of an Internet technology company making $5 million a year plus bonuses. He has the opportunity to merge his company into a much larger company. This will drive the price of his stock up dramatically. His stock options will reward him with many millions of dollars more when the deal goes through. He needs and wants the support of his whole company. Members of his senior staff have incentive enough in stock options of their own, but what will motivate the rest of the employees? They might expect the larger company to gobble them up and spit many of them out as unnecessary duplication. Shall the CEO give them a pep talk about what's best for the company? He might as well tell them they are all stupid. That is in fact the message they would hear. He would be well advised to start by honestly admitting his own self-interest. They will not believe anything else until that truth is out.

Annette Simmons, in her very helpful book *The Story Factor*, tells of a businessman from Lebanon who came to America at age 13. He worked as a busboy in a restaurant while he taught himself a few more English words every day. He admired the Americans with big cars, fine clothes, and happy families. Could it ever happen to him? He did succeed beyond all the dreams of his teenage mind. Today he likes to tell his story. With a glint in his eye, he ends saying he now has "new and improved dreams." Is that self-interest? Of course, but he is honest about it. He is not hiding anything. That enables people to trust him. Preachers too need to learn to tell the personal testimony that tells who we are and why we are here.

This is why so many visiting preachers start with a joke. Especially at conventions where many will hear them for the first time, they begin with a humorous story. Are they suggesting that they need not be taken seriously? Some who listen may think so! Actually they are trying to say, "You may listen to me; I won't bore you. Even if you do not know me, you can trust me." Of course, a speaker might begin in just those words. It would not be as convincing as a story.

Before we move another step, a question needs to be addressed. When does a testimony belong in a sermon? The answer: only when the narrative faithfully presents the truth of God's Word or at least illustrates that divine truth. It is not enough that the narrative is true, interesting, even moving. It is not enough that it be a faithful witness to a vital religious experience. Does it communicate the Word of God? That's what makes a sermon. There are books and magazines aplenty filled with interesting stories in first-person testimony format. Everyone has opinions about religion, and many are willing to tell them. The preacher's task is to keep in mind the question King Zedekiah asked Jeremiah. It is ever the question of those who gather to hear a sermon: "Is there any word from the Lord?" And let the preacher be sure to answer, "There is!" (Jer 37:17).

The Vision Story

After they hear who you are and why you are here, people need to hear from the pastor the vision story. Literature on leadership has much to say about the importance of "casting the vision." This is a task for religious leaders as well as those in business, in government and every other pursuit. Casting the vision is a matter of having a dream of what ought to be done and inspiring others to share the same dream and help make it come true. The leader's vision must become a shared vision.

Nehemiah was a leader who shared the story in such a way as to enlist the aid of others. He was greatly distressed about the news of Jerusalem lying in ruins. In the providence of God, he was able to move King Artaxerxes to care too and to grant Nehemiah leave to do something about it. Not only did the king grant permission for his loyal aid to make the journey to Jerusalem, he also gave him official letters of safe-conduct and authorization to restore the city walls. Once in Jerusalem, Nehemiah was able to share the vision and enlist the help of the local population. The work moved forward in spite of great opposition by Sanballat and other foes. Nehemiah was a leader who had a vision of what needed to be done and the gift of moving others to share the vision and work together to see it done.

A pastor may have a vision of a new church growing to five thousand excited worshippers in a new worship center at the intersection of interstate highways. But that's his vision! Can the people see that happening? As Annette Simmons put it, "Hey, if they don't *see* the vision, it ain't a vision."[4] The pastor's vision must

---

[4] Annette Simmons, *The Story Factor: Inspiration, Influence, and Persuasion through the Art of Storytelling* (Cambridge, MA: Perseus, 2001), 15.

become their vision. How does that happen? Storytelling is one powerful means to that end.

On August 28, 1963, a quarter million people or more gathered near the Lincoln Memorial in Washington. They were there to rally "for jobs and freedom." One of the speakers on the program was a young preacher and civil rights leader named Martin Luther King Jr. Also on the platform at that rally was singer Mahalia Jackson. As she tells it, King was a relatively unknown soldier in the ranks of the Civil Rights Movement. He was laboring that day in a sermon that did not seem to be connecting. Miss Jackson, from her seat on the platform in the second row behind him, called to him, "The dream, Martin! Tell them about the dream!" Whether he had planned to do so or not, King did launch into his I-have-a-dream litany with pathos and passion. He successfully cast the vision of what America could be like in his generation or the next if racial prejudice were overcome.

> Let us not wallow in the valley of despair. I say to you today my friends—so even though we face the difficulties of today and tomorrow, I still have a dream. It is a dream deeply rooted in the American dream.
>
> I have a dream that one day this nation will rise up and live out the true meaning of its creed: "We hold these truths to be self-evident, that all men are created equal."
>
> I have a dream that one day on the red hills of Georgia the sons of former slaves and the sons of former slave owners will be able to sit down together at the table of brotherhood.
>
> I have a dream that one day even the state of Mississippi, a state sweltering with the heat of injustice, sweltering with the heat of oppression, will be transformed into an oasis of freedom and justice.
>
> I have a dream that my four little children will one day live in a nation where they will not be judged by the color of their skin but by the content of their character.
>
> I have a dream today. I have a dream that one day down in Alabama, with its vicious racists, with its governor having his lips dripping with the words of interposition and nullification—one day right there

in Alabama little black boys and black girls will be able to join hands with little white boys and white girls as sisters and brothers.

I have a dream today. I have a dream that one day every valley shall be exalted, and every hill and mountain shall be made low, the rough places will be made plain, and the crooked places will be made straight, and the glory of the Lord shall be revealed and all flesh shall see it together.

This is our hope. This is the faith that I go back to the South with. With this faith we will be able to hew out of the mountain of despair a stone of hope. With this faith we will be able to transform the jangling discords of our nation into a beautiful symphony of brotherhood. With this faith we will be able to work together, to pray together, to struggle together, to go to jail together, to stand up for freedom together, knowing that we will be free one day.

This will be the day, this will be the day when all of God's children will be able to sing with new meaning "My country 'tis of thee, sweet land of liberty, of thee I sing. Land where my fathers died, land of the Pilgrim's pride, from every mountainside, let freedom ring!"

And if America is to be a great nation, this must become true. And so let freedom ring from the prodigious hilltops of New Hampshire. Let freedom ring from the mighty mountains of New York. Let freedom ring from the heightening Alleghenies of Pennsylvania. Let freedom ring from the snow-capped Rockies of Colorado. Let freedom ring from the curvaceous slopes of California.

But not only that; let freedom ring from Stone Mountain of Georgia. Let freedom ring from Lookout Mountain of Tennessee. Let freedom ring from every hill and molehill of Mississippi—from every mountainside. Let freedom ring. And when this happens, and when we allow freedom to ring—when we let it ring from every village and every hamlet, from every state and every city, we will be able to speed up that day when all of God's children—black men and white men, Jews and Gentiles, Protestants and Catholics—will be able to join hands and sing in the words of the old Negro spiritual: "Free at last! Free at last! Thank God Almighty, we are free at last!"[5]

When I was a teenager, I came under the influence of a visionary leader named N. A. Woychuk. He was a Presbyterian pastor and founder of a Scripture memory plan that used a contest and rewards for motivation. It started as a ministry to youth but grew to involve children and adults of all ages. The plan prescribed weekly recitations of Scripture and recognized achievement with regular incentive rewards of Christian books, plaques, and games. A grand reward for all who successfully completed the 12-week course was a week at summer camp. There the campers studied the Scriptures they had memorized. Age-graded classes blended with a full schedule of recreation and other camping activities.

Dr. Woychuk at this writing is in his nineties and still active, and he is still a master of telling the vision story. He still chronicles the history of that early ministry including how God wonderfully provided funds and workers for the building of the first camp in northwest Louisiana in time for the first summer assembly. It seemed God gave one miracle after another, building the cabins around a lake, drilling a well for fresh water and building a water tower, preparing a dining hall and place of assembly. So the camp was named Miracle Camp. In time the work grew with camps in Georgia, Missouri, California, then on across the oceans. Dr. Woychuk would tell the story and move seamlessly from the narrative of what God had already done in this ministry to his vision of what yet remained to be done. He had the ability to inspire others with his dream by telling the story.

A story that we have in common with others makes us one people. In this way story creates community. We have fellowship only if we are fellows in the same ship. And the more we participate

---

[5] Distribution statement: Accepted as part of the Douglass Archives of American Public Address (http://douglass.speech.nwu.edu) on May 26, 1999. Prepared by D. Oetting (http://nonce.com/oetting). Permission is hereby granted to download, reprint, and/or otherwise redistribute this file, provided this distribution statement is included and appropriate point of origin credit is given to the preparer and Douglass. Online at http://usinfo.state.gov/usa/infousa/facts/democrac/38.htm.

in the same history, the greater is our common life together. In a very broad bond we are altogether in the human family. But there is the narrower family unit of husband and wife, parents and children, brothers and sisters. The New Testament church in its local expression is a family of believers called out of the world and gathered around Christ our Savior. We share a common family; God is our heavenly Father (Eph 3:14). We are brothers and sisters to one another (1 John 3:14–18). Together we worship, work, and bear witness as a community with a common story and a common goal—if we catch the vision.

Preachers, like all leaders, need to know where they want to take those who follow. That is the first task of the leader. Then they need skill in communicating that goal and moving others to make the pilgrimage together. The vision story may both inform and inspire.

This chapter has introduced three kinds of narrative that every preacher needs to be able to use. Before moving to the next chapter, complete at least one of these three exercises

Exercise 1. Take the time to put your own personal testimony of salvation into words on paper. Put enough detail to give a stranger a picture of what your life was like before Christ, how you came to know you needed a Savior, how you came to the moment of commitment, and a little of how your life has been different since then.

Exercise 2. Select a story from your Christian pilgrimage. It may be a very recent milestone marker, or it might be the narrative of an earlier turning point that made a major and lasting difference in your life.

Exercise 3. If you have a clear vision of where you believe God wants your church to be going, give some prayerful thought to how you might communicate that vision in a story. It might begin with how you personally came to be a part of this church. Did you come to embrace a vision that others in the fellowship had before you joined them? Or was the fellowship drifting without purpose waiting for a leader to come along? In either case, how will you as a leader inform and inspire the fellowship to unite in pursuit of a common destiny?

Chapter 5

THE PERSUASIVE POWER OF TESTIMONY

A FRIEND OF DOUGLAS ADAMS was on a Royal Commission in England with Aldus Huxley, also a member. They were studying together in a little country town when Sunday came. Professor Huxley said to the friend, "I suppose you are going to church." And when the friend replied in the affirmative, Huxley proposed, "What if, instead, you stayed at home and talked to me of religion?"

"No," was the reply, "for I am not clever enough to refute your arguments."

"But what if you simply told me your own experience of what religion has done for you?" The friend did not go to church that morning; he stayed home and told the famous agnostic the story of all that Christ had been to him. After a while there were tears in Huxley's eyes as he said, "I would give my right hand if I could believe that!"[1]

Most preachers and Bible teachers depend on deductive logic to convince their hearers. Major premise: All that the Bible says is true (usually inferred only). Minor premise: The Bible says "X." Conclusion: therefore, "X" is true. A syllogism is a useful tool for the preacher to *arrive at a truth*, but it is not the best way to *convey the truth*. Stories, however, express truth in a unified package somewhat like a masterpiece on canvas. The truth enters the imagination and finds a home in the soul. As David Michael Phelps put

---

[1] F. W. Boreham, *A Handful of Stars* (Philadelphia: Judson, 1922), 128.

it, "Stories . . . contain a totality of an idea *along with a unifying beauty, an emotional power that snuggles an idea in to the head by way of the heart*."[2] A story holds together and holds ideas in a way that an argument never can. And when the storyteller has led us to the end of his drama, we see the whole he is showing us in a way an argument never could show us.

Some strongly object to a preacher's using anything that might persuade or convince unless it is the quoting of a biblical authority or the cold logic of a syllogism. They consider it manipulation in the tradition of Madison Avenue's "hidden persuaders." This chapter will deal with these critics of effective preaching and offer a distinction between manipulation, which is never acceptable, and persuasion, which certainly is.

The Psychology of Storytelling

Twenty-first century Western civilization is not much moved by logical arguments but does make life-shaping decisions based on emotional arguments. Oxford University Press published Norman Holland's important study in the psychology of communication. He demonstrated "that storytellers possess a powerful tool for communicating as they address significant psychological depths within the reader." Story addresses basic human needs "for gratification, tension management, and self-identification." The typical modern sermon combines a rhetorical structure borrowed from the age of Scholasticism and logical arguments equally out of touch with twenty-first century patterns of thinking. Such patterns today are more likely to stimulate resistance to persuasion. "A story sermon, however, stirs the imagination and invites the listener to become a participant in the preaching event." If we know that the story is make-believe, we are able to relax and "to suspend our disbelief." Ironically, our knowledge that we are entering the world of the unreal makes the message more real. We are free to respond in faith to eternal truth made known to us through the make-believe. Steven Shuster frames

---

[2] David Michael Phelps, "The Leaky Bucket: Why Conservatives Need to Learn the Art of Story," *Religion & Liberty* (Spring 2007): 10–11.

this paradox: "It is a conscious disbelief that becomes suspension of disbelief."[3]

Some object to stories in preaching as condescending and unworthy of the modern congregation's mentality. Shuster argues to the contrary that "the story preacher assumes a less condescending posture than the didactic preacher." The narrative offers "truth as an experience" and invites everyone to share the experience. The alternative is to assume the listener will accept the right beliefs if the preacher addresses the congregation with logic. Shuster argues that "the listener discovers meaning less at the hands of the preacher than from the story itself"[4]

John MacArthur is one who believes that the preacher should only address the congregation with logic and rely on the Holy Spirit to take the Word of God and use it in the transformation of souls. He objects to all storytelling in preaching as unworthy manipulation of people. His theology of preaching has no place for an appeal to emotions. He believes a preacher should work only on the reasoning mind of the hearer and in this only by explaining the meaning of Scripture. Lest anyone be influenced by the preacher's oratorical ability or human wisdom, any "tear-jerking story" is anathema. He appeals to Paul's testimony to the Corinthians: "When I came to you, brothers, I did not come with eloquence or superior wisdom as I proclaimed to you the testimony about God. . . . I came to you in weakness and fear, and with much trembling. My message and my preaching were not with wise and persuasive words, but with a demonstration of the Spirit's power, so that your faith might not rest on men's wisdom, but on God's power" (1 Cor 2:1,3–5).[5] Others of Paul's fellow missionaries at Corinth did make use of their own gifts for public address. Apollos was "a native of Alexandria . . . a learned man, with a thorough knowledge of the Scriptures . . . [who] spoke with great fervor . . . [and] vigorously refuted the Jews in public

---

[3] Steven Shuster, "Story Preaching: The Literary Artist's Gift to Preachers," *The Journal of Communication and Religion* 12 (March 1989): 24. Shuster cites the important study by Norman N. Holland, *The Dynamics of Literary Response* (New York: Oxford University Press, 1968), 66–67.

[4] Ibid., 26.

[5] John MacArthur Jr., "Altar Calls," a message delivered at Grace Community Church Panorama City, California, 1992. Available at www.biblebb.com/files/ MAC/ALTAR. HTM.

debate, proving from the Scriptures that Jesus was the Christ" (Acts 18:24,28). In addition, it seems misguided and shortsighted to exalt human logic at the expense of a channel of communication like storytelling with its distinguished history. If there were no history of storytelling beyond the Bible, that would seem to be overflowing support for the practice. Any form of communication, including narrative, has hazards. We turn attention now to one of the stones in the path of the storyteller with a look at the danger of misuse of testimony.

A Testimony Sermon

There is always a danger that a preacher's use of story may persuade contrary to the truth as it is in Christ. This is a greater hazard when the preacher uses personal testimony as the shape of the narrative. The example that follows is a seminary chapel message. I personally transcribed the recorded address and believe that the synopsis I offer here is a faithful summary only slightly abridged. The speaker was one of my seminary professors whom I greatly respected, but he will be unnamed since he is still living today as are most of the principals mentioned. Also, I wish to conclude this exercise by showing why I believe this is a good example of bad use of testimony. It is an example of the persuasive power of story, nevertheless. All the names of people and places in the address have been changed.

A Chapel Message

I want to read a passage of Scripture, not to exegete it, but to remind those of us whom God has called that we have a hard time loving and ministering to all of the people whom He loves and to whom He ministers. "At that moment the disciples returned and were astonished to find him talking to a woman. But none of them said 'What do you want' or 'Why are you talking to her?' The woman put down her water jar, went away to the town where she said to the people, 'Come see a Man who told me everything I ever did'" (John 4:27–29, NKJV). And I want to remind you this town was full of people who told her everything she had ever done, and she despised them! The elliptical phrase is "Come see a man who's told me everything I ever did and still feels God loves me."

I'm going to share with you from the beginning how we got into a ministry to the formerly married. It was *not* our purpose! We were shoved into it. We were like the chaplain in the airborne division who was asked how many times he had jumped. He said, "None! I was shoved out the door every time."

When I went to old First Church, I began to put together a staff. Ted came to be my associate as minister to students and single adults. Soon our church bought an office building two doors away from us. While we renovated it, Ted enlisted and trained 87 adults in our church for 13 weeks. The plan was to jump two very small single adult departments to six or seven immediately. When we launched, I think we had five hundred single adults, and they asked the strangest questions: "Is the nursery open? Do you have childcare?" Neither of us had anticipated that question from singles. We thought singles were young people who graduated from college and came to the city for a job and were not yet married. We discovered that in our city, four out of ten single adults had been married and were now single again. And they had not found any help whatsoever in dealing with the breakup of their marriage. Many of them had deep wounds that would not heal.

Now I'm telling you this so you will realize that the work I am going to describe to you is not something we sought. It is something that sought us. The question we had to ask is "How will old First Church treat people who have been married and are now single?" I remember exegeting all the passages in the Bible on divorce in my seminary ethics class. But you know, sitting in the library with a bunch of commentaries is essentially different from having a number of wounded people standing before you asking for help. It's like dealing with the death of a mate, except worse. People know how to deal with those who mourn a death. Someone said in one of our first seminars, "Let me tell you something! Nobody brings a casserole to the courthouse! When the relationship died and I was hurting, people backed off."

Here's the decision we made: We would not try to discover the innocent parties and make halos for them. There are enough people working on that! We decided we would not try to discover who was guilty and crochet an "A" for them to wear forever as *Adulterer*; someone beat us to that. People judged them, and they were judging themselves. Here's the conclusion: we will take anyone who is hurting. And in Jesus' name we will seek to love them back to wholeness and to health. And it is the best decision that our church has ever made in its whole life.

I want to explain how we implemented these decisions. First of all, the doors of the church and the Bible study organizations are open to them on the same basis as everyone else—the confession of faith in Jesus Christ and believer's baptism by immersion. We decided not to create a Singles Again organization. We were saying, "We don't think you have committed the unpardonable sin. We don't intend to treat you as second-class citizens."

The second thing we did was move to Wednesday nights to provide special needs seminars. We run most of these things for four or five Wednesday nights, 7:30 to 9:30 p.m. We have a lecture called: "Beginning Again: A Help Seminar for the Formerly Married." We have done it 27 times. We have had over three thousand people in it. Then we do some self-improvement seminars. We have some holiday support groups because holidays are very difficult for people who are trading children back and forth and who miss the in-laws. The outreach potential for single adults has been great by doing these seminars; 85 percent of all people who come to a seminar have never before been to our church.

The church staff began to face the question of marriage again. We decided as ministers we had no alternative but to participate in performing weddings of people who had been married before. Our participation in weddings as ministers is by and large a civil aspect. It has very little to do with our calling. It is more a carryover from the Roman Catholic dominance of marriage. We decided we could not welcome them into the church and its organizations and turn them away from the wedding chapel. You communicate an awful lot in some of the simple little rejections.

We decided that we also had to deal honestly with where the church had shut people out because of a failed marriage—namely, the diaconate. I went to the first deacons' nominating committee when we went to old First Church. And I said, "Now what do we go by?"

They said, "We go by the Bible."

I said, "I think that is a good idea; what part of the Bible?"

They said, "We go from Acts and Timothy."

I said, "That's pretty good when you are dealing with the diaconate because that is about all there is in there about that. Now how do you use those? Do you use them as your model and as your ideal toward which you want everyone to move? Or do you use them like rules—meaning we don't elect anybody who doesn't measure up?"

They said, "We use them as rules."

I said, "You mean you have been able to get deacons that measure up to all that?"

"Yep! We have never once compromised on what God demands of a deacon."

I said, "Hey, I've been looking at our deacons." And they laughed nervously. So I went over to the chalkboard. We wrote down the list suggested in Acts and Paul's letter to Timothy, about 18 things I think. Then I said, "Let's take this one: 'manages household well.' We've got deacons whose kids are juvenile delinquents."

"Well, listen, Pastor, you got to realize that's sort of the *ideal* you know. It would be nice if everybody, you know . . ."

We went on. I said, "Does not love money." It seems to me that is the best way to get on the finance committee—to love money.

"Well, you know . . ." We went down the list one by one while they moved those requirements from the Rules column to the Ideals column until we got to the only thing you can check at the courthouse. They had never let anyone be a deacon who had been tainted by divorce.

That year they ordained a man who had for 20 years been the scout leader in the church and the outstanding teacher of sixth-grade boys but whose wife had been married before. Now hear me: there is an essential hypocrisy in being flexible on everything including being filled with the Holy Spirit and being rigid on divorce!

We learned to distinguish between the *ideal* and the *real* and the *redemptive*. We have never tried to amend the Ten Commandments just because your marriage or mine does not measure up to the *ideal*. God's *ideal* for you and me is perfection. We don't measure up, but God still loves us.

Now in putting this together, we had to decide several things: One, nowhere in the New Testament is there a systematic, thorough teaching on divorce. It's not there. In 1 Corinthians 7 you could make a better case for celibacy than marriage. And two, we do not have good hints in the New Testament on how the early church ministered to divorced people. That verse from Matthew 19 does not make divorce the unpardonable sin. When I do the seminars, I basically stand up there and plead with them to believe that the *ideal* has not changed. Then we discuss realistically what has happened to them and what it is doing to them. I plead with them to believe that God is the one who covers up the prodigal's past.[6]

We take the break and then questions come for at least an hour. I wish you could photograph them coming in and going out. They are completely different people! And I will have been totally drained, but I never walk out to my car without saying, "Thank you, God, for giving us this ministry. Amen."

Examining the Testimony Version

Though the chapel speaker never says so explicitly, he implies in many statements that the new position on this ethical issue he and his church adopted is the only loving and compassionate position. Anyone hanging on to the old traditional model is hypocritical and void of sympathy for those hurt by divorce. Suppose instead of the testimony shape chosen by the seminary chapel speaker, it had been cast into the typical structure favored by most preachers. His thesis might be: *Ministers, you should abandon your old convictions against blessing second marriages for these seven reasons*:

First, you can't really take the Word of God seriously on this issue and other ethical issues. After all, there's not much in there about this issue anyway, just a questionable passage in Acts and Paul's advice to Timothy. Besides, the Bible spoke to a special need of the first century and not to our twenty-first century. And

---

[6] The texts referenced but not quoted are 1 Corinthians 7:10, where Paul counsels the abandoned spouse to "remain unmarried or be reconciled," and Matthew 19:6b where Jesus says, "What God joined together, let no man separate."

what Paul said to the Corinthians and what Jesus said in Matthew's Gospel was idealistic and legalistic. It was not very real and not very redemptive.

Second, this more liberal stance is the only one that you can maintain consistently without hypocrisy. It's utter hypocrisy, for example, to qualify or disqualify deacons on the basis of the biblical standard for marriage. We don't use the Rule Book approach on other qualifications on the list such as being filled with the Holy Spirit.

Third, this new position is also practical. Once you take this position, you can ordain some fine deacons who have been unreasonably disqualified before.

Fourth, if you will change your convictions and lead your church to change its policy you can reach hundreds of people you will never enlist otherwise. Divorce is a reality of modern, urban life. We must admit it and adjust to it.

Fifth, hurting people don't think of traditional pastors and churches as particularly compassionate or helpful. If you and your staff will decide to officiate at the weddings of rematched couples, you will help make them happy and avoid making them unhappy with you.

Sixth, our ministerial function at weddings is a civil duty anyway—not a religious function. It's just a hangover from the days of Roman Catholic domination of the institute of marriage.

Seventh, you will help a lot of hurting people with this model and feel really good about yourself as you do so. Amen.

The Trouble with Testimony

Obviously, few evangelical pastors, while wrestling with the complex divorce issue, would find the argument compelling couched in such an outline. Both forms of this argument use the particulars to reach a general conclusion. Testimony, however, is a convincing form of inductive logic and almost impossible to refute. If you are telling me what happened to you, I may object that my experience is not the same, but I can hardly say, "That never happened to you."

As far as its function logically, testimony is an appeal to the authority of the speaker. The speaker testifies to what he or she has experienced.[7] Testimony may not be, strictly speaking, a logical argument. Some logicians classify it among the fallacious arguments with good reason. Still, in the world of marketing, "testimonials" are standard fare. If the speaker is a recognized public figure, an entertainment celebrity perhaps, the public gives more weight to his or her words. She may have no expertise at all evaluating the cosmetic she is endorsing, and that is just one reason it tends to be a fallacious argument. As long as it was legal to do so, tobacco advertisers used champion athletes and movie stars to endorse their products. The Marlboro Man was a huge winner for his brand of cigarettes until he developed lung cancer and died. So what if a rugged cowboy or an airline pilot has no particular expertise with the product endorsed? Television viewers do not have to be logical or particularly discriminating.

When I was growing up in Louisiana, one of our state senators, Dudley J. LeBlanc, developed a tonic a lot like other patent medicines and named it Hadacol. It was a brew of foul-tasting vitamins and minerals in a base of honey and 12 percent alcohol. The big difference between his product and others was promotion. He advertised big time with a heavy concentration of testimonies on the radio. Typical is this ad featuring Mrs. L. E. Mitchell of Wadsworth, Texas: "I have been suffering from nervousness, weak spells, lack of energy, and never felt like working. After taking Hadacol, I am doing my work better than I have in years. I don't have weak spells; I eat well; and I sleep like a log. My little girl didn't eat very much. After Hadacol, she eats two helpings every meal. We just can't praise it enough. I just wish more people knew how wonderful Hadacol is."[8]

---

[7] While writing this chapter, my copy of *Christianity Today*, July 2007, 30–32, arrived with an article by White House press secretary Tony Snow. The article is poignant because it is personal testimony. Its persuasive power flows from the authority of the speaker's first-hand experience—not because he is a specialist in any field of medicine or philosophy or religion. Snow had colon cancer in 2005. After surgery and chemotherapy, he joined the Bush administration in April 2006. In March 2007, he announced the cancer had returned. We listen to him on this subject because we feel he has earned a hearing. Who wants to hear about the blessings of cancer from someone who has never been there? Tony Snow, "Cancer's Unexpected Blessings," *Christianity Today*, July 2007, 30–32.

[8] Colin Escott, William MacEwen, and George Merritt, *Hank Williams: The Biography* (New York: Little, Brown, 2004). LeBlanc's "Hadacol Caravan" was the last of the

With so many giving such a bad rap to testimony, it is no wonder that some outsiders criticize the use of testimony in religious speech. Nor is it any wonder that some preachers also are loath to use it. Let us respond to the critics with three observations. First, it is interesting that those who most object to persuasive speech in preaching do so in the name of ethics. It is unethical, they say, to use persuasion of any kind in matters of religion. Never mind that those critics use their most persuasive arguments against the use of persuasion in religion.

Second, we are not advocating manipulation but legitimate persuasion. To manipulate someone is to control them especially in a devious way. To persuade employs legitimate reasoning, pleading, or urging to bring someone to believe something. The apostle Paul made that distinction. The power to convince in Paul's preaching did not come from any rhetorical art of human skill. He says, "My message and my preaching were not with wise and persuasive words, but with a demonstration of the Spirit's power" (1 Cor 2:4). Of course, Paul did labor to persuade people but never with any devious means of manipulation. In Ephesus, Paul visited the synagogue "and spoke boldly there for three months, *arguing persuasively* about the kingdom of God" (Acts 19:8). And Paul himself wrote to the Corinthians, "Since, then, we know what it is to fear the Lord, *we try to persuade men*" (2 Cor 5:11).

The command of Christ is clear: "But you will receive power when the Holy Spirit comes on you; and you will be my witnesses in Jerusalem, and in all Judea and Samaria, and to the ends of the earth" (Acts 1:8). A witness is one who tells what he or she knows in experience. That means giving testimony. That so many have misused testimony is no reason to ban it on the streets or in the courts of law or in church. We might just as well ban all persuasive speech for good because Hitler used it effectively for evil.

---

big-time medicine shows. He hired Hollywood celebrates of the day including Milton Berle, Lucille Ball, Mickey Rooney, Bob Hope, Carman Miranda, and George Burns and Gracie Allen among others. These stars were often outshone by rising country singers like Hank Williams Sr. and Minnie Pearl. In the 15-month period ending March 1951, LeBlanc sold more than $3.6 million worth of his tonic at $1.25 per 8-ounce bottle and $3.50 in 24-oz. size. When the FCC called the senator to accounting for his claims, the glow soon faded for Hadacol.

How to Use Testimony in Preaching

The best way to use testimony in the pulpit is the most direct way: tell your own story. The previous chapter dealt with that matter, so here we treat use of the testimony of others. First, a preacher may cite the word of a biblical witness. Jesus once gave sight to a man born blind. When the man came home, his neighbors were divided in opinion as to whether he was the same man. He testified, "I am the man." And when they demanded how it happened that blind eyes could see now, he testified further, "The man they call Jesus made some mud and put it on my eyes. He told me to go to Siloam and wash. So I went and washed, and then I could see." Thus far he bears witness to what he knew in personal experience. When they asked him where Jesus was then, he did not speculate; he said truthfully, "I don't know." The Pharisees entered the discussion and asked the same question about what happened and got the same answer: "I washed, and now I see." Then the Pharisees and the man's neighbors got into a theological debate as to whether someone from God would break their Sabbath taboos. When they pressed the formerly blind man for an opinion, he gave one. In fact the more they pressed him, the more his testimony honored Christ. He pronounced Jesus a prophet. When the Pharisees could not pin his parents down, they turned to the man again and pushed him to agree that Jesus must be a sinner. His testimony now became, "Whether he is a sinner or not, I don't know. One thing I do know. I was blind and now I see." They kept badgering him, and he kept giving his personal testimony. They escalated to insults, and he answered with bold irony. "Now that is remarkable! You don't know where he comes from, yet he opened my eyes. . . . If this man were not from God, he could do nothing" (John 9:1–33). John's Gospel gives John's own witness to Christ and records the testimony of many others like the blind man. That is a good pattern for preachers.

Occasionally the pastor of our church turns aside during his sermon to introduce someone in the congregation who has a fresh testimony. He brings that person to the platform (by prior arrangement) to bear witness briefly to God's dealing in his or her life that week. The speaker becomes a living sermon illustration. It may be someone who just became a Christian, or it may be a longtime member of the fellowship who has a testimony of recent and remarkable answered prayer or some other great blessing. It is an effective use of testimony.

At other times a preacher may relate the experience of others from his reading or his personal knowledge. If it is someone the pastor knows, it should be a story the pastor knows to be true. Sometimes the preacher may be a part of the story; at other times not. There are some cautions that the preacher should keep in mind. For one, in using testimony, especially the testimony of others, the character and reputation of the witness is important. We want witnesses known to be truthful who are in a position to make an informed judgment. This is especially important in testimony to matters of fact. In addition, a distinction must be made between matters of opinion as distinguished from matters of fact. Many witnesses, for example, have testified to sightings of UFOs and "crop circles." That is fact. That either of these phenomena suggests visitors from beyond our planet is in the realm of opinion. Religious opinions, likewise, are legion and varied.

Biblical witnesses are authoritative, even though postmodern listeners tend to regard them as just another religious opinion. Let the preacher continue to proclaim the testimony of God's Word and trust God to see that it does not fall to the ground impotent. God's Word still has the power to accomplish His purpose (see Isa 55:10–11). It is still like fire that consumes the worthless chaff and purifies precious gold, and it is like a hammer that breaks a rock in pieces (Jer 23:29). Certainly the secularists will think you strange to continue to appeal to an authority they reject. Never mind that; they are still subject to the law of gravity, whether or not they know it or like it.

Finally, it is well to note that the unintentional testimony of adversaries is frequently of value. In the Gospels the word of pagan and Jewish opponents to Christ attributed his miracles to magic or to the supernatural power of Belzebub. Indirectly they attest to the fact that Jesus did indeed do miracles.[9]

---

[9] Contemporary homiletical texts do not offer much guidance on logical arguments in preaching. There is an extended treatment in the classic by John A. Broadus, *On the Preparation and Delivery of Sermons*, rev. ed., ed. J. B. Weatherspoon (New York: Harper & Brothers, 1870, 1944), 167–96.

In this chapter we have highlighted the persuasive power of testimony in preaching. We have noted that critics object to the use of any persuasion in religious matters and object to emotional persuasion most of all. We have sought to make the case that persuasion is legitimate and necessary in preaching. Manipulation is a different matter and has no place in the ministry of God's Word or any other part of the gospel ministry. Noting that modern Western minds are moved more by emotional arguments than logic, we have suggested some guidance for acceptable use of testimony to convince without coercion.

Thus far in the book we have been mostly laying a foundation for storytelling in preaching. Now we turn to how to build the house. Part 1 dealt much with understanding concepts. Part 2 will get us using the power saw and nail gun. We start with a practical blueprint for constructing a sermon with strong narrative content—step-by-step to the sermon.

Exercise 1. If you have not done so earlier, take time to write out your personal testimony of salvation. Tell what your life was like before you became a Christian, how you came to know you needed the Savior, and what your life has been like since then. Notice that testimony does not require any urging of your personal experience on anyone else.

Exercise 2. Take an index card and write "testimony" across the top. Put it in your pocket and listen for examples of testimony in personal conversations, in broadcast and print advertising, and wherever it may appear. Jot a note as you notice it. Then think critically about it. Is it legitimate? Is it manipulative?

Exercise 3. As you prepare your next sermon, give consideration to an appropriate use of personal testimony. Our pastor sometimes inserts into his Sunday morning sermon a personal testimony of someone he has enlisted to come from the congregation and tell of a decision for Christ in recent days.

part two

GETTING THE
STORY STRAIGHT

Chapter 6

STEP-BY-STEP TO THE NARRATIVE SERMON

"WHY IS THERE SO MUCH narrative in the Bible and so little in our sermons?" Ralph Lewis and son Gregg Lewis ask this question in one of their books, *Inductive Preaching*. And they answer, "Our sermons follow Greek rhetorical patterns rather than Bible models."[1] This chapter will begin by defending narrative as a proper shape for biblical sermons. Then we will move to a step-by-step chronology for preparing sermons with more storytelling. It is possible to preach a sermon that is totally narrative, but most of us could afford to do more storytelling in our preaching.

Taking Our Cue from Jesus

Every preacher who wants to preach like Jesus will want to master storytelling arts. Of course Jesus used other patterns. He preached and taught in metaphor and simile. He exhorted and encouraged. He rebuked and warned, but mostly he told stories. The parables, obviously, are narratives almost exclusively. But Jesus also illustrated his teaching and preaching with stories of current events. There were the "Galileans whose blood Pilate mingled with their sacrifices" mentioned by his listeners, to which

---

[1] Ralph Lewis and Gregg Lewis, *Inductive Preaching: Helping People Listen* (Wheaton, IL: Crossway, 1983), 58, 64.

Jesus added a reference to "those eighteen who died when the Tower in Siloam fell on them" (Luke 13:4).

Jesus used a number of other rhetorical structures in public speech also. He could hurl denunciation and diatribe. "Woe unto you scribes and Pharisees. Hypocrites!" And besides narratives such as parables, note the many visual images evoked by the teaching and preaching of Jesus. In the Sermon on the Mount, there is only one parable proper. That is the parable of the two houses, one built on the rock and one on the sand. But look at how many vivid images are evoked with just a few words. In the Beatitudes our minds see people mourn and comforted. Some mental image is evoked by words like "they persecuted the prophets who were before you" (Matt 5:12). Can you see the city on a hill? My mind imagines it in the late evening or at night with windows and doors aglow from lamps and candles (5:14). Visualize a lamp under a bowl and another on a lamp stand. What strong imagery is in the phrase "until heaven and earth disappear" (5:18). Then he prompts each hearer to see himself or herself "angry with his brother." See the worshipper offering his gift at the altar and then remembering the need to be reconciled to a brother. Watch him as he leaves his gift there and goes to seek reconciliation before returning in peace to complete that act of worship in his offering (5:23–24). The scene changes suddenly to a court of law, an adversary, the judge, the bailiff, the prison! (5:25–26). In a flash the image morphs to a man looking at a woman lustfully. And this is followed by the grotesque hyperbole of the guilty gouging out an eye and throwing it away or cutting off a hand and throwing it away. And we are hardly through half of the first of three chapters! If we were not so familiar with the words, we would be shocked by the scenes evoked.

If, as most New Testament scholars believe, these three chapters are compiled summaries of much longer teachings of Jesus, we can imagine Jesus giving much more detail in these evocative images. A narrative is one specific type of inductive communication. The details taken as a whole make the point. The preacher does not state a proposition and then prove it; he shows the congregation a vision that he sees so they too can see it.

Can a preacher construct a biblical sermon that is totally narrative or almost totally narrative? No exhortation? No logical arguments? No application stated? H. Grady Davis more than a half century ago said a sermon may take five "organic forms": (1) a subject discussed, (2) a thesis supported, (3) a message illuminated, (4) a question propounded, and (5) *a story told*. Haddon Robinson refined and reworded the list, but his *Biblical Preaching* recognized essentially the same five "shapes sermons take" including *a story told*. The story is the only completely inductive form of communication in the five, though Robinson shows how the most common form, a subject completed, may be given a twist that makes it part deductive and part inductive. A preacher may have a problem to be solved in his sermon. To begin with, he may chase several common solutions and show how each is not the answer we need. That is inductive method. Then in the middle of the sermon, the preacher may arrive at the answer the text supports and develop the rest of the sermon deductively. The only truly inductive form in either list is the story told. It is hard to do any sermon well, and inductive sermons are especially freighted with problems. Yet advantages make inductive sermons worth the risk. People learn better when they are able to discover the truth for themselves rather than have the pastor discover it for them and spoon feed it to them. A story sermon enables the preacher to outflank the hostile listener, and the typical congregation today shelters many hostiles. The Bible is a book of stories; how can we not tell stories in the pulpit?[2]

A Four-Stage Chronology for Preparing Narrative Sermons

Let's assume that you are a preacher convinced by now that storytelling should be a more important part of your ministry of the Word. How do you go about preparing a sermon that will depend more on storytelling? The procedure for preparing sermons as a storyteller is the same in most stages of preparation as the familiar

---

[2] H. Grady Davis, *Design for Preaching* (Philadelphia: Fortress, 1958), 139–62. Haddon W. Robinson's five shapes sermons take are (1) an idea to be explained, (2) a proposition to be proved, (3) a principle to be applied, (4) a subject to be completed, and (5) *a story told*. Haddon W. Robinson, *Biblical Preaching*, 2d ed. (Grand Rapids: Baker, 2001), 115–37.

deductive structure of other sermons. In the narrative, inductive plan, the details taken as a whole make the point. The preacher does not state a proposition and then prove it; he shows the congregation a vision that he sees so they too can see it.

Let's examine the four-stage procedure with attention to becoming a better narrative preacher. The first thing to do is to anchor your preparation early in a text of Scripture. Then, second, with that decided at least tentatively, let the preacher diligently study that text. The third stage is organizing the sermon. The principal focus of the second half of this chapter will be to explore a number of narrative options for shaping the sermon. Then a fourth stage is to give time for the sermon to grow and mature, to polish it, and to ready the preacher to deliver the sermon.

Stage one: anchor your preparation early in a text of Scripture. I say "a text" fully aware that many preachers do not know how to do this. They select a theme and match it with a launching point in Scripture which they call their text. Then they develop the theme topically. If the text happens to catch their attention first, they want to categorize it into this or that topic before going further. They may bounce all over the Bible selecting cross-references and proof texts for the various subthemes in their sermon plan. Topical preaching may be one legitimate way to preach. Many people like it, perhaps because it is easier for the preacher to give a clear outline in a topical sermon. Nevertheless, it is a poor second or third choice for those who really want to minister the Word and feed Christ's sheep. The great weakness of topical preaching is that the preacher shapes the sermon without due submission to the text. The same is true of most textual preaching organized topically.

Let the preacher listen to the voice of God in the biblical text. This is no leisurely duty. Exegesis of the Scripture demands diligent attention. Let the preacher determine to engage prayerfully and thoughtfully one passage of Scripture until it yields the very voice of God who gave it. Reading the observations of scholars in commentaries and other Bible study tools will be helpful, but don't turn to them before you have read the text for yourself many times with pen and notebook before you. If you have facility in the original languages, by all means make your own translation. Then compare the translations of experts who labored before you.

As you study, ask God to speak in the text to your own heart first. Where does the text intersect with your own life story? Engage the text as if the sermon you are preparing will be for an audience of one. Yourself! Then when that message is clear, read and study, also remembering the hurts and heart cries of those who will sit before you in the pews when you preach. Where does the story in the Bible intersect with their stories? What hopes and hungers will this text touch? And what *unfelt* needs of your congregation does this text address? Preaching to felt needs is fine; it gives the preacher a head start on connecting with the congregation. But there may be some very real needs that the preacher should not neglect. Many "seekers" come to church seeking a salve for their spiritual sickness. If they are lost and need to know the Savior, the preacher needs to bring that to their attention. If they are baby believers who are not moving toward maturity, who will help them beyond that immaturity? If the text addresses that need, let the preacher do so as well, arousing awareness of the need all along the way.

What if the text does not really address the need the pastor feels needs to be addressed? Then this is the time to change texts or change the focus of the sermon to follow this text. Imagine three lines converging. One line represents the Word of God reaching down from heaven to earth. Another represents the life of the preacher reaching up from earth toward God. The third line is the experience of the congregation crossing both lines horizontally. Where those three lines converge marks the zone where the Word of God will touch the lives of people. Perhaps the preacher finds the text speaks to the great indifference to eternal values in contemporary culture. There the sermon seed will sprout and begin to grow. Or perhaps it seems to the preacher that members are stumbling too much and too seldom advancing in grace. Is there too little seeking of the Lord and too much seeking the pleasures of the world? What life need does this text address? Once a germinal idea from the text grips the preacher's heart, the sermon begins.

What if the text is not a narrative text? When I was a college and seminary student, Donald G. Miller of Union Theological

Seminary wrote a book that advocated every sermon have a theme and that the theme of the sermon be the theme of the passage on which it is based. We should say amen to that. Furthermore, Miller went on to teach that the sermon's emphasis should match the emphasis in the text and the structure of the sermon should follow the structure of the text. So much the better! More than that, Miller said the aim or purpose of the text should determine the aim or purpose of the expository sermon. Miller went even one step further; he taught that the mood or atmosphere of each text of Scripture should be preached in the same mood. If the text is diatribe or invective, then the sermon should be likewise. That may be going a bit far, but if the text is not one long condemnation of sinners, then certainly the sermon should not seek to be one.

Miller did not address the question of literary *genre*, for he wrote before that emphasis arose to prominence in homiletical literature. If the text is narrative, should the sermon be narrative? This question is certainly worth considering, but the text need not be a narrative text before the sermon can be narrative. Notice that Jesus used parable to answer the theological question, "Who is my neighbor?" (Luke 15). If the text comes from the Psalter, should the preacher sing his sermon? What should we do with a text from the Proverbs? Obviously, this counsel of perfection is not quite perfect.[3]

Stage two: interpret the text. This requires a thorough study of the text. This is just one reason marshalling 20 proof texts to prop up a topical sermon is not wise. Can the preacher study 20 texts in their various contexts enough to deal faithfully with each? I fear many preachers are content to decide if their use of the text suits the preacher's purpose. Is what God intended us to hear in this text of lesser importance? Surely not!

Reading Numbers 8:1–3 recently, it seemed curious to me that the lamps were arranged in the tabernacle to "give light in front of the lamp stand." How can the lamps do this? Did they have reflectors that cast the light forward more than behind? If so, why is this detail important? Was it a practical matter? Is there some symbolic

---

[3] Donald G. Miller, *The Way to Biblical Preaching: How to Communicate the Gospel in Depth* (Nashville: Abingdon, 1957). Miller wrote another popular text for preachers that was a hot topic among homileticians of his era. *Fire in Thy Mouth* advocated what became known as the "sacrament of preaching."

or typological significance in that detail? Or take a text in the next chapter. On the wilderness trek the new nation Israel was commanded to move when the cloud moved and to stay as long as the cloud stayed. Imagine the thoughts of one on that pilgrimage, learning about divine guidance. Every day was a new day. One never knew at night if in the morning they would work in camp or strike tents and continue the march. Does that say something about the pilgrim nature of Christian life?

In another text from the wilderness wanderings (Num 14:20–25), Israel put God to the test "now these ten times." If I were preaching that text, I think I would be obliged to check the record in Exodus and Numbers to see if I could find all ten in the history. Who can examine such detail in ten or 20 proof texts for a topical sermon? Biblical preaching requires serious Bible study. After the preacher has examined the text personally, there are commentaries to compare, word studies to consult, yes, cross-references to trace, and other theological references to read. A preacher should study a text until he can state the central idea of that text in a single clear and plain sentence. In a narrative text, admittedly, this may be impossible. Still the preacher should be able to capsule the story in a brief descriptive statement. We call this labor *exegesis* because we draw *out of* the text what is there rather than use it as a buttress for ideas we bring with us to the text. The preacher needs to study the text prayerfully and diligently until he can be sure that he understands its teaching. Ideally, the preacher should be able to give a simple answer to the question, what is the point of this story? But as mentioned earlier, a story that can be boiled down to a proposition probably has been abridged too much. Nevertheless, the preacher has no more important task than to become a master of the Book. No sermon is ready to preach or even to organize until the preacher has mastered the chosen text.

Stage three: plan the general organization of the sermon. Since we are going to deal in some detail with the narrative options in sermon structure later in this chapter, let me mention here that other options are open to the preacher. For one, the preacher may develop one idea and organize it with what Broadus called "the functional elements of preaching." There are four functional elements for preaching. They are explanation, illustration, argument, and application. Theoretically a sermon might have these four divisions. More likely, these four functions will be mixed in the sermon plan. The preacher might begin by explaining the text, then illustrating it once or more. Then it might be helpful or even necessary to introduce logical arguments. Logical arguments in preaching are not as useful in this century as when Broadus wrote his classic *Treatise on the Preparation and Delivery of Sermons.* We are brainwashed to believe that a sermon must have three points or divisions. Why not try a one-point sermon, or "jewel sermon"? A "jewel sermon" holds up one thought, turning it this way and that, to see different facets, as one would turn a diamond or other precious stone in the light. Explanation and application will dominate. Illustration may serve either of these functions or stand alone. Include argument only if the sermon requires it. Of course, many preachers will prefer the familiar rhetorical structure of sermons that divide the text or the topic into so many parts or points.

Stage four: give time for the sermon to grow and mature. This stage of sermon preparation may continue over several days. In long-range planning such as a series of expositions through the book of Romans, this stage will last for months. And it should overlap the earlier stages. The preacher will be gathering materials on several sermons. Some of it will be found in a deliberate search; some of it will find the preacher while engaged in other ministry. Other chapters deal at length with the gathering of narrative illustrations, so we will be brief about it here. The decision to use a narrative shape for the sermon will govern what other narrative illustrations may be needed.

Suppose the preacher decides in step three to use a narrative shape for the sermon. Then what specific storytelling point of view will the preacher assume? Some of the Bible is written in first person; Ezra and Nehemiah, for example, use first-person pronouns, *I* and *we* mostly. Some books use direct address and are filled with second-person pronouns. Think of the book of Proverbs and the New Testament letters as examples. The most common point of view is the third-person observer as storyteller. Most of the stories in the Bible are told from this point of view. The preacher as narrator tells who did what and said what. Abraham did this and that, said such and such, went here and there.

But there are other choices. Storytellers distinguish between two point-of-view options, the omniscient and the realistic. The *omniscient* storyteller knows not only the words and deeds of each character but also the undeclared thoughts and motives. The preacher is not omniscient; he knows only such as the text reveals. In the case of a story created by the preacher to illustrate the text, the storyteller has this choice to make. In the more *realistic* point of view, the storyteller knows the mind of no more than one person in the story. The others are known only as they reveal themselves in word or deed. Even in a story of the preacher's own creation, the realistic point of view comes across as more credible. In this case the storyteller still has three choices. The preacher may be telling his own story. This becomes, like a testimony, a story using first-person pronouns. It is what *we* did or what *I* did or said. Second, the storyteller may be an uninvolved third-person narrator. *They* did this and that. *He* said something; *she* answered. Dealing with the text, the preacher narrates, for example, what Paul did and said, where Paul went and what happened next. A third option in the realistic point of view is for the storyteller to be a third person who participates in the story. In this case the storyteller knows his or her own mind at most. It is not realistic for you to know what your neighbor thought, said, or did when you were not present. Even if you have someone in the story tell you what happened, you are not able to get inside your neighbor's thoughts. Part three of this book gives ample examples.

Seven Models for Organizing Narrative Sermons

Let us suppose that the preacher decided in stage three of preparation to preach a narrative sermon, not just embellish the rhetorical outline with spots of narrative illustrations. What are the options? They are numerous, but we will offer here a few models for organizing a narrative sermon.

1. *The Bible lesson model.* We all know some preachers who are strong on exhortation and weak on exposition. Others are

stronger at explaining Scripture than exhorting. Chuck Swindoll is an expositor who is a worthy model of opening his text and making it plain. A common structure for narrative sermons in this model spends most of the time in telling the biblical story with such explanations as may make it plain. The last few minutes of the sermon are reserved for such "lessons" as may be drawn from that text. This was a common homiletical pattern in earlier days. The preacher explained the text and in the end of the sermon enumerated "uses" as the application used to be called. It is still well received when well done.

2. *The story without stated application.* The application may be implied by the story but not stated. Sometimes Jesus did this with his parables. Later the disciples would beg for an explanation, and Jesus would interpret the story. That is the strength of this approach. When the listeners cry out for the meaning of the story, they are more ready to receive it. The parable of the soils is an example. Jesus described four different kinds of hearers in the crowds who heard His teaching. Some, like the hard-ground hearers, gave an immediate and unqualified *no* to the gospel. Others, like the rocky-ground hearers, made a shallow response to the Word that did not last. I call that a *yes-if* response. They want the kingdom of God if it is an easy road. Others, like thorny-ground hearers, gave a distracted reception. It was a kind of *yes-but* response. They want Christ but don't want to give up the world. That seed also was soon choked out by things that prevented it from going on to maturity and fruitfulness. But some, at last, did give an unqualified *yes* to Jesus. They are like seed sown on fertile ground.

As stated elsewhere, I do not think it is usually a good idea to tell a story and leave it to whatever understanding the hearer may bring to the story. There are exceptions. Jesus sometimes pressed the point of His parables. "Which of these three do you think was a neighbor to the man who fell into the hands of robbers? . . . Go and do likewise" (Luke 10:36–37). At other times, at least to the mixed multitudes, He left the application unstated.

A missionary to an African village told about undergoing a time of personal difficulty that became known to his friends in the village church. Three of the elders paid him a visit. After customary courtesies of hospitality, the oldest man began telling a story. It did not take long for the missionary to realize that the story was meant to speak to his personal struggle. When the story was ended, the missionary waited politely to be told the application. Instead, the three men stood and spoke their good-byes and left.

The missionary wanted to stop them and cry out, "What was the point? I need the point of the story!" Every Westerner can identify with that. But his friends did not tell him the meaning. They left him to reflect on it and find the truth in it for himself in his situation. The story did not leave him alone. It stuck in his mind until suddenly one day the moment of epiphany came. The way through his personal problem became clear. The story was the point![4]

Sometimes the preacher must make the point clear and unmistakable. At other times, such as when our more direct preachments may encounter resistance or rebellion, we must trust the Holy Spirit to work indirectly. It will take a brave preacher to create a parable and not tell the congregation what it means. Fred Craddock is a storyteller brave enough and adept enough to do it well. Since he retired from teaching New Testament Greek and preaching at Emory, he has continued to preach as pastor of a village church in Tennessee.

Probably all who read these lines are acquainted with Charles Sheldon's novel *In His Steps*. You probably know that Sheldon was a minister. Do you know that he read the chapters as his sermon on successive Sunday evenings? One hundred years after its introduction, something close to a cult following of the theme of the novel arose: "What Would Jesus Do?" One could buy bracelets, stationary, wall decorations, and all kinds of premium merchandise printed with WWJD.

The principal character in the story, Henry Maxwell, is also a pastor. First Church of Raymond was as typical as any small-town First Church could be. In the opening scene the pastor sat at his desk finishing his sermon for Sunday. His text becomes the text for the whole series of sermons in the novel it became. "To this you were called, because Christ suffered for you, leaving you an example that you should follow in his steps" (1 Pet 2:21). The

---

[4] This incident was related by an unnamed missionary to John Walsh, host of the very helpful Web site, www.christianstorytelling.com/past_stories_tips/ 2005–02_storytelling_tip. html.

fictional pastor had planned a traditional three-point sermon on following Jesus. He was working on the third point, which would develop the steps for following Jesus. Just then a young man in shabby clothes interrupted his preparation. He needed help finding a job. On the next Sunday the same young man appeared at church and asked to say a few words to the church. While telling a bit of his tale of woe, he collapsed and died at the altar. This so stirred the pastor and church that on the next Sunday the pastor challenged the congregation to try asking, before every decision they face, the question, "What would Jesus do?" The chapters that follow show what a difference it made as one after another of the members of First Church did exactly that. One chapter follows the editor of the local newspaper as he decides whether Jesus as editor would devote two pages to reporting a prize fight. It was radical social action preaching in 1897, but the shape of the sermon was also radical. It was completely narrative. In fact it was a whole series of sermons, every installment a new story that advanced the overarching narrative. The series was a powerful way to ask people to consider what it would mean to follow seriously in the steps of Jesus. I don't know of anyone who has tried anything just like that since then, though I have shaped children's sermons in ongoing serials with a cliff-hanger ending of each Sunday's installment.[5]

3. *Retelling the story model.* Some years ago Patrick J. Willson wrote a sermon titled "Getting the Story Straight." It was a Thanksgiving sermon based on Deuteronomy 26:1–11. Jacob gave his testimony in terms of his heritage: "A wandering Aramean was my father. . . ." The point of the sermon is that we show whether we are truly thankful people by how we tell our story. The preacher suggested other ways the story might have been told. "My father was a clever conqueror. With cunning and personal strength, he won the battle for the land." A third way the story might be told: "My father, well, was just always lucky. Even when we were slaves in Egypt, we managed to sneak away, and luck was on our side. . . ." We reveal our philosophy of life by how we tell our story. Is your life a gift from God? Or is ours a totally secular and humanistic narrative? How we see ourselves and those around us,

---

[5] Charles L. Campbell, "A Not-So-Distant Mirror: Nineteenth Century Popular Fiction and Pulpit Storytelling," *Theology Today* (January 1995): 574–82.

and especially how we see or don't see God—these shape the way we tell our story.[6]

Dozens of texts in the Bible might be preached with the retelling-the-story pattern. Consider the story of David, Bathsheba, and Uriah. Nathan the prophet confronted the king with a parable about the wealthy man who seized his poor neighbor's one pet lamb to entertain a guest. David repented and found forgiveness and restoration. But suppose he didn't repent. A preacher might recast that story two or three ways simply by retelling it from the point of view first of an unrepentant King David blaming Bathsheba. "She set a trap for me! Bathing out there in plain view of the palace in broad daylight! Besides, I am the king, after all. In such matters, the king is king after all. The whole nation owes me. Uriah owes me," etc.

Then the preacher might recast the text as Bathsheba's story. "Of course, they don't stone men for adultery. It's always the woman to blame. Men can fool around. Even married men can play the field and get away with it. And if you happen to be the king, you can do no wrong. It's not as if I had a choice in the matter. When the king summons you, you go." Then maybe even Uriah's story. The preacher will need to decide whether Uriah knew all along what was going on between David and Bathsheba. In either case the text portrays Uriah as an innocent and loyal soldier. He was the most victimized in this whole sordid affair. After retelling the story two or three times, the preacher might match the Old Testament text with a New Testament text such as the call for Christian confession of sin in 1 John 1:8–10 or the promise of power to overcome temptation in 1 Corinthians 10:13.[7]

4. *Alternating the story.* This is a variation that intersperses the biblical story with application. If our text is the story of Jonah, we may tell of Jonah's rebellion against the call of God and then apply that part of the story. Then we continue with the story of Jonah asleep in the storm at sea and rebuked for his prayerlessness by the pagan shipmates. Application might take several direc-

---

[6] Patrick J. Willson, "Getting the Story Straight," *Pulpit Digest* (November/December 1991): 44–49.

[7] Frederick Buechner in "The Truth of Stories," *Pulpit Digest* (January/February 1992): 7–12, does a similar retelling of the parable of the prodigal son. He tells it from the prodigal's point of view, then from the perspective of the older brother.

tions in this part of the story. Then the story continues with Jonah cast overboard and praying to God from inside the great fish or whale. More application follows. Finally, Jonah gets a second chance and runs to Nineveh, and so on. James Cox suggests this pattern. So does Eugene Lowry, who gave it the name "alternating the story."[8]

5. *Delaying the story.* This is another model named by Lowry. Here the preacher begins the sermon with a concern of those who listen in the congregation. After this introduction the story begins usually with the sermon text. Through the text the preacher leads the listener to discover the solution to the problem or concern. Eugene Lowry analyzes an example of this pattern in a sermon preached by Leander E. Keck, academic dean at Yale Divinity School. His sermon entitled "Limited Resources, Unlimited Possibilities" was preached in chapel at Candler School of Theology. The text is not mentioned until about six minutes into a 16-minute sermon. He spent the first 38 percent of his sermon identifying the listener's "gnawing, demoralizing sense of inadequacy" for ministry. Then comes the text traditionally called "the loaves and the fishes." Not until the last page of the eight-page manuscript does the preacher state what we might call the proposition, the thesis, or the big idea of the sermon: "When I face the world with my limited resources I need not panic because Christ can make them adequate by blessing them."[9]

6. *Suspending the story.* This time the preacher begins with the story, usually the text. Then the preacher moves away from the text decisively, perhaps to a problem of his hearers that needs to be solved. Then the sermon returns to continue the story of the text and concludes it while solving the problem. The story might be the parable of Jesus about the workers in the vineyard. Lowry uses a sermon of his own as an example of suspending the story. The owner went out first at dawn to hire laborers. He agreed with them for the usual rate of a denarius for the day. Again he went out at mid-morning, at noon, and at mid-afternoon to find others. An hour before quitting time he was still adding to his labor force. Lowry always likes to find the bind in the story that upsets

[8] Eugene Lowry, *How to Preach a Parable: Designs for Narrative Sermons* (Nashville: Abingdon, 1989), 142–70.
[9] Ibid., 79–88.

the equilibrium. This time he summarizes the story in just a few paragraphs all the way to the grumbling of those who were hired first and paid last. They were unhappy that they were paid only what they agreed to accept when they were hired. The owner had demonstrated amazing generosity to the latecomers. They thought they might be paid more. There he suspends the story and defends the complainers. He gives several examples in current economic systems where they would certainly have a cause for complaint to the Labor Relations Board. Lowry ends the sermon saying, "So you see, it doesn't matter whether the invitation comes at seven, or nine, or noon, or three, of five, or two till. To be invited into the vineyard is to be invited home. Who could ask for anything more?"[10]

7. *Running the story*. Clarence Macartney suggested two ways to preach a Bible biography sermon. One way is to relate the story of a biblical character and make the points of the sermon as you go through the story. An example is Macartney's own sermon on Daniel. First he talked of Daniel's youth and how he fitted himself for his great career by a moral stand. He purposed in his heart that he would not defile himself with the king's meat. Then he turned to Daniel's manhood. He applied Daniel's courage and fidelity in his prayers to God and his deliverance from the lion's den. Finally the preacher ended with Daniel's honor and reward. God never forgets those who honor him.

Macartney's other method for biographical sermons we have treated above in what we call "the Bible lesson pattern." Here the preacher tells the whole story and then lists several applications. Macartney gives an example from his sermon files of a sermon on Abigail, the woman who married the wrong man. She was married to Nabal, a fool for real. David would have killed Nabal but for the wise intervention of Abigail who eventually did become David's wife. The three "lessons" Macartney extracted after telling that dramatic story dealt with first, a woman unsoured by adversity; second, God's providence in our lives as we are altogether "bound in the bundle of life;" and third, the regrets we have

---

[10] Ibid. I recall the only sermon I ever heard Grady Davis preach. It was on this text. He found the point of the parable in the sovereignty of God. God does not have to answer to us for all His mysterious ways. I like the Davis perspective on the text.

missed, and those we can miss if we listen to the pleadings of the Holy Spirit.[11]

Exercise 1. You should be ready now to construct a narrative sermon. It will not be a deductive sermon propped up with anecdotes to fill out each sermon point. Plan a sermon of one point anchored in a text of your choice. Follow the four chronological stages advocated in the first half of this chapter.

Exercise 2. If you are a pastor or other minister with regular preaching duties, look ahead on your preaching calendar and plan sermons that will use two or three of the seven ways to organize a narrative sermon.

Exercise 3. The best way to develop the skills presented in this chapter will be to try each of them until you are comfortable that you know all seven ways to organize narrative sermons. That may take a long time and a lot of practice. Meanwhile select one you think might become your favorite approach to narrative preaching. Work on that one until you make it your own. Just don't wear out one congregation with that favorite.

---

[11] Clarence E. Macartney, *Preaching without Notes* (New York: Abingdon, 1946), 132–34. Lowry would call this "running the story" and use this pattern for narrative sermons from any text—not just Bible biographies.

Chapter 7

TELLING THE BIBLE STORY

MARTIN BUBER'S GRANDFATHER WAS PARALYZED so that he could not stand or walk at all. One day he was asked to tell about his great teacher, the famous and holy Baal Shem Tov. The grandfather was telling how the holy man used to jump up and down and dance around as he prayed. Swept up in the fervor of his narrative, the storyteller himself stood up and began to dance in demonstration of the holy man's custom. At that moment, said Martin Buber, his grandfather was completely healed of his paralysis. No doubt there is power in a story to change the storyteller who gets personally involved in the narrative. It is also true that stories have power to change those who receive them. This is above all true of the stories in the Bible, for God has promised that His Word has power to achieve His divine purpose wherever it is sent (Isa 55:10–11).

Preachers are servants of that life-giving Word. We have no greater duty than to tell the story of the Redeemer. This is not a story we create but one we faithfully pass along. This chapter begins with the storytelling tradition reflected in the Hebrew Bible. Then we will consider the apostolic use of the stories in that Old Testament. And we will give special attention to how much creativity should be acceptable in retelling of the biblical stories. Finally, the chapter will give a synopsis of a classic biographical sermon from a late nineteenth-century Anglican worthy of attention.

Storytelling in the Hebrew Bible

Storytelling has always been a vital part of Hebrew tradition. Early Christian tradition never mastered the Master's example of teaching in parables. In Plato's *Republic* poets and storytellers were forbidden. Though he himself was a successful storyteller, as much as half of *The Republic* aimed at attacking the power of poetry and narrative. A further blow to storytelling came with the rise of scientific method with a new and objective way of verifying truth. So Francis Bacon and other scientists are blamed with belittling narrative. But in Hebrew history, story has enjoyed an unbroken heritage of esteem as the teaching method supreme.

> Listen my people, mark each word. I begin with a story.
> I speak of mysteries welling up from ancient depths,
> Heard and known from our elders.
> We must not hide this story from our children
> But tell the mighty works and all the wonders of God.
> . . .
> Let future generations learn
> And let them grow up to teach their young to trust in
> God (Ps 78:1–4, 6–7a TS[1]).

"I begin with a story," says the psalmist. The title of Psalm 78 tells us it is an example of a *maskil* or song for instruction in godliness. It is one of several psalms that encourage Israel to continue to rehearse the story of God's dealing with His people so that they do not continue to repeat the sins of their fathers. The children need the instruction; the adult generation needs the constant reminder. Other psalms of instruction rehearse the story of God and Israel including Psalms 105 and 106, a pair of lengthy psalms that

---

[1] From *The Psalter: A Faithful and Inclusive Rendering from the Hebrew into Contemporary English Poetry, Intended Primarily for Communal Song and Recitation* (Chicago: Liturgy Training Publications, 1995).

belong together. These are songs of praise with a strong reminder to "remember the wonders he has done" (see v. 5) and a reminder that God "remembers his covenant forever" (v. 8).

Nevertheless, Israel "did not remember" the Lord's many kindnesses, "but they soon forgot" (Ps 106:7, 13). The narrative bids us keep in mind God's protection and providence. God sent Joseph ahead of them to Egypt. A family grew to be a nation there. With the plagues, God made Pharaoh willing to let them go. Recall, then, how God led them and provided for them. In the wilderness He sent "bread of heaven . . . He opened the rock, and water gushed out; like a river it flowed in the desert" (105:40,41). But they soon forgot. Songs and stories are divinely ordained ways to correct that forgetfulness. And songs that tell a story are best of all.[2]

The Apostolic Use of Sacred Stories

It should be instructive to the Bible teacher and preacher of today to notice how Jesus and the apostles and evangelists used stories from the Hebrew Bible. Stephen's defense before the Sanhedrin is an interesting case study (Acts 7). It is a remarkable summary of Hebrew history. Like any history it is selective, and the selection is purposeful. Stephen selected those stories that demonstrated Israel's tendency to reject God's spokesmen, even to the point of violence against them. Examples were not hard to find. He started with Abraham, of course, because the nation started with him. God warned Abraham that his descendants would be enslaved and mistreated four hundred years. So it was. As his narrative unfolds, however, it becomes increasingly plain that the abuse was as likely to come from brothers as from strangers. The patriarchs were jealous of Joseph and sold him as a slave into Egypt (v. 9). But God was with Joseph and rescued him and made him the instrument of rescue for the whole family. In time another king became ruler in Egypt. This Pharaoh had no love for Jacob or Joseph or any of their rapidly multiplying clan. "He dealt treacherously with our people and oppressed our forefathers by forcing them to throw out their newborn babies so that they would die" (v. 19). Next came Moses. He too was rejected by those he came to defend and liber-

---

[2] Another example of rehearsing Israel's story is Nehemiah 9:5–37.

ate. Stephen made the point explicit in his narrative: "This is the same Moses whom they had rejected with the words, 'Who made you ruler and judge?' He was sent to be their ruler and deliverer by God himself" (v. 35). Though God did use Moses to deliver them from slavery, said Stephen, "our fathers refused to obey him. Instead they rejected him and in their hearts turned back to Egypt" (v. 39). It is a vest-pocket sketch of Israel's sacred history. It features their record of rejecting those God sent to save them. To these who make a big pretense of honoring the sacred temple, Stephen reminded them of what they well knew: their fathers had the tabernacle under Moses and Joshua. Then David planned the temple and Solomon built it. All this led up to his key text from Isaiah 66:1–2.

> "'Heaven is my throne,
> and the earth is my footstool.
> What kind of house will you build for me?
> > says the Lord.
> Or where will my resting place be?
> Has not my hand made all these things?'"
> (Acts 7:49–50).

Stephen's defense turned into a charge against his accusers. It is not just a story, nor is it simply selected narrative. It is holy history recounted with details chosen to make one point. It is inductive preaching, not deductive. He begins with the traditional and respectful direct address: "Brothers and fathers listen to me." The message is narrative in genre and filled with visual imagery, with dialogue and other inductive elements. The point is made in the narrative but not stated until the end of the address. There Stephen states it bluntly. "You stiff-necked people with uncircumcised hearts and ears! You are just like your fathers: You always resist the Holy Spirit! Was there ever a prophet your fathers did not persecute? They even killed those who predicted the coming of the Righteous One. And now you have betrayed and murdered him—you who have received the law . . . but have not obeyed it" (vv. 51–53).

What if Stephen had started with his "big idea" or sermon thesis? He would never have made it through the sermon. A young

Pharisee named Saul of Tarsus was listening to that sermon. He found no rest until he found Christ.

An example of Paul's use of the sacred story is his address in the synagogue of Antioch of Pisidia. When recognized to speak, he began with the customary request for a hearing from the two kinds of people there, "Men of Israel and you Gentiles who worship God, listen to me!" (Acts 13:16). Then Paul summarized their holy history. God chose our fathers. They were strangers in Egypt, but God brought them out. For 40 years He put up with their waywardness in the wilderness. Deftly Paul sketched the narrative: "God gave them their land," then gave them judges, Samuel, a king, Saul, David, through whom "God has brought to Israel the Savior Jesus." He featured the endorsement of John the Baptist as he brought the story up-to-date. Finally, Paul applied the story: "It is to us that this message of salvation has been sent." He continued with a narrative of the life and ministry of Jesus. "The people of Jerusalem and their rulers did not recognize Jesus." They had him executed. "But God raised him from the dead." Paul used several Scriptures from their scrolls to show that Messiah's resurrection was anticipated and that through Jesus is offered forgiveness and justification. He ended with an admonition to take seriously God's gracious offer (Acts 13:26–41).

It is clear that New Testament speakers and writers made selective use of the stories from their Bible. They summarized and interpreted. Most notably, their purpose in telling the story shaped their selection of material. This raises a vital issue.

The Question of Creativity with Bible Stories

What is legitimate use of imagination in telling the biblical stories? Preaching in the black church tradition can enlighten many of us on this skill. Henry H. Mitchell's 1970 book, *Black Preaching*, earned him an invitation to deliver the Yale Lectures on Preaching in 1974. Those lectures, published as *The Recovery of Preaching,* proposed to help white preachers learn to move away from a style directed too exclusively to the intellect and to move instead toward a style that spoke to the whole person.

Mitchell made a valid point in saying, "White middle-class Protestant preaching . . . has been carried on in an academically oriented counterculture to the folk idiom of America's majority." But where do we draw the line between unacceptable liberties with Scripture and legitimate use of imagination in preaching?[3] Mitchell compared stories as they are found in the Bible to "dried milk: they do not become palatable until they are mixed with an ordinary substance like water."[4]

Vivid retelling of the story is the rule rather than exceptional in the Black church tradition. In a sermon on the providence of God, Henry Mitchell dramatizes Joseph's brothers pleading with him for their lives. They have buried their father Jacob and are sure that it signals their brother to repay them for all their wrong against him. The black preacher puts these words in the mouth of their spokesman: "But like Daddy said, we know that you must have done some of this so Daddy wouldn't be so upset and now that he's gone, we feel like a chicken running in an open field before a hawk. It's just a matter of time."[5]

The Black church tradition is not alone in the use of creative imagination in preaching. In H. A. Ironside's exposition of Paul's letter to Philemon, "Charge That to My Account," the preacher supposes, as do many other interpreters, that Onesimus must have stolen from Philemon before he ran away. Paul did suggest that Onesimus might owe Philemon something. Maybe he was a thief, maybe not. The slave himself was property belonging to the owner/master. When he took himself away, he defrauded his master of his service. It is not necessary to read more than that into Paul's words; "If he has done you any wrong or owes you anything, charge it to me. . . . I will pay it back" (Phlm 18–19).

Surely there are limits to the liberty a preacher may take in embellishing Bible stories. The question is where to draw the line. I will propose three standards that might be helpful as we deal with embellishing biblical stories. First, keep your imagination servant to the biblical writer's purpose in the story. Suppose your sermon text is the feeding of the five thousand (Matt 14:13–21).

---

[3] Henry H. Mitchell, *Recovery of Preaching* (New York: Harper Collins, 1977), 74–95.
[4] Ibid., 47.
[5] Quoted in Richard Eslinger, *A New Hearing: Living Options in Homiletical Method* (Nashville: Abingdon, 1987), 62.

You might imagine a couple of local entrepreneurs watching the crowd gather to hear Jesus. They chat with one another and begin to estimate that there will be a need for the crowd to eat before they start for homes around the Sea of Galilee. They will need lots of bread. They do some calculations of the crowd and what it would take to feed them. They calculate how much time and money it will take and plan to provide the meal. They see a legitimate business opportunity. For them it is a find-a-need-and-fill-it moment. So they hurry to the money lender with their plan. They need to buy wheat and barley, to enlist grinders and bakers, to gather firewood for ovens, to enlist carts and donkey drivers, vendors and miscellaneous helpers. They need it all in a hurry!

They get it all done at significant expense in time and money. They arrive with their caravan of bread and fish just in time to learn that Jesus has performed a miracle and fed the crowd before sending them home. Do you think they might be angry? *Mad* is the word! What can they do with a surplus of day-old bread and fish? One says: "I could kill Him! I could just literally kill Him! Somebody probably will! We are ruined! And if He keeps going, our whole economic system is ruined."

The other entrepreneur adds: "I hear that the zealots are ready to declare Him their Messiah. No wonder! Imagine a leader who can feed the whole army! Then if you have casualties, He can heal their wounds and, some say, even raise the dead." Is this legitimate imagination? Perhaps so, if it is presented as supposition.

The decision should hinge on whether this flight of fancy is in keeping with the New Testament writer's purpose in including this miracle story. Generally, in the miracles, the Gospel writers want to showcase the mighty power of Christ. There are other texts to show when and why opposition to Christ arose. Perhaps a preacher might start with one of those texts and use this one to illustrate how some opposition might have started and grown. Matthew presents Christ as Israel's King and Messiah who fulfilled the prophecies of old. Mark portrays Him as the Suffering Servant of Jehovah who came to seek and to save all the lost. Luke's two-volume work may highlight those stories that show Christ as Savior of all classes and Christians as bearers of that saving message. John's Gospel unveils the eternal Word who invaded our time and space to bring us salvation. New Testament scholarship continues with interpretations that revise and refine the church's understanding of the subtle emphases of the various Gospel accounts. Let the preacher or teacher keep the big picture in mind in interpreting each story.

A second standard deals with whether the preacher communicates that he is stepping into the realm of creative imagination. The congregation should know where and when the line is crossed. What does the Scripture plainly say, and what does the preacher imagine might be a legitimate reading between the lines? The preacher may give verbal cues. "Let's imagine that it happened this way." Or, "Do you suppose that it might have happened like this?" Words like *imagine, suppose, see,* or *envision* suggest that the preacher is going beyond pure exegesis into imaginative speculation. The sermon now tells how the action *may* have moved and the kind of dialogue that would be reasonable in that case.

A preacher may be personally convinced that Judas was a well-meaning zealot who entered into the Passover plot to expedite the glorious unveiling of the Messiah. Or as one recent book proposes, Judas and Jesus were in this together from the beginning. Never mind that the Gospels assign less noble motives to Judas: he was a thief who carried the money bag and was moved by Satan to betray Christ. If a preacher insists on a right to his opinion, at least let it be labeled as opinion. Perhaps people will go home from church saying, "Isn't that amazing? I never saw that in the Bible before!" That would be nice if they would all be like the Bereans and get out their Bibles and search to see if these things are so. A preacher may be allowed a little more room for creativity if he can make clear to the listener that his imagination is on steroids. This is not so easy to clarify, however, if the preacher is casting the whole sermon in a narrative, whether third-person or first-person storyteller.

A third standard deserves notice. When we see Jesus and others in the New Testament cite Old Testament references, we do not find them taking liberties with the sacred record. Even Jesus, who claimed the Creator's prerogative as Lord of the Sabbath, interpreted the Law. He did not embellish it. Paul might justify his Christology on the basis of the singular noun "Seed" as reference to one person,

Christ, rather than the collective reference we would suppose as reference to the whole nation Israel. Paul, however, did not yield to an unbridled imagination and rewrite the stories in his Bible.

So is creative imagination in interpretation ever valid? Sometimes it may be an aid to explaining or applying the text. Occasionally the Bible introduces a character and then tells us less than we might like to know about her or him. Fiction writers cater to such cravings. The first Bible-based novel I ever read was about Barabbas. The Bible does not give us much on him, and there is nothing for sure in the annals of secular history about the one whose cross Jesus occupied. How can anyone tell his story without using mostly imagination? That is what Bob Jones Jr. did in his historical novel *Wine of Morning*. It is a story that follows Barabbas from the crucifixion he was spared by Christ, his substitute. He was legally set free from a physical death penalty as the story opens. Not until the last scene in the book does he find true and everlasting liberty in Christ. Is this a valid way to communicate the gospel? The issue is not whether the Bible says that Barabbas was later converted to Christ. The gospel is in the imagined story of someone who ran from God in rebellion but finally came to surrender to Christ. Then this larger-than-life Barabbas of the novelist, like those Spirit-filled believers on the day of Pentecost, may be thought drunk on new wine in the middle of the morning.

An Example of a Story Sermon

Henry Scott Holland (1847–1918) was an English clergyman and author, born at Wimbleton, schooled at Eaton and Oxford, where he was renowned for learning and for character. While still in his thirties, he was appointed canon of St. Paul's Cathedral, London. He served there until the last eight years of his life, when he was professor of divinity at Oxford. Here is a digest of his classic biographical sermon on the apostle John.[6]

---

[6] Henry Scott Holland, "The Story of a Disciple's Faith," in *The World's Great Sermons*, Grenville Kleiser, compiler (New York: Funk and Wagnalls, 1908), 9:147–64; see also http://books.google.com/books?id=3F5EFsSdoMgC&pg=PA145&lpg=PA145&dq=henry+scott+holland+%22story+of+a+disciple's+faith%22&source=web&ots=XMS4HFIOiT&sig=cDcQT4JyrVyfCUGCGdcaBCg78So#PPP7,M1/. The sermon traces John's personal testimony through his Gospel. It is a manuscript of some 4,700 words but here is a synopsis of about one-third that.

The Story of a Disciple's Faith

by Henry Scott Holland

*"Then went in also that other disciple which came first
to the sepulcher, and he saw and believed."*
—John 20:8

John the beloved disciple, has given his witness. What he once touched, and tasted, and handled, that he has declared unto us. It was the epiphany of God the Father which he and the twelve had discovered, tabernacled close at their side in the body of Christ. "We saw his glory, the glory as of God himself." So he pronounces. Yet still his listeners sit on about his feet. They must reproduce in themselves the living story. "Let us hear it all," they say; "tell us of that day when it first came to you that something wonderful was there. Tell us how you slowly learned the great mystery. Tell us, that we, too, may say with you and ten thousand times ten thousand: 'Worthy is the Lamb that was slain.'" This St. John sets himself to do, and you can see that he begins his gospel with the day on which the disciples began to believe on Him; and he ends it with the first completed confession of Jesus by an apostle—the confession of Thomas.

The Fourth Gospel tells us how the apostolic faith was established. The apostle unlocks his soul to us that he may help us mount up into his assured peace, so calm, so sure, so strong. He can recall every tiny detail of that first critical hour. Even the Pharisees of Jerusalem felt the excitement and shared the hope; and it was to their deputation that the Baptist made his repudiation; "No, I am not it, not the Christ; no, nor Elias, nor a prophet. I am nought but a flying cry in the wilderness. Not I but another that comes after me. . . . I am not the Christ."

And then came the great moment. It was the very next day—so exact in the apostle's memory. The very day after the great confession, John saw Jesus coming toward him, and a wonderful word broke from him: "Behold the

Lamb of God, which taketh away the sins of the world."
Taketh away the sin! Oh, the peace of such a promise!
They had been washed in the Jordan, and had repented,
and had confessed, and yet found their burden of sin as
miserable as ever! The words haunted them. And when
the day following, John uttered them again, two of them
at least could not rest. Their hearts burned to know more.
Who is this strange visitant—so silent? He does not even
stop to look. He just passes by. In another moment He will
be gone. They must act for themselves then. So two of
them that heard John speak followed Him. And John the
beloved, who now tells us the story, was one of the two.
He turned and saw them following, and it was then they
heard His voice first speak—"Whom seek ye?" That was
all. They hardly knew what to say and they stammered
out: "Rabbi, where dwellest thou?" And He said: "Come
and see."

Come and see! It was all so quiet and natural. No one
could have seen anything unusual. Just three short sentences. And yet they sealed their lot for eternity. That was
the moment of decision. "Come and see." They went and
saw. So intense is the apostle's memory of that blest hour
that he can never forget the very hour of the day. It was
ten o'clock when he got to the house. They stopped there
with him that night, and in the morning they were sure of
what they had found. So sure were they that neither could
rest until he had hurried off with the good news to find and
bring his brother. Andrew found his brother Peter before
John could find James. Both were prepared to assert, "We
have found the Christ." So it all began.

"And what next"—so the listeners ask—"what was the
next step made?" Three days later, at Cana, for the first
time, came that strange secret of which the apostle had
spoken. The glory shown out with a sudden flash from
the deeps within him; a word of power leapt out—very
quietly. Very few saw or knew it. But as the few saw the
white water redden into wine, they felt the wonder that

had passed over their own being. There his disciples first believed in him.

And what next did they learn? It was at Jerusalem, the Passover feast. The Master made first entry and startled them. He who was so quiet and reserved burned with a sudden fury as He looked upon the Temple of Jehovah. Very, very rarely did He show Himself excited or disturbed, but then He was terrible. He bound together a scourge of small cords. He drove the cattle in front of Him. He dashed over the money-changers' tables. And John can recall still the look of the coins as they poured upon the pavement. The disciples wondered at the violence of the emotion, until a word from an old Psalm came into their minds, that the zeal of the Lord's house should be in a prophet's heart like a devouring fire.

And how can we follow the apostle through all the wonderful story? Yet just one thing we cannot pass over—the crisis in Galilee. Just when all looked brightest, when the people were rushing round Him, and would have made Him a king. But He—He threw it all away to the winds. He hurried off the twelve across the lake. He scattered the crowd; He fled back Himself alone in the dark hills, and on the morrow at Capernaum, He broke it all down by a word which staggered the rising belief. It was a saying about His body and His blood—a very hard saying. The Pharisees were furious; His own disciples were dumfounded. They fell away and walked no more with Jesus.

"And you, O disciple dearly loved, what of you and your brethren? Will ye also go away?" The very tenderness of the reproach recovered us. Peter's lips broke the words which sealed us to Him forever: "Nay, Lord, to whom shall we go? Thou hast the words of eternal life." So they followed and clung, the trembling band, through all the harrowing days in which enmity hardened itself into hate.

Two points John singles out for himself as marking epochs of his own conviction. He stood below the bitter cross, and saw the nail beaten through the hands and feet, and he heard the last loud cry, and yet still his despair hung heavy as death upon his soul, until just at the touch of the soldier's spear, there broke from the dead side a little jet of blood and water. What was it he saw and felt? What so startled him? Why should it haunt him sixty years after? We cannot tell. Perhaps he could never tell. Only just at that little pivot moment, he must break off all his story to declare with abrupt and quivering emphasis: "This is the disciple that wrote these things. He it is who saw the water and the blood, and he knows that his record is true."

And once again, in the haste of the resurrection morning, what was the moment and what was the scene which turned his despair to belief? It was the moment at which he stooped down and saw within the empty tomb the folded napkin and the linen clothes. What did he notice? Why, that the napkin that had been round the Master's head was not lying with the linen clothes, but was rolled up in a place by itself. A tiny, tiny thing! Yet somehow it was that which he saw and never forgot. A key was turned and a bolt shot back somewhere within his breast, and a secret flashed upon him, and his blindness fell off, and a quiver of hope shot up like a flame, and a new light broke over him, and he passed at one bound out of death into life. "Then entered in, therefore that other disciple . . . and he saw and believed."

My brethren, where do you stand? How far have you come in this pathway of faith? Consider it. What an assurance! Who is there that has ever been brave enough to accept such a salutation without a whisper of protest? Who is this that dares to stand up and say "Come, all who are weary and heavy-laden—come, all who are burdened sorely with sin—come all to me—I will give you rest?" Who is He? Look at Him. He is passing even now before you. Follow him.

O Jesus, Lord and lover of souls, there are many of us laden with sickness and sin, sad and with doubt and fear, that are asking: "Master, where dwellest thou?" Oh, let

them even come home with thee and see. Go and see.
Abide with Him, talk with Him. Go and see.

Exercise 1. Canon Holland's sermon on the beloved disciple deserves diligent study. John 10:8 is posted as a text before the sermon introduction. Is this single verse the text? Or would you consider the many biblical references from the Gospel of John the true biblical authority? How many such references do you find? Count them.

Exercise 2. What technique does the preacher use that keeps the whole sermon a narrative besides telling a number of stories from John's experience of Christ? Who are these "listeners" who sit at the aged apostle's feet?

Exercise 3. A great many details of this sermon reveal thoughtful and diligent attention to the Gospel of John for what it says about John's personal experience of Christ. How appropriate is the sermon title?

Chapter 8

REMEMBERING THE CHILDREN

PASTOR PAUL HAD BEEN CALLED to Shady Suburb Church and was in his first staff meeting. Two secretaries, a minister of music and a minister of education gathered around. A part-time youth minister was in college and not available for this meeting. This was not Pastor Paul's first pastorate, so he came with an agenda for the meeting. There were some things he was eager to settle right from the start. After a time of prayer and a Scripture reading, the first item on the agenda read, "The Children's Sermon."

Pastor Paul had noticed in some recent copies of the Order of Service that there was a time early in the Sunday morning service called "The Children's Sermon." The pastor's secretary had already told him that it was a perennial problem to get someone to take the assignment. Some of the staff felt strongly that it would be well to discontinue the feature. It had been a long tradition as part of the Sunday morning service, however, and there were always one to two dozen children from kindergarten to third grade who came to the front at the time for this feature. So the big question remained not *if* but *who*? What a surprise for the staff when Pastor Paul announced, "Well, I thought I might work into this slowly, but if I am not taking away someone's job, I will plan on doing the children's sermon regularly beginning next Sunday."

This chapter calls on the pastor to be the number one storyteller for children in his church. Children need to hear from the pastor at three places in particular, and they will hear if what the pastor says is cast in a story. First, children hear every sermon whether the preacher keeps them in mind or not. They pay attention to the stories, and they remember them. Remember the children when you are preparing your Sunday sermons.

Second, the children's sermon is a special opportunity to minister to children in their most impressionable time of life. And third, stories are also wonderful pathways to helping and healing children in one-on-one counseling and other therapeutic ministry. In this chapter we will give special attention to the children's sermon and to the use of story in counseling with children.

The Children's Sermon

Why do a children's sermon? A pastor can easily find plenty of reasons to skip it. It takes time to prepare to do it well. How can the pastor add one more preparation to his overloaded agenda every week? Some complain that children are bored with it. They won't sit still for a sermon; that's not the way to communicate to children in the twenty-first century if it ever was. Some people consider it a distraction and a disruption to the dignity and decorum of the worship hour. "If we could put the children in a separate children's service, it would be better for them and for us."

The pastor certainly has good reasons to proclaim the Word to children, whether in their own service or in their own special part of the family worship service. God has promised to bless the proclamation of His Word. (Remember Isa 55:10–11, for example.) The Word of God has the power to change lives and save souls. When we stand at the judgment seat of Christ, he will not ask us how many children we were able to gather and how much fun they had. Jesus will ask us if we fed the little lambs. Children deserve more than entertainment. They deserve the life-giving Word.

Some churches that still include a children's sermon, assign the task to an assistant, to a volunteer children's worker, or to whoever can't say no. The pastor should consider accepting this assignment for several reasons. Children are ready to receive spiritual truth from the pastor. They do not yet have the resistance or cynicism of youth and adults. These are their most formative years. In addition, the pastor is called and commissioned to preach the gospel. God's Word commands us to keep in our hearts God's gracious dealing with us as His people. We are to teach these things to our children and grandchildren (Deut 4:9). And while we never want to make the mistake of using the children to say something to the adults, the adults often say, only half joking, that they get more out of the children's sermon than from the main message. This is often true. In any case, the Word of God goes where God directs it and does what God deigns for it to do.

What about a children's worship service? Much can be said in favor of a separate worship space for children. Even if it seems to be the wise choice, the pastor should consider taking seven to ten minutes from the family worship service to join the children long enough for a five- or six-minute children's sermon. Some growing churches need the space for adults in the auditorium. The parents are able to give their undivided attention to their worship if someone else is supervising their children. Some churches still bring busloads of children without parental supervision and without a tradition of how to behave in church. These are all good reasons to have children in a separate service, but they are not necessarily good reasons for the pastor to delegate the children's sermon to someone else.

If the church decides to segregate children from the family worship setting, let them make a separate decision about the children's sermon and who should present it. In one of my pastorates, we had a separate children's service but filed the children into the sanctuary while the congregation sang a hymn. They heard a brief children's sermon and in a recessional returned to their own space for the rest of the time. It was the better of two worlds for the children. They had some experience of worship with the choir and congregation and still had a service planned appropriate to their learning readiness.

Planning the children's sermon. Question: How many points does a children's sermon need? Answer: At least one, and most of the time at most one. That is not a bad rule for any sermon to any age group, by the way. The ideal children's sermon has three essentials but not necessarily three points. First and foremost, the message needs to be anchored in the Word of God. The preacher has no message of his own to deliver; he is a messenger of the King of kings. Let the apostle Paul's charge to Timothy be our commitment: "I give you this charge: Preach the Word" (2 Tim 4:1–2). Second, let the Word be clearly applied to the appropriate age level. And don't sell children short because they are young. And third, keep the narrative quality in every sermon. The story may be an attention-getter for an opening to the sermon. Of course, it needs to do more than gain attention. It needs to focus the attention of the children on the text and the goal of this brief message. H. C. Brown Jr. used to remind us in preaching class, "It's not an advantage to be known as 'Brother Obvious.'" Vary the approach, but ensure narrative quality in every children's sermon; just don't let that be the only way you begin one. Suppose the text is a narrative passage from one of the Gospels; then a narrative illustration may be unnecessary. In any case, it's good to keep the narrative quality in children's sermons.

It is not enough to have some object lesson to gain the attention of the children. Most object lessons I have heard or read fall far short of the essential goal of explaining and applying the Word of God. Besides, many young children may not be able to make the connection between the concrete object and the abstract truth it is supposed to illustrate. The leap of logic is lost on small children, no doubt.

Children's sermons in series. Long-range planning is essential for children's sermons as well as for the pastor's entire pulpit plan. Include the selection of texts and sermon aim as you plan the Sunday morning services. Often the same Scripture reading will provide a text for the children's sermon as well as guidance for the full sermon. Long-range planning makes for efficiency of study time. Many pastors have based their first children's sermon on Luke 2:52. "Jesus grew both in body and in wisdom, gaining favor with God and men" (TEV). Instead of one sermon with four points, why not make that a series of four sermons with one point each Sunday. It takes about as much time to plan all four messages as to plan one. Besides, children (as well as adults) learn and remember more with the aid of combined units.

Once while browsing in a Christian bookstore, I found a little sock puppet with the face of a little lamb. I got the idea for a series of children's sermons on the theme "His Sheep Am I." The children came to the front for their special part of the worship while we all sang the chorus by that name. With the help of dialogue between the pastor and the puppet, the series asked and answered four questions from Scripture. First "How Does a Sheep Get Lost?" In question-and-answer dialogue with the puppet, I asked "Sammy Sheep" if he had ever been lost? "Oh, yes! It was awful! I couldn't find my mommy or daddy. I didn't know the way home. It was awful!" Then I asked, "How does a sheep get lost? Is he a bad sheep fighting the other sheep? Does he jump over the fence and run away? Does he butt the shepherd and run and hide?" Each time Sammy answered, "No-oo." Then how did you get lost? "I just wandered off." Then I went to the text Isaiah 53:6 and had Sammy help me read it. "All we like sheep have gone astray; we have turned every one to his own way." That is enough for one installment. Let the children get their minds around what it means to be lost. Then tell them that next week we will talk about who came to find the lost sheep. The answer is in Luke 15:1–7 and 19:10. The third Sunday we turned to Psalm 23 to answer the question, "Who Cares for the Sheep?" The final installment asked, "Whom Do the Sheep Follow?" The answer is in John 10:27–28.

On another year we returned to Psalm 23 with the children for a whole series on the Shepherd's Psalm. And the "I Am" sayings of Jesus in John's Gospel are good for a series of six meditations on Christ. "I am the bread of life" (6:35), "I am the light of the world" (8:12), "I am (God)" (8:58). And I chose to present a separate meditation on each of the three metaphors in John 14:1–8, "I am the way and the truth and the life." The series rounded out with one brief meditation on John 15:1–8, "I am the true vine." Others have made a whole series of sermons or Bible studies on that passage.

Jonah provided a completely narrative series in four installments, one for each of the four chapters: Chapter 1, "You Can't Run Away from God." Chapter 2, "God Answers Prayer." Chapter 3, "When you Follow Directions." And chapter 4, "The Prophet Who Pouted."

Sometimes I like to do a "cliff-hanger series" like the old Saturday matinee features of my childhood. A series, for example, on David the shepherd boy was a continuing story, but each installment ended with David in some crisis that was not resolved until the next Sunday. Then he went to the next crisis. Some of the texts and titles for these eight installments were "God Looks at the Heart" (1 Sam 16:10–13); "Little David, Play on Your Harp" (1 Sam 16:19–23); "David, the Lion Slayer" (1 Sam 17:34–35), and "The Eye of Envy" (1 Sam 18:6–11). The first installment told the story of God's sending Samuel to anoint one of Jesse's sons to be the next king of Israel. Would it be Eliab? Abinaadab? Shammah, or one of the other seven sons of Jesse? Finally they sent for the boy David, who was out in the fields with the sheep. The Lord told Samuel, "Man looks at the outward appearance, but the Lord looks at the heart" (1 Sam 16:7). Since that is the truth we want to convey to the children in this sermon, we interrupt the story right there with David before Samuel. "Is this the one to be anointed king? How can we know? We will find out next week!" In another episode the lad protects the sheep from a lion and a bear. Then there is the dramatic and familiar story of combat with Goliath. Another installment features David and Jonathan, "Friends Forever." Each episode ends with a cliff hanger. In one, King Saul, the madman, hurls a javelin at David aiming to pin him to the wall. That's a good place to break off the story with the javelin in mid-flight toward the young court harpist. Is this the end for David? The series ends in the ninth episode with David crowned king. When God makes a promise, it will always come true sooner or later.

Once I did a series on "Hymn Writers You Should Know." Six selected writers were introduced with a brief story from their childhood matched to a text of Scripture. Fanny Crosby wrote poems when she was just a little girl including a verse which said: "O what a happy girl am I/ Although I cannot see/ I am resolved that in this world/ Contented I shall be." Philippians 4:11 makes a good text: "I have learned to be content whatever the circumstances." Another was Isaac Watts, who also wrote poems while still a little boy. In fact, one time it got him in trouble during family devotions. His father had become weary of the boy always speaking in rhymes and warned him that the next time he did so, he would get a spanking. Young Isaac saw a mouse on the grandfather clock and chuckled during family prayers. His father wanted to know what was so funny. He told him about the little four-legged visitor in a spontaneous verse: "There was a mouse for want of stairs ran up the clock to say his prayers." That was the last straw for his father, so out came the rod of correction. Young Isaac pleaded pitifully: "Oh Father, Father, pity take, and I will no more verses make!" Other hymn writers included Charlotte Elliott, who was converted when a family friend showed her how to come to Christ just as she was. She wrote, "Just as I am without one plea,/ But that thy blood was shed for me,/ And that thou bidst me come to thee,/ O Lamb of God, I come." Revelation 22:17 was a fitting text. "The Spirit and the bride say, 'Come.'" Similar treatment from the stories of William Cowper, William Bradbury, and Francis Havergal rounded out this series.

Also good for a series of children's sermon are the seven virtues in "The Armor of God" series from Ephesians 6:13–17. And children need to know the Ten Commandments. A worthy goal would be to encourage the children to memorize the Decalogue during the ten weeks. In this series the preacher will definitely need to have all ten planned before starting. Preaching to children on "Thou Shalt Not Commit Adultery" requires forethought whether the parents are listening in or not. I handled that one with a story from Corrie ten Boom's autobiography. When she was a little girl, she asked her father once, "Poppa, what is sex sin?" The wise old man thought a long time before he answered: "Corrie, you know when we go on the train, Poppa carries your suitcase because it is too heavy for you? Well, sex sin is like that; some things are too heavy for the mind of a little girl. Until you are old enough, Poppa will carry it for you." Then the preacher can go on and tell the children as much as they are ready to know. You might tell them that this commandment is meant to keep their mother and daddy true and faithful in love with each other as long as they both live.

Once I did a three-part series on "Big Words for Little Folk." Children like to learn big words, and it is sometimes helpful to have some big words to talk about our great big God. I taught the children how to pronounce *omniscience, omnipotence,* and *omnipresence.* The texts for these three were John 21:17, "Lord, Thou knowest all" and Matthew 18:20, "There I am," and Philippians 3:21, "He is able."

Later I did a longer series on "Big Words to Talk about Our Great Salvation." This time, to help with pronunciation, I cut 28-inch poster board into strips to accommodate four-inch block letters. They easily learned the pronunciation by breaking the words into syllables, starting at the end of the word, and adding syllables all the way to the beginning. The words were all metaphors for salvation—*redemption, reconciliation, propitiation, regeneration, justification, adoption,* and *assurance.* After learning to say the word, a New Testament verse that uses the word was explained with an appropriate story. For example, explaining *redemption* took me way back to a story I first heard in my own childhood. A little boy made a little wooden boat with a mast and a sail. But it got away from him in the stream near his home and was lost. Later he saw his little boat in the window of a second-hand store. He went in to reclaim his boat, but the store owner told him he had bought the boat from someone else. If he wanted it, he would have to pay the price. The little fellow went home, gathered the price from his piggy bank, and went back to buy his boat. As he left, he was heard to say, "Now, little boat, you are doubly mine. You are mine because I made you, and you are mine because I bought you."

At Christmastime the pastor may do a series on "Name the Baby" and use the significance of names like Jesus, Emmanuel, Wonderful Counselor, Mighty God, and Prince of Peace. Christmas carols also make a good series in another Advent season. And I once did a series on Christmas traditions and explained the biblical justification for traditions that some think should be discarded because of possible pagan roots. Why not teach the children that we give gifts because God so loved us that He gave the greatest gift of all, Jesus? And let the Christmas lights remind us of the star that led the magi to Bethlehem and of Jesus, the Light of the world. Of course, better than tinsel and toys would be a manger scene with more explicit link to the Scripture narrative.

Notes on delivery of the children's sermon. A conversational tone rather than an oratorical declamation is fitting for talking to children. If at all possible, get on their eye level, even if you need to sit down with them. This does not mean passionless speech.

Children will know if you are putting on a manner hypocritically. They want you to show excitement when it is real and appropriate. Though painted fire never burns, genuine enthusiasm kindles the flame in tender hearts.

Therapeutic Stories for Children

One morning soon after the terrorist attacks of 9/11 a six-year-old girl told her mother about a dream. "I was on a ship, and it crashed. There were a lot of skeletons around, and then some people came who were trying to kill us."

Because the mother, Karen Carter, had learned about storytelling as a healing art, she said decidedly to her child, "That sounds like a story. It just isn't finished yet." They snuggled close together, and then the mother began.

Once upon a time there were 1500 people on a big strong ship. It sailed out into the ocean with great hope and courage. It sailed on very well, but one day a storm came. The sky darkened, and the ocean swelled higher and higher, then plunged down low. Up and down the sea tossed the boat as the rain rained, and the thunder thundered, and the winds howled. The people on the boat looked out but couldn't see what was ahead of them or what was behind them. They were lost. They tossed here and there until they crashed hard into a rock. The boat broke apart. The people swam and tried to hold onto bits and pieces of the boat. They tried to help each other, but the stormy sea kept them going under and coming back up and going under and coming back up until they also crashed into the rock. And there they saw skeletons. And there they saw a band of pirates who came toward them with daggers in their hands. The good people of the ship feared that the pirates would kill them. This was the Island of Bones. The pirates wanted more people to build their island bigger. They

wanted to kill those good people and have more
and more skeletons.

At last another ship came. It was a ship that needed
no water. It sailed right out of the stormy sky. Sailing
the ship was an enormous angel with tremendous
power. With a bolt of lightning, he stunned the pirates
so they could kill no more. Then he gathered the people of the ship. Some of them he brought to heaven
so that they could be made whole again. And others
he brought to different places all over the world. He
gave them the power of peace. And so strongly did
they carry it that when other people saw them, they
became peaceful too. They felt it right in the middle
of their hearts. It was the peace that can live in one's
heart of hearts, and it is helpful for all men and all
women and all children whenever they are troubled
and whenever they are not. And that is the story of
"The Ship That Needed No Water."'

Her daughter pondered the story and was satisfied. Afterward
she had a good day of playing with friends. Nancy Mellon, the
storyteller, encourages parents and others to help their troubled
children with healing stories. She recommends a plan for the
storyteller.[1]

First, listen carefully to your child's fears and troubling dreams
with openness and respect. Pay attention to detail. If your child is
experiencing nightmares like the one in the story above, you might
say, "That dream sounds like a story. It just isn't finished yet."

Second, slow down and relax. Take time to snuggle close
together in a comforting place. Mellon suggests strumming a few
chords on an open-stringed instrument or playing a few notes
slowly and thoughtfully on a xylophone to encourage a soothing
pace and mood.

---

[1] I have followed Mellon's plan with a few modifications which seem more appropriate
for Christian storytellers. For more help on therapeutic stories for children see www.heal-
ingstory.com. Shortly after the 9/11 attack, Nancy Mellon posted this remarkable offering on the Web site called "Healing Story." See Nancy Mellon, "How to Create Stories
for Children Who Are Having Fears and Nightmares," http://www.healingstory.org/crisis/
nightmares/ fears_and_nightmares.html, accessed September 21, 2001. Used by permission of Healing Story and Nancy Mellon.

Third, listen to your heart and your child's heart. Take a few moments to prepare yourself and the troubled child.

Fourth, dedicate yourself to offering a healing gift. Ask God to use your imagination and intuition to create a story to meet the needs of your child or children. Dismiss any fears and doubts of your own about your creativity and abilities as a storyteller.

Fifth, frame the story in your mind. You might find it helpful to follow the cycle of the Plot Movements Worksheet in chapter 3. Let the story move from the opening situation to the stress of the storm and shipwreck to the searching struggle of the survivors, to the solution of the rescue ship and the new situation of peace and security restored. Use the crisis expressed in the child's nightmare. Keep the story structure simple. The classic plot structure moves through tests and trials toward greater strength, wisdom, and love. In the mother's resolution of the child's nightmare, the child's account of the stress situation is accepted. The situation is escalated by a triple crisis: the storm at sea, the shipwreck, and the Island of Bones with menacing pirates. The solution did not depend on any physical strength of the child but in the coming of the heavenly ship to rescue the good people.

The mother who made up the story "The Ship That Needed No Water" accepted her child's dream-picture of a ship. She chose to emphasize a mood of hope, courage, and clear sailing at the beginning of her story. She did not change the imagery to airliners crashing into twin towers. She chose the image of a storm with waves tossing the ship up and down. The characters in her story wanted to see beyond this storm but could not. That is a healthy admission. The child would know that her mother was aware of her feelings of fear and helplessness. She did not label these feelings lest that reinforce them. Instead she let the flow of images in the story deal with her child's terror. At the same time the storyteller's calm strength spoke to the child's fear.

Children can usually handle scary scenes in an entertaining monster story such as Hansel and Gretel, but a therapeutic tale is not the time to reinforce fear. The mother was probably wise to avoid saying that the people were very afraid. More important than whether the fear is named is the storyteller's calm voice. Even if the fear is named, it need not be fortified. In the mother's story the boat broke, and the people found themselves in great distress. Like the child's dream the story unfolds in powerful and mysterious images.

Notice that the storyteller admitted the presence of evil people in the world; the child knew that much. The new story, however, stressed the goodness of people. "The people tried to help one another." She presented the murderous people in a matter-of-fact way. Her child had met pirates with daggers in their hands in other stories so the mother kept that familiar imagery. It took candor and courage for the mother to introduce the Island of Bones in the tale. Again, there are evil people in their world.

In fairy tales and wonder tales through the centuries, help always comes to good people in trouble—often through magical or mysterious ways. In Nancy Mellon's report of the story, the ship that needed no water was such a rescue. About as close as she came to a wise and loving Heavenly Father was the image of a "colossal Angel whose power comes from beyond ordinary consciousness." The powerful angel gathers the people of the shipwreck to make them whole. Some he takes to heaven. Others he sends with the power of peace around the world.

As her story draws to a close, the mother speaks of peace in the heart of hearts that is "helpful for all men and women and children whenever they are troubled and whenever they are not." This helps the child feel that she and her playmates are cared for and loved. Children need this assurance especially in times of national crisis. Children become judges of honesty very early. The story closes with evil and frightening events transformed mysteriously into wholeness and goodness.

Because the mother started with her child's dream image, she used such images to bring the stress to solution. Terror is not the final word; peace and security prevail. Blessed are the children who have a parent or a pastor or someone who can help them find peace in the storm and strength in the trial. Shouldn't pastors cultivate such skills in ministry to children? And shouldn't ministers see that children's workers in the church learn the power of storytelling and help equip parents for this ministry as well?[2]

---

[2] Karen Carter is the mother who told this story to her daughter. They lived in New York when 9/11 came. Now they live in Iowa. For more on Nancy Mellon's work with children, see Nancy Mellon, *Storytelling with Children* (Gloucestershire, UK: Hawthorn, 2000).

Exercise 1. Start a seed file of texts and ideas for children's sermons. Anything that children need to know about God is in the Bible. The pastor's challenge is learning to communicate God's Word to the little ones.

Exercise 2. Consider the dramatic monologue for at least one children's sermon. Most pastors will never in their career attempt a dramatic monologue at all. That's OK, but the children's sermon is a great way to try one on for size. It need not be a full costume drama with stage setting. Just put on a turban and pretend to be a Bible character telling your story in first-person testimony style.

Exercise 3. Think of a recent one-on-one counseling encounter you had with a troubled child. It may have been one of your own or one in a church setting. How might you have been more helpful with a therapeutic story?

Chapter 9

TEN WAYS TO SHARPEN
STORYTELLING SKILLS

PASTOR PAUL PUSHED BACK FROM his desk and gathered up the stack of papers representing the first draft of his sermon. He had wrestled with the text and the doctrine of the incarnation of Christ. He had organized his presentation toward a goal of understanding and celebrating that doctrine. But as he reviewed his work, he knew something was missing. For such a doctrine, it seemed so abstract! He was confident it was orthodox and anchored in his text, but would it connect with the congregation? How could he bring it down to earth?

He let his mind chase the problem for a while and then picked up a clean sheet of paper and started his sermon introduction this way: "If you knew that by becoming a sparrow you could bring the gospel to the world of sparrows, would you do it? But wait a minute. If you knew that by taking on the body of a sparrow for this mission, you would remain a sparrow for all eternity, would you do it?" He felt now he had his sermon starter, but the doctrinal sermon still needed more narrative quality.

The thought of sparrows reminded Pastor Paul of a story he had heard in his childhood. A farmer declined as usual his wife's invitation to go with her to church. He was not a believer and was agnostic about anything supernatural. It was Christmastime. The idea of God's becoming man made absolutely no sense to him at all. As he went about his chores in the ice and snow covering his barnyard, he noticed a fluttering of sparrows vainly searching for a crumb to keep them alive. The man was not without compassion so he decided to get a few cups of feed grain and scatter it on the ice. The birds were not long in finding it. Then he thought: *They are going to freeze to death before dark if they don't find some shelter.* He decided to open his barn doors wide and spread some feed inside. Then if they would go in, he could close the barn and give them a safe place from the gathering storm. As hungry as they were, most of the sparrows would not go in the barn. Those who did, flew away as soon as he tried to close the door. The farmer looked at them wonderingly. Didn't they know that he only meant to help them? How could he ever communicate his intentions? Then it dawned on him that the only way he might do that would require that he himself become a sparrow.

Pastor Paul wondered how many in his congregation might have already heard the anecdote. He thought of one dear sister in particular who always let him know if he used a story she had heard before. Only she never said, "I've heard that story." The way she put it was always, "We've heard that sermon before." Never mind that it was a completely new sermon; if it included an old anecdote, it was an old sermon.

Pastor Paul's problem was the problem of every preacher: how to enhance the narrative quality in our sermons. Instead of resorting to omnibus volumes of stale anecdotes, try these exercises. For a preacher serious about sharpening storytelling skills, a worthy goal might be to try a different one of these ten suggestions in each of the next five or six sermons you prepare.[1]

Summarize a Short Story

A short story or even a whole novel may be reduced to one or two hundred words. Keep the plot in place. Here is a summary of a story by Guy de Maupassant that many of us read in high school. It illustrates the destructive power of the tongue warned of in James 3.

A little old man stooped on the dusty road to pick up a piece of string. He was embarrassed to note that someone saw him do so,

[1] Some of this chapter was previously published in Austin B. Tucker, "Enhancing the Narrative Quality in Your Sermons," *Proclaim: The Pastor's Journal for Biblical Preaching* (June-August 1997): 46–48, and more recently in Austin B. Tucker, "Seven Ways to Boost Your Storytelling Power," *Preaching* (September-October, 2006): 20–22.

and he quickly hid the innocent scrap. By the time he got to town to discover that a wallet was lost, he was already accused of finding it. His denials and explanations about "a piece of string" seemed only to confirm growing suspicion. Then a week later someone did find the wallet and return it. Instead of clearing the old man, this gave the rumors momentum. Shortly after that he died. Talk killed him.[2]

If your sermon can afford twice the space for this illustration, add dialogue, names, and other details from the story.

Turn a Cartoon or Comic Strip into a Narrative

Comic strips have something of a story line built in, but even a cartoon can provide a bit of narrative with setting, characters, and plot. A *Forbes* magazine cartoon shows a grandfatherly gentleman in an oversized easy chair talking to a little girl seated opposite him in a matching chair. Around them in the elegant sitting room is ample evidence of wealth. He is answering her question about how he made his fortune.

"It was really quite simple. I bought a pencil for a penny, sharpened it, and sold it for two cents. With this I bought two pencils, sharpened them, and sold them for four cents. And so it went until I had amassed $10.24. It was then that your Great Aunt Selma died and left us $10 million."[3]

The cartoonist probably never meant that to illustrate spiritual truth, but it might. Think of the testimony of one who does not really appreciate salvation by grace. "I joined the church and was baptized. I started working in the church and giving to the church. Oh yes, and Christ died for all my sins."

One edition of the comic strip *Dilbert* pivots on the use of a metaphor. In the first frame of the comic strip, Dilbert's pointy-haired boss meets him in the hall and asks: "Can you bring me up to speed before we go to the meeting?" In the second frame Dilbert answers: "No. You can't fit two gallons in a thimble no matter how fast you pour." The third frame is around the conference table obviously in the meeting room where it suddenly dawns on the pointy-haired boss to ask: "Wait a minute . . . which one of us is the thimble?"[4]

---

[2] Guy de Maupassant, "A Piece of String," 1884.
[3] B. J. Killen cartoon in *Forbes*, July 15, 1985, 20.
[4] *Dilbert* comic strip in *The Times of Shreveport-Bossier* (LA), July 27, 2006.

Place a Quotation in Its Historical Context

As a diamond is shown to its best advantage in the right mounting, so a familiar quotation sparkles more in its historical setting. A preacher citing Martin Luther might be surprised how many in the congregation think he is quoting a mid-twentieth-century civil rights leader rather than the seventeenth-century reformer. I was in college and had heard the "Here I stand" statement many times before I learned the Diet of Worms was a general assembly of the empire and not what Luther had to eat in prison. Let the preacher give a thumbnail sketch of Luther's life, focusing on that crucial scene. If you need help with the biographical data, you can do an online search and find more than you ever wanted to know. Just be sure to use a reliable source.

Glean from Leisure Reading and TV Time

Sometimes a scene in a secular book, movie, or television show will be useful for presenting Christ as the hope of the hopeless. Get the notebook habit. I keep a few index cards handy while relaxing with TV or leisure reading. A telling scene in the 1986 movie *The Trumpet of Gideon,* still seen on TV from time to time, speaks volumes to the impasse of hostility that continues between Arabs and Jews as well as the larger problem of terrorism and war in the world. Steven Bauer plays a young Israeli secret service agent named Avner. He and his select team are on a mission to avenge the Munich massacre. They have traveled the world killing Arab terrorists. This, of course, stirs Arab retaliation. One after another of Avner's team members are killed. They are blown up or shot or stabbed until he alone is left. In a return visit to his commander in Israel, Avner expressed his misgivings, "We cannot go on this way—'an eye for an eye'—pretty soon the whole world will be blind!"

The commander retorted: "What is the answer then?" To which Avner replied: "I don't have the answer!" We who know Christ claim that we do have the answer.

Quote a Verse of a Hymn or Other Poetry in Its Narrative Setting

A number of good books tell about authors and composers and the circumstances surrounding the writing of our hymns.

John Fawcett was born and raised in poverty in eighteenth-century England. At age 16 he came to Christ through the ministry of evangelist George Whitfield. Ten years later he became an ordained Baptist minister and pastor of an impoverished congregation in Northern England. As the years went by, his family grew but not his salary. But then a call came from the large and influential Carter's Lane Baptist Church in London. When the day of departure came, the saddened congregation gathered around the wagons. Mrs. Fawcett finally broke down and said, "John, I cannot bear to leave. I know not how to go!"

"Nor can I either," said the pastor. Soon the happy congregation was unpacking the wagons. In a sermon some time later, the pastor shared the four verses of a poem he had written which began:

> Blest be the tie that binds
> Our hearts in Christian love!
> The fellowship of kindred minds
> Is like to that above.

Pastor Fawcett stayed in the poor parish the rest of his days, but a wider recognition and usefulness did come to him.[5]

The poet Edwin Markham, as he approached retirement, discovered that the man to whom he had entrusted his financial portfolio had spent every penny. Markham's dream of a comfortable retirement vanished in an instant. Of course he was furious, and with time, bitterness grew by leaps and bounds. One day Markham found himself trying to calm down by drawing circles on a piece of paper. Looking at the circles moved Markham to write the following lines:

> He drew a circle to shut me out,
> Heretic, rebel, a thing to flout;
> But love and I had the wit to win,
> We drew a circle to take him in.

Those words today are by far the most famous among Markham's hundreds of poems. They helped the poet give up his anger and find grace to forgive the man who stole his lifelong savings.[6]

---

[5] Kenneth W. Osbeck, *101 Hymn Stories* (Grand Rapids: Kregel, 1982), 45–46.

[6] David Jeremiah, "Turning Point Daily Devotional," November 17, 2005, www.lineone.net/~andrewhdknock/StoriesA-H.htm.

Use One of the Elements of Narrative
to Brighten Exposition

To have a complete story, you will need a plot that moves, characters, and a setting—all with some controlling purpose. But if that seems too much, just imagine a bit of dialogue to illustrate your sermon text. This may clarify, restate, or emphasize a thought in the Scripture. Suppose, for example, your text is James 1:9–11. "The brother in humble circumstances ought to take pride in his high position. But the one who is rich should take pride in his low position, because he will pass away like the wild flower. For the sun rises with scorching heat and withers the plant; its blossom falls and its beauty is destroyed. In the same way, the rich man will fade away even while he goes about his business."

Whose life is transitory? Is it the rich man or the poor man? Attention to the text makes us know that both alike are fading. Imagine this conversation:

"I'm just like so much grass growing on a Galilean hillside," says the poor man. "I grow for a while and then burn up."

"My life is like a glorious lily!" boasts the rich man, "Splendid and magnificent like the lily or anemone."

"You are both the same," says James. "Rich man or poor man—leaf or petal—all alike are time-bound and fading. Like the Mediterranean spring, life may be brilliant or not, but it will be brief. Very brief!"

When the text is narrative *genre*, such as in 1 Samuel or Acts, adding dialogue may be unnecessary. If you are in Leviticus, however, or in some New Testament letter, a little narrative, with or without dialogue, can help you hold attention and make the message clear.

Try Your Hand at Creating a Parable,
a Fable, or an Allegory

Søren Kierkagaard did this masterfully, but it is not easy to do. In one of his briefest parables, a fire broke out backstage in a theater. The clown came out to inform the public. Everyone thought it was a joke and applauded. He repeated his warning; they shouted even louder. Kierkegaard told the story to say that he thought the world would come to an end amid general applause from all the wits, who would believe it all a jest.[7]

Suppose your text is Amos 1–2, where the prophet denounced each of Israel's neighboring nations in order: Syria, Philistia, Phoenicia, Edom, Ammon, Moab, and even Judah. Then using the same formula he promised judgment also on Israel. It must have been a shock to those who first heard Amos. Perhaps the preacher can make that point with a make-believe story.

One of Kierkegaard's most often used parables illustrates the danger of a Christian's decline from living on a high level and how subtly that decline may overtake one. As I recall a wild duck came down in a barnyard in the Danish countryside. The corn for the domestic fowl was easy and plentiful. He stayed for a while, and this while turned into spending the winter there. In the spring when his own kind passed overhead, he heard their calls and with a great flapping of wings tried to rejoin them. But he had grown fat and weak from not flying. He got about as high as the eaves of the barn before settling back down in the barnyard. The next time he got to the top rail of the fence. Still later he hardly looked up when a flock passed overhead.

Narrate in a Few Sentences Your Own Thoughts on the Passing Parade of Life

Bumper stickers, for example, are often thought provokers. Who of us has never played mind reader with the cues people placard on their autos? I passed an eighties-era Chevrolet on the interstate that looked about used up. It was so rusted you could hardly tell the original color. The bumper sticker, too, was almost faded away, but I managed to read it: *Jesus Christ, the Great Provider.* I nodded a smile of affirmation to the young man driving it and wondered what his life was like. "Not a very great Provider, is He?" jabbed the devil. But then the old clunker was transportation, after all. It was getting him there about as well as my nicer car. And maybe he was learning a most valuable lesson of stewardship: live within your means. I would almost bet his car was paid for. The Word promises: "My God will meet all your needs" (Phil 4:19).

---

[7] Thomas Clark Oden, ed., *Parables of Kierkegaard* (Princeton, NJ: Princeton University Press, 1998), 3.

Another bumper sticker was on a modest pickup truck in Baton Rouge, Louisiana. In the cab between his parents was a boy about 10 or 11 years old. The father was driving and had a close-cropped crew cut and a T-shirt just like his son's. On the other side was the young mother. All three were sandy headed. The bumper sticker proudly announced, "My son can whip your honor roll boy."

Driving time is a fertile opportunity for preachers to sharpen their powers of observation and of description. Not all observations will show up in a sermon, but the exercise will be a good stewardship of drive time. If your background is urban, as most of mine is, work on noticing the agriculture as you drive through. What is that crop? Some kind of grain? What kind? Look at those tight rows of stalks; is that corn or sugar cane or sorghum? How does a city boy tell soybeans from cotton? Sometimes it is worth a brief detour and a question to a local. In south Louisiana fields are flooded for growing rice and crawfish. Jesus quoted Isaiah's prophesy of people who would look and look and not see. It cannot hurt our powers of spiritual perception to sharpen our skill observing the physical world.

Use Your Testimony or the Testimony of Others

We have treated testimony in another chapter, so we will simply add a reminder of the importance of telling your own story. This may be a testimony of your conversion or of some more recent work of grace in your life. Many believers have learned to compose their testimony by following a simple four-step plan. Tell first what your life was like before you met Christ; second, how you came to know your need of a Savior; third, how you came to conversion; and finally, what your life has been like since then.[8]

Recast a News Story

Journalism students are taught to write a lead sentence with the answer to all of "Kipling's six honest serving men: What and Why and How and When and Where and Who." Then the editor further

[8] D. James Kennedy of Coral Ridge, Florida, is probably the source of this often-copied plan for personal testimony. See Kennedy, *Evangelism Explosion* (Wheaton, IL: Lyndale, 1970).

summarizes the lead in a headline. Read the following story, and then we will see how the newspaper reported it.

Dianne Mitchell of Blalock's Beauty School in Shreveport, Louisiana gathered her students at the beginning of the day and gave them a pep talk. "We have to stay together as a team," she told them. She encouraged them to watch out for one another, never imagining how soon they would need and how dramatically they would heed her admonition.

A little before noon the students and workers were cleaning up. In walked a man wearing a handkerchief over his face and a skullcap over his hair. He carried a large caliber revolver. He walked right past a sign on the door that read:

WARNING
This property protected by
JESUS CHRIST

The man with the gun was Jared Gipson, age 24, five feet, eight inches, 140 pounds. He put the gun in the back of instructor Dianne Mitchell who is much taller and considerably heavier. At first she thought it was a joke when she heard, "This is a holdup." Then she "saw that big old gun" and heard him order everyone to get down on the floor. "Get down, big momma," he barked at Mitchell. She didn't yet know what court records would show: Gipson had a history of armed robbery and other crimes. Some of the thirty students and staff on the floor started crying as they saw their grocery money and rent money taking wings. When the robber had gathered all the cash, he took the one male student in the class and pushed him with the pistol toward a door. Mitchell thought, *Oh, my God, he's going to shoot him!*

As the robber stepped over his prone victims, Mitchell saw a bare moment of opportunity and stuck out a foot to trip him. The robber tumbled into a wall and dropped his gun. Someone shouted, "Get that sucker!" And that is exactly what they did. The women pounced on him with curling irons, chairs, a wooden table leg, clenched fists, shoes, and a flood of pent-up anger.

The police took the bleeding culprit to the hospital for treatment of numerous wounds, especially lacerations to the head. At his arraignment the next day he wore a white bandage across the right side of his forehead. His right eye was blackened and swollen shut.

He hung his head when the judge set his bond at $100,000, but he may have considered the jail a safer place than the neighborhood.

The newspaper, however, did not tell the story in chronological order. It never does except in an occasional feature article. The headline tells it all: "Beauticians stomp, stop armed robber." The first sentence or two gives a little more detail. "An armed robber brandishing a revolver and some rough talk entered Blalock's Beauty College demanding money Tuesday afternoon. He left crying, bleeding and under arrest, after Dianne Mitchell, her students and employees attacked the suspect, beating him into submission."[9]

Now a reader can skip the other 60 column inches. We need newspapers to be written that way. We scan the headlines. If they interest us, we read the lead. If we are still interested, we may read more. If not, we have the synopsis. We would never get through the newspaper if the stories were not capsuled in the headlines and summarized in a lead sentence or two. But that's not the way of the storyteller! No one would read a mystery entitled *The Butler Did It!* Who would tell a joke with the punch line first? Newspapers are a great source of narrative support for a sermon, but preachers need to take care to revise the story in favor of a true narrative with a genuine plot.

Did this chapter give you some ideas for adding narrative to your sermons? Make them a part of your regular sermon preparation plan by trying a few until they become second nature to you.

Exercise 1. Clip an interesting article from your newspaper. Use the Plot Movements Worksheet to return the story to chronological order. Then rewrite the narrative starting with the original situation and moving to the opening stress that creates a crisis in the story. Trace the searching stage and the ultimate solution all the way to the resolution in the new situation.

Exercise 2. Select two or three of the other suggestions for experience in structuring narrative for sermon illustrations. Try a few of them this week in your sermon preparation. A good goal would be to try two or three each week until you have tried them all at least once.

---

[9] "Beauticians Stomp, Stop Armed Robber," *The Times of Shreveport-Bossier* (LA), June 15, 2005, 1A, 3A, and follow-up story, "Bond Set," June 16, 2005, 2A.

Chapter 10

AN ENDLESS SUPPLY OF STORIES

THE PROBLEM WITH ANECDOTES IS they keep coming around again and again like a merry-go-round. If a good story comes up at a preacher's convention, it finds its way into hundreds of sermons the next week or two. Stories circulate even faster on the Internet, but they are still shopworn; they are still shoddy in the verification department, and they are still admired by preachers more for their power to rivet attention and tug at the heart strings than to shed light on any sermon text or topic.

Grady Davis compared the ideal sermon to a tree. Pilfered stories are "brightly colored kites pulled from the winds of someone else's thought." They get "entangled in the branches." More appropriate illustrations will be "like blossoms opening from inside" the branches and twigs of that sermon.[1] Can preachers learn to craft worthy narrative illustrations that are original, interesting, and fitted exactly to the sermon? We can. Is there an alternative to pre-owned sermon illustrations bartered like used cars? There is. This chapter shows a preacher ten ways to create narrative illustrations for sermons that grow right out of the text of the sermon, even if the text is not a narrative.

---

[1] H. Grady Davis, *Design for Preaching* (Philadelphia: Muhlenberg, 1958), 15–16.

Word Studies Are Full of Stories

William Barclay excelled in drawing stories from the background of Greek words. All of his Daily Bible Study series of commentaries abound in the clearest of Greek word pictures. In his volume on the letters to the Corinthians, he notes that in different letters and speeches, Paul used no fewer than nine different words to describe the collection he was gathering for the destitute saints in Jerusalem. He sketches a bit of the background and history of each word. Here is his paragraph on one of them.

> Sometimes [Paul] uses the word *leitourgia* (2 Corinthians 9:12). In classical Greek this is a word with a noble history. In the great days of Athens there were generous citizens who volunteered out of their own pockets to shoulder the expenses of some enterprise on which the city was engaged. It might be to defray the expenses of training the chorus for some new drama or some team to compete for the honour of the city in the games; it might be to pay for the outfitting and manning of a trireme or man-of-war in time of the city's peril. A *leitourgia* was originally a service of the state voluntarily accepted. Christian giving is something which should be volunteered. It should be accepted as a privilege to help in some way the household of God.[2]

Calvin Miller recommends word studies as a way to bring strong narrative presentation to what he calls "precept passages." First, let the preacher dig in the reference books in study of the words of the text. Second, once the preacher has settled on the theme of the sermon and the thesis, or "motif" as Miller prefers, the English

---

[2] William Barclay, *The Letters to the Corinthians*, Daily Study Bible (Philadelphia: Westminster, 1975), 164. Barclay wrote two volumes of word studies published alphabetically in English transliteration of the Greek words. The first was called *A New Testament Wordbook*. It was followed by *More New Testament Words*. Both volumes were combined in *New Testament Words* (London: SCM, 1964). They include 61 words or word families. Herschel H. Hobbs was another preacher who excelled in shedding light on a text from Greek word studies. See his *Preaching Values from the Papyri* (Grand Rapids: Baker, 1964). This volume treats 40 specific words or word groups with insight not available until the translation of papyri in the twentieth century. For examples of word studies in his sermons, see *The Crucial Words from Calvary* (Grand Rapids: Baker, 1958).

words may suggest narratives. For example, the theme of a sermon about Balaam's donkey is obedience, and the motif will be "Disobedience to God is a reckless path." The three English words *disobedience, recklessness,* and *path* may each suggest narratives. The *definition* of disobedience is "to fail to obey a command." Does that suggest a story, perhaps from military life?[3]

Two come to my mind immediately. One is the story of Lord Nelson, who put his spyglass to his blind eye in the Battle of Copenhagen when he looked at the admiral's signal flags. He knew they would be telling him to come out of the battle, and he had no intention of doing so. He got away with it and came out a hero. The second story that comes to mind does not end so well. A colonel disobeyed orders recently and resorted to what he considered his better judgment in Iraq with most unfortunate loss of life to a number of those under his command. This story is not finished yet, but at this writing it appears this marine will not come away a hero.

There Are Stories in the Context of Your Text

If your text has no narrative, look into the setting or background of the text. Paul's Corinthian correspondence is heavy with ethical and theological instruction. But behind those letters, as any good survey or introduction to the New Testament will show, is a virtual travelogue of journeys back and forth from Ephesus to Corinth as Paul sent Timothy to deal with the issues. Then Paul himself left his work to make the 250-mile sea trip personally. There is narrative in that background. You might need to read a few pages and decide which scenario you will endorse, but that's good. It is much better to spend time searching the Scriptures than rummaging through musty collections of sermon illustrations that have nothing to do with your text.

Suppose your sermon text is Psalm 130. There is no narrative in the psalm. Your study shows that this is one of the "Psalms of Degrees" or "Psalms of the Going Up." You learn that pilgrims sang

---

[3] Calvin Miller, *Preaching: The Art of Narrative Exposition* (Grand Rapids: Baker, 2006), 136–38, 152–55. See also Miller's *Spirit, Word and Story* (Dallas: Word, 1989). Both are excellent guidance for those wanting to become storytellers. I haven't read all of Miller's 40 plus books, but every one I read makes me want to read the rest.

these 15 psalms on the journey to Jerusalem. It is an uphill climb from any direction. They are also called "Pilgrim Psalms" (Pss 120–134). If we place ourselves in the time and place of ancient pilgrims, we may visualize a story such as the following.

Imagine yourself, if you can, a pilgrim in a caravan traveling from Galilee down the Jordan Valley on the way to Jerusalem. We are on our way to the festival of Pentecost. The first day is nearly all downhill, but we sing the songs of "the going up." The day is soon gone as the sun disappears over the Judean hills. Gathering darkness will soon settle over the whole Jordan Valley. It is time to camp. From the scrubby underbrush in the thickets by the Jordan, we find plenty of fuel for a campfire. Some among us will need to take turns staying awake to guard against bandits and wild beasts.

When dawn finally comes, it seems to come all at once. A red streak over the hills of Moab drives away the darkness and soon floods the river road with light. The voice of the watchman sings, "My soul waits for the Lord more than watchmen wait for the morning . . . for the morning!" (Ps 130:6). Our minds turn to Jerusalem and the temple where we know that the first light of dawn signals the moment for the morning sacrifice.

After a breakfast of cheese and bread, we resume our southward trek. We are still many miles from Jerusalem. Soon some of us pilgrims take up again the pilgrim psalms. We sing them on the journey in anticipation of singing them soon in the temple.

Just-Suppose Stories

Adolph Monod was an eloquent evangelical among early nine-teenth-century French preachers. Here is the way he began a sermon from 1 John 4:8, "God is love."

> In a small town of Italy, which, eighteen hundred years since, an eruption of Mount Vesuvius buried beneath a flood of lava, some ancient manuscripts, so scorched as to resemble cinders more nearly than books, have been discovered, and, by an ingenious process, slowly and with difficulty unrolled. Let us imagine that one of these scrolls of Herculaneum contains a copy, and the only one in the world, of the

epistle from which the text is taken; and that, having come to the fourth chapter and the eighth verse, they have just deciphered these two words, "God is," and were as yet ignorant of what should follow.

A paragraph follows in which the answer is held in suspension, and then he goes on:

> At length the momentous word *love* appears! Who could desire a better? What could be conceived comparable to it by the boldest and loftiest imagination? This hidden God, this powerful God, this holy God—He is love! What need we more? God loves us. Do I say he loves us? All in God speaks of love. Love is his very essence. He who speaks of God speaks of love! O answer, surpassing all our hopes! O blessed revelation, putting an end to all our apprehensions! O glorious pledge of our happiness, present, future, eternal![4]

To study the whole sermon would be a grand exercise, and so would a study of the preacher. Our interest at present, however, is to see here an example of "let us imagine." This is a narrative illustration created by the preacher. Notice that he started with a brief sketch of history. The translator of the sermon put these six lines of the original French into one long and complex sentence as was the fashion of the day. The story of Mount Vesuvius in Italy and the eruption of AD 79 that buried the whole cities of Pompeii and Herculaneum was no doubt more familiar to Monod's congregation in Paris around 1850 than it is to us today. The major excavations of that marvel of Mediterranean archeology began in Monod's early years. The wise preacher knows we do not need a history lesson; we need to *image* or *imagine* the text in a new and fresh way. We need just enough of the real history and just enough of the imaginary history to rediscovery the familiar text. Notice also that the preacher draws a clear line between the paragraph of history and the imaginary scene that he sketches. He says, "Let

---

[4] Edwin C. Dargan, *A History of Preaching* (New York: Armstrong, 1905), 2:462. Adolf Monod lived 1802–1856. After this sermon introduction the preacher developed the theme by answering two questions: What impression would this statement, "God is love," make upon one who had never heard it before? And what impression ought it make on Christians who have heard it often?

us imagine." A preacher might on another occasion create a completely imaginary scene with no reference to history. Still he needs to use such markers as *suppose*, *imagine*, or *what if.*

Write Your Own Story

This is not a wish drifting in the winds. You can do it. Robert Louis Stephenson said there are three ways and three ways only of writing a story. First, you may take a plot and fit characters to it. Second, you may start with a character and choose incidents and situations to develop that character's story. Third, you may start with a certain atmosphere or idea and create actions and persons to express that idea. The preacher will most often need to start with the idea he needs to illustrate. Then use imagination.[5]

In high school one of the seniors told a few of us underclassmen a personal story that kept us with our mouths open while we were all cleaning our rifles in the Junior ROTC armory. He met this beautiful young lady dressed like a fashion catalog model. She expressed interest in him, and he was definitely interested in her. He had our undivided attention all the way to the end of the story when, said he, she pulled out of her handbag a .38 caliber Beretta and shot him in the heart! Where did we lose such imagination?

I was a daydreamer, and I bet you were too. I still am at times. When did we discipline ourselves to stifle such creativity? I will never forget the comment a teacher wrote on my English paper in fifth or sixth grade. The writing assignment was to make up a story. I just let my 13-year-old imagination go and described a daydream as if it really happened. While I don't remember my story now, I recall the setting. It was the downtown bowling alley and nearby streets and railroad tracks in my hometown. And I vividly remember the comment of the teacher while she handed back the graded assignments. She stopped at my desk and pointed out her comment at the bottom of my story, "Very credible." She asked me if I knew what that meant, and I did not. She said, "That means it is a believable story." That was enough affirmation to last me all day at least. And there! I've told two stories from my school days.

---

[5] Cited in Ian Macpherson, *The Art of Illustrating Sermons* (Nashville: Abingdon, 1964), 137.

Don't they remind you of something from yours? That brings us to another source of stories without end.

Use Stories from Your Personal Pilgrimage

Someone has said that the uninteresting autobiography has never been written. People are interested in people. Parishioners are interested in their pastor. If you do not talk about yourself often, their ears perk up when you begin to tell something about yourself. Of course, no one wants to be subjected to a windbag full of himself in the pulpit or elsewhere. One church suffered too many years a pastor who endlessly bragged about himself and his achievements. When he finally retired, his replacement unfortunately chose as the text of his first sermon, "A greater than Solomon is here." The poor fellow didn't know that his predecessor's nickname was Solomon.

The topic of testimony is treated in an earlier chapter with examples, so we will let this reminder suffice. Just keep in mind that your testimony did not end when you were baptized. What has God done in your life lately? And what is he doing now. Dare to be vulnerable.

Stories Can Mix Fiction with Reality

Garrison Keillor is what I consider a natural storyteller. His *A Prairie Home Companion* stories impress us as something he is making up as he goes along. Yet they captivate us. For all who happened to see a certain news item, Keillor gave a valuable lesson in storytelling. It was an off-the-cuff interview during a visit to the Iowa State Fair. While munching on a pork chop on a stick and chatting with fairgoers, Keillor said, "All fiction comes from a little bit of reality, otherwise it would have no relevance. The fun is in innovation: take something real like this fair and make something larger than life." Keillor loves to create small-town characters who have a thread of commonality with everyone we meet. He mixes humor and subtlety with fiction and reality. In his off-hand comments of that visit to the fair, he observed that eating a pork chop on a stick gave him an opportunity to eat with his fingers, something his mother never would have allowed. When we listen to his narratives about Lake Wobegon days on the weekly radio program, we get caught up in the flow of the story. It is so real and so unreal all at the same time.[6]

There are two things for the preacher to remember in mixing fact and fancy. One, if you use an example from pastoral ministry such as family counseling, you must never betray a confidence or even seem to do so. Some of your best stories will have to go untold. Even if you disguise the principals, you cannot relate the story as if it is your ministry with one of your parishioners. Who will trust you with their sins and secrets after that? You might know a similar story from some other pastor that will illustrate the point. Even so, a double portion of caution is in order. Your credibility is at stake as sure as your ability to guard a confidence. And two, if the story is not obviously apocryphal, you will have to convey somehow that it is not a true story. That alone weakens the value of the telling.

Think of Your Most Unforgettable Characters

Tom Ratcliff is a director of missions in Texas. He served as a pastor, a church planter, and a foreign missionary to the Dominican Republic. When he became a director of missions in Florida, he was called on constantly to help ordain pastors and deacons. In his ordination sermons he began to include brief character sketches of deacons, pastors, and others he had known. Here is one sample.

> My wife and I first met Rose Vielma when we visited a Spanish-language congregation in a small town west of Corpus Christi, Texas. She had just finished high school and taken a job in the local variety store. We saw potential in her for so much more. She loved Bible study and sprinkled her conversation with biblical support for her opinions. We encouraged her to enroll at the nearby junior college, which she did.
>
> Then perhaps the best thing that ever happened to her and the worst thing both came in one day. She was in Nashville, Tennessee, at a missions conference and

[6] "Keillor Finds Inspiration for Show at State Fair" *The Times, Shreveport-Bossier* (LA) (August 16, 2005): 5D.

made a decision for full-time Christian service. But when she called her mother and told her about the decision, her mother informed her that if she planned to do this with her life, the family would no longer help her.

Rose continued to pursue her dream. She financed her own education by working as a secretary. She studied hard, graduated from junior college, and went on to take her baccalaureate degree at Howard Payne University. Then she went on to seminary in Fort Worth. She became active in a local church where she met and married David Zamora. After seminary she moved to Birmingham, Alabama to become the Spanish language representative for Woman's Missionary Union.

Rose was determined to serve the Lord in missionary work, little realizing that God would also use her in teaching about missions, in promotion and praying for missionaries around the world as well as in doing missions work. She and her husband David are now pioneering as missionaries to the ever-expanding multihousing populations in the middle of the Dallas-Fort Worth multiplex.

For years *Reader's Digest* included the "Unforgettable Character" feature. If you read those popular sketches, you will note that narrative is the biggest part of them. How better can you present a personality than show what he or she says and does? A character sketch will include some description, but action words still speak louder than a load of description.

Mr. S. C. Stephens was my Sunday school teacher when I was about nine years old. He seemed like a very old man way back then, though I recall visiting him and his wife years later in a nursing home where they shared a room and took care of each other. One day in Sunday school class one of the nine-year-olds stood up and asked, "Mr. Stephens, do they pay you for teaching us?"

"No, Roger," said the teacher. "No Sunday school teacher is paid."

"Why do you do it then?"

The teacher said, "Because I love boys and want to see them saved."

"That's what I thought," and the nine-year-old sat down.

A character sketch can convey a lot about a person in a few sentences of dialogue or a few lines of narrative. It is not necessary to characterize a person with labels. Nouns and verbs say much more than adverbs and adjectives. Here is a sketch of the pastor of the church of my childhood.

I set down a book the other day and instinctively turned back to move it. I had put it on top of my Bible! I never do that without thinking of my earliest impression of T. C. Pennell. There was an aura of expectancy that Sunday morning years ago as the primary superintendent fairly beamed her introduction: "Brother Pennell is going to come and present the Bibles to everyone being promoted."

I suppose he told us we should read the Bible daily and other things, but only one thing stuck in my mind. I still see Brother Pennell holding one of those hardback Bibles and telling us never to stack anything on top of it. If it is in a stack of books, the Bible should always be on the top.

That stuck with me. The Bible was the heart of his ministry. He was above all a preacher of the Word. His commanding presence as a man among men inspired awe. But it was when he stood to preach that Word with resonate tones—now marching deliberately—and now thundering in sincere pathos—every soul was alert to him.

Long before God laid His hand on me to preach, I thought the greatest thing that could happen to me would be to grow up and make Bible characters live and speak as did "The Preacher." Start your list now of unforgettable characters in your life.

Sharpen Your Observation Skills of Everyday Life

Oh, if we could only use stories from our children and grandchildren without offending them and without trying the patience of our congregation! We would instantly double our supply of narrative and memorable sayings. Stories are going on all around us all the time. We just have to open our eyes to see. Observation is a skill that can be developed. A serious fisherman soon notices things that work in catching bass. Are they lurking under the logs and near the tree line or out in the open water? Do they like a spinner or a plastic worm or something new? Are they on top or down deep?

Scientists, including social scientists, know that there are many ways to collect data and do research. We may use questionnaires, interviews, content analyses, samplings, and observation. Yes, observation! This is an important way to do research. Untrained observers are notoriously unreliable as conflicting testimony in court often demonstrates. The value of observation depends much on who is looking. Louis Pasteur discovered immunization, some would say by accident.

> Robert A. Heinlein, a science fiction novelist, somewhere said, "No storyteller has ever been able to dream up anything as fantastically unlikely as what really does happen in this mad universe."

While he was on vacation, a cholera serum grew stale. Later birds injected with that serum failed to develop the disease. Then when exposed to a fresh culture, nearly all of them withstood the deadly disease. It was not an accident that Pasteur was a careful observer. Penicillin was discovered likewise when bacteria in a petri dish happened to die after accidental exposure to that agent. Paying attention is essential in science and helpful in all of life.

In a logic class at the University of Wisconsin, the professor deliberately staged a disruption of his class while collecting papers. Two of his 75 students started a scuffle. Immediately a third tossed two silver dollars into the air and scrambled to recover them. The professor asked all three students to leave the room. Then he asked the class to write a fair and complete statement of what happened. The class reported greatly differing accounts on such objective facts as the physical position of the teacher at the time of the incident. Twenty-two could swear he was in front of the class; 21 were sure he was in the rear, and 12 placed him in the middle. Five students could swear that the professor was picking up their own papers when it started. What actually happened was just as confused by the impartial observers.[7]

Dare to Try a First-Person Narrative Sermon

A first-person narrative sermon, also called dramatic monologue, presents the truth of the biblical text from the perspective of an

---

[7] W. I. Beveridge, *The Art of Scientific Investigation* (New York: Norton, 1950), 98; and C. Luther Fry, *The Technique of Social Investigation* (New York: Harper, 1934), 45–46.

eyewitness or a participant. With or without costume the preacher may play the role of Simon Peter and take the congregation back to some New Testament happening such as the transfiguration. The narrative takes the shape of an I-was-there report of the witness. This way of presenting biblical truth works for several reasons. It is a fresh approach to preaching that gets attention and sticks in the memory. People are interested in other people and not likely to be bored with this approach if done well and not done too often. Personal testimony is convincing. The Bible lends itself to this kind of drama. It also has the advantage of persuasion by indirection.

Do I have to set a stage and wear a costume? Certainly not. If you think wearing a headdress or a tunic will help you get into character, go ahead. The thing that makes it a monologue is one person doing all the talking—just as you always do. The thing that makes it a dramatic monologue is the preacher speaks as if he were the biblical character.

You are already halfway there and don't know it. Your sermon is a monologue, right? Just add a bit of drama![8]

Collect Family Stories

Everyone has some interesting stories up the family tree. Don't fail to collect them before they are lost forever. I have used the following to encourage churches to be open to new ideas and new methods.

Granduncle Bill Garner went to town to buy his first T-Model Ford. He drove it home with intense pride and extreme caution. He steered it between the beckoning doors of the new garage. The beaming family looked on. Man and machine disappeared into the garage. "Whoa!" demanded the driver, but the automobile did not obey. Amid crashing timber and flying splinters, man and machine reappeared on the other side.

It was a costly way to learn that the old way may not serve the new day. Just because a church has always worshipped at 11

---

[8] Help for the adventurous preacher in this area is available. See Haddon W. Robinson and Torrey W. Robinson, *It's All in How You Tell It: Preaching First-Person Expository Messages* (Grand Rapids: Baker, 2003). An earlier advocate who has written several articles and sermons and at least one how-to book on first-person narrative sermons is Alton H. McEachern, *Dramatic Monologue Preaching* (Nashville: Broadman, 1984).

o'clock on Sunday morning does not doom a church that has good reason to assemble at another time.

Scribes and Pharisees confronted Jesus because His disciples did not go through a ceremonial washing before eating. They demanded: "Why do your disciples break the tradition of the elders? They don't wash their hands before they eat!" (Matt 15:2). In answer Jesus pointedly warned against letting tradition—even religious tradition—make void God's Word. He added a stern rebuke about too much concern with outward form and ceremony and too little concern with religion of the heart.

I wish our churches could display more of the initiative of Mr. Garner. When he rebuilt the back wall of the garage, he installed an extra set of doors. Then he just drove his car around in a circle until he made it whoa where he told it to whoa. I wonder if anyone ever told him, "We've never done it that way before."

You can break your dependence on borrowed stories and omnibus collections of horse-and-buggy anecdotes. Start now. For learning exercises on this chapter, take any three of the examples above and create three illustrations of your own. Let at least one of them be for the sermon you are working on for your next preaching assignment.

Exercise 1. Did you do an exercise in the last chapter? If so, you are on your way to developing skills for creating your own narrative illustrations. If not, start with this chapter. Select two or three ways described above for brightening your discourse. Use at least one in each sermon you preach until you have tried them all.

Exercise 2. Do you have the notebook habit? Do you remember hearing something a week or two ago or seeing something you intended to remember? It was timber for your homiletical sawmill, but now you can't remember what it was! I recommend you carry a single four-by-six file card, folded and in the same pocket as your pen. Make it a habit. Stop to take notes when something captures your imagination. Don't fret about where it might be used; record it while fresh in your memory. You will be amazed at how it grows.

Chapter 11

IT'S ALL IN HOW YOU TELL IT

A YOUNG MAN WENT AWAY to college, the first in his family to finish high school. His hardworking parents had never learned to read and were very proud of him. One day a letter came from their boy in college. Eager to get the news, the father waved down a neighbor on the road and begged him to read the letter from his boy away at the big university. The neighbor was impatient and rude and ran through the letter as if it had no punctuation: "Mom-and-Dad-School's-hard-I'm-making-the-grade-Running-short-of *money.* . . . Send some! Your son, Tim."

The neighbor tossed the letter back to the father and hurried on his way. The old man shuffled slowly back to the house with his chin on his chest. "If that's the way he talks to his parents now, I don't know if college is such a good idea. Maybe I won't send him any money." When he told his wife the gist of the letter, she too was hurt but thought there might be a mistake. She persuaded her husband to ask another neighbor to read it.

He made his way to a nearby farm where lived a more helpful neighbor. He read the letter in a slow and tender voice, pausing as the punctuation required. "Dear Mom and Dad, School is hard, but I am making the grade. Right now I am running a little short of money though. I would be very grateful if you could send some. Your loving son, Tim."

"Now that's more like it," said the father, as he brushed away a tear. "When my boy talks that way, I'd give him my last dime!" In storytelling, too, it makes a difference how you tell it.

This chapter offers guidance on sermon delivery as it relates to storytelling. In a fine restaurant the chef gives diligent attention to presentation of the meal as well as to ingredients and cooking. Let the preacher take care to serve his feast in the most appealing way. Here you will find a suggested method for preparing a story for telling. Next you will find a number of suggestions that will help you with an approach to a storytelling style. Then arises the question of whether a certain story is appropriate for the pulpit. What enters into that decision?

Preparing for the Pulpit

The moment of delivery is the moment of truth. Part of sermon preparation is planning for delivery. As an old proverb says, a good story ill told is a bad one. Prepare the story well enough that pulpit notes do not become a barrier. Here is a deep mystery: a capable pulpiteer is not otherwise bound to sermon manuscript or pulpit notes except when he pulls out a clipping and reads a narrative to the congregation. A story is the easiest part of the prepared sermon to recall; why read it? An exact quotation of an important person might need to be read verbatim, but a narrative is too easy to learn to justify reading.

How does a storyteller prepare to tell the story? Advance preparation involves the selection of the story, even if it is a story of your own composition. It needs to be one that you are eager to tell. If you have put it into your sermon, may we assume you have the conviction that God wants you to tell it? Once you have settled on your story, there are basically five steps to getting yourself ready to tell it. The goal is not to memorize the story but to absorb it until you can retell it without use of notes.[1]

First, read the story for its own sake. Let the story make its impression on you without pausing too much to reflect critically on what

---

[1] You may have notes in the pulpit if they comfort you and spare you the anxiety that may cause you to freeze up and go blank. But I warn you, until you have become comfortable with your own method of sermon delivery, having notes will be like an alcoholic carrying a little bottle in his pocket just in case he needs a little drink.

that impression is or how it is made. Just enjoy the story and otherwise appreciate it. The second step is to read the story several times more. Read it aloud as well as silently. At this stage you want to fix the story as a whole in your mind before dealing with the parts.

Then in the third step, begin to think about the parts. Think about the beginning, the middle, and the end. Notice the setting of the story if it is important. What is the starting situation? Is there a stress or conflict that arises? What search for a solution follows? And how is it resolved? In looking at the details, spend time with the characters. It may take time for them to become real. Give them time.

A fourth stage is to visualize the story. This may be combined with stage three, but it is a separate matter. See the sights. Hear the sounds. Imagine the aromas and textures and tastes that may be in the story. What colors do you see in your vision? Take time to fix them in your mind. You may not mention any hue or scent in the telling, but whatever is vivid to you will more easily stick in your memory.

Finally, practice telling the story. Tell the story orally as many times as necessary to fix it in your mind and assure yourself that you have it. It can be frustrating to be telling a story and recall late in the plot that you left out an early and important detail. It will happen. When it does, may you have presence of mind to work it in ad lib without saying, "Oh, wait a minute! I forgot to tell you. . . ." Flashback can be useful at such times. At other times, avoid backing up the plot. Keep the narrative in the natural chronology.

You might find it helpful to follow this plan with a two-minute story before moving on to five- and ten-minute stories. If you have a longer story such as a sermon that is one long narrative, here's another hint for getting ready to tell. In addition to the five stages above, practice with pen and paper, jotting down key words or symbols that will help you recall in order the whole with all of its parts.[2]

An Approach to Style for Storytelling in Preaching

Style is a preacher's characteristic way of expressing himself. Your style is your own personal way of using the resources of

---

[2] Margaret Read MacDonald, *The Story-Teller's Start Up Book* (Little Rock, AR: August House, 1993) offers a similar plan in chapter 1, "Learning the Story in One Hour."

language to accomplish the objective of your address. To communicate a message from God ought to be every preacher's overall purpose in every sermon and in every story. How well you do that depends much on your attention to clear, interesting, and forceful speech. This includes your choice of words, their arrangement, and finally speaking them. Some choices help gain the goal; others get in the way. With practice and attention to detail, a preacher can evolve an effective style for pulpit or platform. The following is not a list of rules but some matters that might help you toward becoming an excellent storyteller.

Place yourself in the background. Keep in mind that your goal is to express God's Word, not to make a good impression for yourself. Someone said, and I'm not sure who, "No preacher can convey the impression that he himself is clever and at the same time that Jesus Christ is mighty to save." Stories that promote and puff the preacher should be judged in the pastor's study and never make it to the pulpit so that they will need never be judged at the judgment seat of Christ. It is possible to overdo the ego bit and to underdo it. You should be the first to notice if you are saying "I" too often, but some preachers are too sensitive here. As the classic definition by Phillips Brooks says, "Preaching is truth through personality."

Write and speak in a way that comes naturally. Some people write in a style entirely different from their speaking style. If you write your sermons, as I strongly recommend for at least the first ten years of your ministry, take care to write in an oral style. Write as you speak. The late Charles Allen, a preacher who occupied the greatest United Methodist pulpits in the late twentieth century, used to write his sermons longhand. He paused to speak every sentence out loud before he penned it. When he finished his first draft, he rarely changed a single sentence before he preached it. Then very much of what he preached found its way into one of his books of sermons published with little or no editing. Cultivate an oral style in writing stories.

Stimulate the senses. Help the listener see and feel and even smell the story as well as hear it. Fifty years ago I heard N. A. Woychuk at Bible Memory Camp relating an incident from his childhood. He described the arrival in the mail of a book he had ordered. He carefully unwrapped the package until the volume lay open in his hands. "I can close my eyes," he said, "and still remember how it smelled." That was enough to connect with us, for everyone has experienced that special mix of printer's ink and binder's glue or whatever it is that gives a new book its unique aroma.

Tell the story; don't read it to the congregation. The story sermon makes preaching without notes a realistic goal. Personal stories and experiences are especially easy to tell without notes. A number of preachers have turned to narrative in sermons in the quest to preach without notes—that goal which seems to be the holy grail of every pastor and is without a doubt admired by those who gather to hear sermons. Clarence Macartney is one who turned to biblical stories and Bible biography sermons as the way to learn to preach without notes.[3]

It's not a good idea to memorize and recite the story. It will almost always sound recited. We want to hear a preacher tell a story, not perform one. The protocol suggested above will help a preacher absorb the story and tell it *to* the congregation rather than perform it *before* them.

What about gestures in storytelling? Let them be unplanned, spontaneous, natural. Planned gestures run the risk of coming across as planned. They are likely to be just a bit off timing. Then they become comic gestures since missed timing is a staple of slapstick comedy. Eye contact is also an important use of the body. I recall a preaching professor describing how he makes use of eye contact by looking away from the congregation while telling the story, then turning decisively to look directly at the congregation in making the application. Any such planning is likely to appear planned. If you get involved in the story, as you should, you will feel the story and convey those feelings by your body language. If a passage is pensive, there is likely to be a diversion of the eyes naturally, perhaps looking down while talking. Or there may be a far-away look that conveys thoughtfulness. In any case, planning any such gesture is not recommended. Nevertheless, we do speak volumes with our eyes.

Dialogue is an asset in a story. It breaks up the narrative, but when told orally, it does not take much dialogue to turn this asset

---

[3] George M. Bass, "The Story Sermon: Key to Effective Preaching?" Paper presented at the annual meeting of the Academy of Homiletics, Princeton, NJ, December 5–8, 1984, 2, 5.

into a confusing liability. Remember that the listener does not have the advantage of a printed page before him or her to give a glance of review. How do you avoid the confusion of who-said-what in oral transmission? One way is to use less dialogue. Use few extended passages of direct quotes or none at all. Another way is to let the narrator summarize some of the conversation and include only such direct quotations as may be helpful. A variation of this is to use direct quotes for only one of the speakers while narrating a synopsis of the other speaker.

What about imitating the tone or dialect of different voices in dialogue? It's better not to try. A male preacher, for example, trying to impersonate a female voice is another opportunity for the preacher to make himself ridiculous. And unless you have a really good ear for dialect, don't try that. Black dialect, Latino accent, and imitation of other racial or ethnic minorities is unacceptable.

Keep your younger listeners in mind. That you use stories at all is a big step in that direction. Children listen and love the story even though the theological truth may escape them for now. Don't talk down to them; they can follow a story line when they are two and three years old. This is an amazing fact of the human brain. We will know we have developed artificial intelligence when a computer can create and appreciate a story.

It is better not to introduce a story. Just tell it. If the story cannot stand on its own in a sermon, perhaps it does not belong there. For the same reason, it's better not to "apply" the story. Belaboring the point of the story becomes "preaching" the illustration. The story is a wonderful servant but an oppressive master. If you have to explain the story, it is not helping you explain your biblical truth.

Some Stories to Avoid

A few common mistakes regularly appear in pulpit storytelling. Just a word of caution may keep you from making some of them.

Avoid implausible stories. A preacher story I first heard in my childhood has resurfaced several times in my recent research though it may not be familiar to the reader. It seems a pilot was on a transoceanic flight when he heard the distinct sound of a mouse gnawing on metal. He was sure the creature would gnaw through a control cable and the plane would crash. What could he do? The pilot was too far into his flight to turn back. There was no place to land. He decided to climb to a higher altitude where the air would be too rare for the mouse to survive. Thus did he save himself, his plane, and his passengers.

Most of us will cock our head at that story and know that something is just not right in there. Is it the mouse gnawing on a steel cable? Any pilot will know right away why it never happened. In my younger days I flew a variety of small planes from the J3 Piper Cub to a World War II Navy Trainer. Anything with an airplane engine will make too much noise for the pilot to hear any mouse gnawing. Once I even flew a Schweitzer Sailplane with no motor at all. Even then, except at the top of a climb or a loop when airspeed approaches zero, the sound of the wind whistling past the smoothest canopy would make that mouse too quiet to be heard. Ian Macpherson credits to John Gray this cautionary couplet: "Lest men suspect your tale untrue, keep probability in view."

Lay worn-out stories to rest. A visiting preacher got a word of advice from a lay leader about doing the children's sermon when he visited a pastorless church. The layman told the visitor that in the past 12 months no fewer than ten preachers had used the same worn-out tale of the little boy who gave his mother a bill for chores done.

Avoid stories that are crude, course, or offensive to sensibilities. Bedroom and bathroom are best left out of sermons. This applies to attempts at humor as well as serious narrative. And we can do without stories that make us cringe at some crucial detail. A Clovis Chappell story that I would not tell in a sermon and will only describe for the purpose here is about a great bell that was cast and recast repeatedly until the bell maker's daughter threw herself into the molten bronze and made it work. It was meant to illustrate God's sacrifice of his Son. I'm afraid the message is marred more than illumined. Guard the dignity of the pulpit.

Avoid stories that hijack the sermon. Sometime you will find a story that is so compelling that you just have to use it. You may prepare a whole sermon just to fit that story. That is not bad if you really do wed the story to the right text and theme. The danger is double here, however. You may end up with the tail wagging the dog. The story must never draw attention to itself. The other danger is that the preacher will count on the strength of one story and not give due diligence to searching exegesis of the Scriptures and submission of the story to the divine truth in the Word. After that, it is an advantage to have a story that the preacher really feels strongly about.

Finally, it's not just old preachers who tell the same old stories over and over. Repeating favorite stories is tempting to us all. Most preachers know they can repeat a sermon to the same congregation if the narrative illustrations are different. On the other hand, the preacher can deliver an entirely new sermon, different text, different title, different organization; but if the preacher repeats a story in that sermon, numerous members of the congregation will remark about having heard that sermon before.

If you repeat a story, introduce it in a way that acknowledges it is a story revisited. "You might remember the story of Mr. X, Olympic swimmer, etc." Or, "I told this story to some of you a couple of years ago, but it is worth hearing again in the present context."

Keep records on when and where you told this story. And go easy on that "old preacher" stuff. If you live long enough, you will be an old preacher yourself someday!

Exercise 1. Perhaps you have a collection of stories you saved from among the mass of e-mailings forwarded to you. Take a look at some of the recent ones. What made them worth sparing the recycle bin with all the other spam? What did you like about this story? In making the decision to spare the story, can you tell how much value you gave to the content or subject matter? How much to the sentimentality in the story? To the elements of narrative included?

Exercise 2. Where can a preacher gain experience and sharpen storytelling skills? Other than the endless demand of the next sermon or Bible class for a minister, look for opportunities to tell stand-alone stories that are not in a sermon. Visit the children's Sunday school often and tell them a Bible story. Retirement homes will welcome you. Senior citizens will gather to listen to a few stories. Plan a few just for fun—like Peter Rabbit in addition to serious Christian stories.

Exercise 3. If you do not have a story file and index, start one today. Keep it simple.

part three

LEARNING FROM THE MASTERS OF STORYTELLING

Chapter 12

GOTHAM IN THE GOLDEN AGE

THE FIFTY YEARS IN AMERICA between the Civil War and
the First World War saw a nation coming of age. Before the Civil
War the nation was a rural republic; soon it was an urban industri-
alized nation. Steel mills, transcontinental railroads, urban facto-
ries and mills became the new order of the day. Before 1860 a total
of 36,000 patents were registered in the United States. In the next
thirty years, 1860 to 1890, we added 440,000 more. The internal
combustion engine was invented in 1860. Alexander Graham Bell
gave us the telephone in 1876. Marconi's wireless dates to 1895.
The Wright brothers flew their first airplane in 1903. Six years later
Ford's Model T was in mass production. Soon streets and roads of
dirt and mud gave way to pavement. Horse and buggy made room
for the horseless carriage. This was the Industrial Revolution. It
was also an age of moral and religious revolution.

Great and growing churches multiplied as the cities drew people from rural America and from foreign shores in ever-increasing
numbers. The leader in this era of urban expansion seemed to be
New York City. Churches in cities were able to attract the ablest
preachers. Henry Ward Beecher came to lead the newly established Plymouth Congregational Church of Brooklyn in 1847. He
started with a membership of 21. This would grow to gatherings
of a hundred times that and more. He would continue there until
his death 40 years later. His younger contemporary, T. De Witt

150

Talmage, began his 26-year pastorate at Central Presbyterian, Brooklyn in 1869. The Brooklyn Bridge was long under construction but would not open until 1883 when Talmage was 50 and Beecher was 70 years old. Meanwhile, ferries, popularly called "Beecher Boats," brought hundreds from Manhattan to hear the pulpit stars in the rapidly growing churches of Brooklyn. The community would not be annexed into New York City until 1898. In 1870, Beecher mortgaged his home to provide funds for Theodore Tilton, a younger friend and member of his church, to start a religious newspaper called *The Golden Age*. Mark Twain's novel two years later would be titled *The Gilded Age*. There is justification for either name.[1]

In this chapter we will give attention to two princes of the pulpit. Both of them made extensive use of narrative in their sermons. Beecher skillfully wove narrative illustrations into the warp and woof of his sermons. Talmage was an outstanding preacher of Bible biography.

What might we gain from this approach to study of pulpit storytelling? Ed Young Jr. makes an important distinction: "You can learn what to do and what not to do by studying others. Notice I said *study others*, not copy them. . . . Don't imitate another speaker." Preachers ought to accept themselves as the unique persons God made each of us to be, but they should also "learn some tips and techniques from others." That's good advice on both points: don't ape anyone, but study other preachers. Ed Jr. had a fine model in his pastor-father, and no doubt he learned a lot just growing up in that family and church. But of course, no one who knows them both will think that Junior is just a chip off the old block.[2]

We learn from emulation probably more than we realize. Small children acquire language by mimicking the sounds of their parents and others around them. We also absorb information and useful skills from others around us. This is plain to everyone when an infant of one culture is adopted into a different culture. Preachers,

[1] For details on this interesting history, see Austin B. Tucker, "What Do You Mean 'Truth Through Personality'? The Phillips Brooks' Definition of Preaching in Historical Context," a paper presented to the annual meeting of the Evangelical Homiletics Society, October 2004, Wake Forest, NC. See at http://www.ehomiletics.com/.
[2] Ed Young Jr., *The Creative Leader* (Nashville: Broadman & Holman, 2006), 108, emphasis added.

too, for better or worse, learn to preach from the models available. This emulation is mostly unintentional. Without abandoning our own unique gifts and personality, why not make a deliberate effort to study the best of preachers so that we might become better preachers? The rest of this book does just that. From thousands of notable preachers in history, here are some of the most skillful in storytelling. We will place each preacher in the context of his life and times with special attention to his narrative method. As space allows we will give at least one example of the storytelling method of each. Artists learn from the masters, and artisans serve an apprenticeship, but rarely do they have more than one mentor. We can explore the best of Christian preachers across two centuries.

Henry Ward Beecher: Describing the Passing Parade

Blessed by birth into the illustrious Lyman Beecher family, Henry was one of 13 children. All seven of the Beecher sons who survived to adulthood became ministers, but Henry was by far the best known. One of Henry's six sisters was Harriet Beecher Stowe, author of *Uncle Tom's Cabin* and one of America's most famous storytellers. She and her sister Catherine both became antislavery activists.

When Henry was but a child of three, his mother died. The loss to him was profound. Through childhood he struggled with shyness and a speech impediment. He also struggled greatly to grasp the doctrines his family taught him. One biographer at least feels this was the root of his later determination to make religious truth plain and simple to others. His speaking and writing made use, almost exclusively, of the simple, expressive words from the Anglo-Saxon branch of English. He used stories and narrative examples to make abstract truth clear and concrete.

By the time Henry got to Amherst College in 1830, the timid boy had grown into a fun-loving and outgoing young man. After college he became a pastor in Indianapolis and attracted a great deal of attention. Then the new Plymouth Church in rapidly growing Brooklyn enlisted him to be their first pastor. There he built a great church on his pulpit ministry. Annual pew rentals, in the custom of the day, made it possible to build a great edifice to gather the multitudes who wanted to hear Beecher. He urged members who came on Sunday morning not to return on Sunday evening so that nonmembers might occupy their rented pews. People came from all over America to hear Beecher.

One who reads Beecher's sermons should not expect many stories with well-developed plots. Beecher preferred to describe the passing parade of life in historical present tense. The listener understands immediately that this is not a particular person in a certain episode of life; this is Everyman. It may be you. In his sermon on "The Fruits of the Spirit," for example, he described each of the nine graces listed by Paul in Galatians 5 with the help of skillful slice-of-life vignettes. The following is an illustration of *long-suffering*.

> Whoever saw a wife—of all tragedies bloodless, but the most horrible—marrying in the freshness of her early life an ideal husband, only to find out little by little that she was worshipping an idol—gambling, drunken, licentious, removed further and further from her in moral character. Yet she must needs cling to him, and of all lying outside of hell I know of nothing so loathsome as for one to lay side by side with a brutal beast, whose every sense gives evidence of rottenness. Yet how many holy women there have been who have borne it in the morning, at noon, at night, in youth, in middle life, and further on, and when at last the wretch dies, and everybody thanks God that he is gone, there is one that sheds tears over his dishonored grave, and remembers only the things that she had thought of him. When one looks upon such heroism as that, who can say that he does not believe in long-suffering?[3]

After Harriet Beecher Stowe gained fame for her novel depicting slave life in America, Henry tried his hand at writing a religious novel. *Norwood* was published serially first, then in book form. It

---

[3] Henry Ward Beecher, "The Fruit of the Spirit," in *The Essence of Religion* (London: James Clarke & Co., n. d.), 65–80, reprinted in Clyde Fant and William Pinson, *Twenty Centuries of Great Preaching* (Waco, TX: Word, 1971), 4:316–29. Nineteenth-century spelling has been updated.

never enjoyed the acclaim afforded his sister's storytelling. Beecher, however, made effective use of narrative for sermon illustrations. He delivered the first three years of the Yale Lectures on Preaching in 1872, 1873, and 1874. That famous lecture series, endowed by a member of his Plymouth Church, is more precisely named the Lyman Beecher Lectures after the illustrious patriarch of the family.

In preaching, Beecher was not a theological thinker. His mind was more tuned to concrete than abstract thought. On moral and ethical issues he took his stand. All his life the slavery issue was a matter of concern. Indeed, his whole family felt strongly about the "peculiar institution." The new theory of evolution became a burning issue in his day. Beecher lost some support by taking a stand favorable to the new explanation of origins. Debates over Calvinism were also common then as they are in many circles again today. The labor movement was just gaining ground and gaining enemies. Beecher gave no support to labor unions. He spoke against them. He was a strong supporter of the temperance movement of the day and an opponent of gambling and of alcoholic beverage. In a sermon to young men requested by the fledgling organization called YMCA, he warned against the dangers of the city: alcohol, tobacco (smoking or chewing).

Our special interest in the pulpit work of Beecher and of all others in this series is their power of storytelling. Beecher did not use anecdotes, nor did he regularly glean stories from history or literature. Mostly he used what we might characterize as imagined examples or as we termed it above, describing the passing parade of life. In a sermon on "The Christian Life as Growth," he used an analogy to illustrate rising levels of Christian life.

> The experience in many men of what they call *reconversion* is a genuine experience. And yet they may not have been the less truly converted before. I think there are many persons that are converted, as it were, as boats go on a canal. They run along on one level till they understand all about that level, and they are familiar with all the scenery that is visible from it; and by and by they come into a lock. There the water is let in beneath them, and they rise; and as they rise they are banged and scraped against

the sides. At length they get upon another level. And they see what they did not think of before they went into that lock of sorrow, and distress, and troubles, that lifted them up higher. . . .

When, after two or three years have passed away there comes another revival, a new descent of the Holy Ghost into their hearts, they say, "Brethren, I thought I was converted several years ago; but I was not, and God has converted me now." They go on from that point five or ten years longer, when they are lifted up again; and they say, "Twice I have been fooled; at different times I supposed I was converted; but now my conversion is real." No, you were not deceived either time. You were converted when you started in the Christian life, later you were converted again, and now you have been converted the third time.

Beecher added it would not hurt them if they were converted two or three times more.[4]

T. De Witt Talmage, Flamboyant Pulpiteer

In his student days T. De Witt Talmage was told he would never be fit to preach the gospel in any American pulpit. When he was 37 years old, in 1869, he found himself in the enviable predicament of being offered four of America's most prominent pulpits in one day! Invitations from Chicago's Calvary Church, Boston's Union Church, San Francisco's First Presbyterian Church, and the Central Presbyterian Church of Brooklyn came simultaneously in February of that year. On one morning in February 1869, three committees waited in three different rooms to visit with him. Mrs. Talmage moved from room to room between committees from Chicago, from Brooklyn, and a committee from his Philadelphia church. She worked to keep them entertained and apart since "it would have been unpleasant for them to meet," he said in his autobiography.

Though perplexed, he resolved to stay in Philadelphia unless God made plain that he was to go and where he was to go. He took a train that night to a speaking engagement in Harrisburg,

[4] Fant and Pinson, *Twenty Centuries*, 4:341–42.

Pennsylvania, with his mind cluttered by the pleadings of the four committees. The bewildered pastor stretched himself out upon the seats for a sound sleep praying: "Lord, what wilt Thou have me to do? Make it plain to me when I wake up." He awoke as the train entered Harrisburg, and as plainly as though the voice had been audible, God said to him, "Go to Brooklyn." He went and never doubted that it was the right thing to go. "It is always best," wrote Talmage later, "to stay where you are until God gives you marching orders, and then move on."[5]

Brooklyn was the center of his stellar pulpit ministry for the next 26 years. Before that, he was educated at schools now called New York University and New Brunswick Theological Seminary. After graduation in 1856, he served Dutch Reformed churches in New Jersey, New York, and then Philadelphia, Pennsylvania. When he became a pastor in Brooklyn, he also became a Presbyterian. The church had less than 20 active members when he started but drew increasingly larger crowds as he grew and matured. The first wooden tabernacle was built in 1870 with seating for four thousand. A fire destroyed it two years later. The church rebuilt it to seat five thousand. This one survived 21 years before being turned to rubble by a windstorm. The third time it was relocated and rebuilt.

During the Civil War, Talmage was a chaplain in the Union Army and added the lecture circuit to his busy schedule, as did a number of other famous preachers such as Henry Ward Beecher and Russell Conwell, subjects of other sketches in this series. Widespread rumor supposed him to be a millionaire from all his speaking and writing income. He never reached that level but did admit to being paid as much as a thousand dollars for a lecture. He calculated the average to be about five hundred dollars per night. But this was in an era when the average family income in America did not reach five hundred dollars in a year.

The decision not to respond to his critics and their wild guesses about his wealth served him well. When the New York papers printed an attack, the reporters gathered next Sunday at the Tabernacle to hear his response. They heard only a sermon which

---

[5] Thomas De Witt Talmage, *T. De Witt Talmage as I Knew Him* (New York: Dutton, 1912). (Final chapter written after his death by Mrs. T. De Witt Talmage). Also available online but in unedited digital copy at least two places including: http://www.gutenberg.org/catalog/world/readfile?fk_files= 180422&pageno=6.

they took down and published. This gave Talmage the idea that his sermons might be well received in print. He began to syndicate them. Eventually his sermons reached 20 million people each week in three thousand newspapers around the world. This from the man who was told in his student days that he would never be fit to preach the gospel in any American pulpit.

What made Talmage so popular? His eloquence and his flamboyance are often mentioned. Some called it "showmanship." He was an energetic preacher, pacing back and forth on stage or platform. He had an expressive face whether smiling or scowling. He developed a powerful speaking voice by practice in the woods. Someone estimated he could be heard by five thousand people even outdoors. His eloquence shines in vivid descriptions of scenes and skillful storytelling. Illustrations came naturally to him. Most preachers struggle to find one fitting; he labored to thin out his supply.

His printed sermons show a speaker who was bold and relevant. Talmage never shirked to deal with controversial matters. During the labor strife of the 1880s, he preached a series of sermons on labor and capital. Published in 1886 under the title "The Battle for Bread," each of the six sermons in the series began with a brief text. Like most of his sermons, these addresses are more like popular lectures than true expositions of Scripture. The first one is on "The Labor Question." Genesis 1:2 is the text. "The earth was without form, and void; and darkness was upon the face of the deep. And the Spirit of God moved upon the face of the waters" (KJV). The preacher asserted that the God who brought order out of the "anarchy of the elements" could do the same in the threatened social chaos. The church must be peacemaker, ever alert to the peril of the times. He gave pointed advice to three classes of laborers: First, to those who are at work, stick to it. Second, to those who have resigned work (or joined a strike), go back immediately. Then the third "word of brotherly advice to the nearly two million people who could not get work before this trouble began, [is] go now and take the vacated places."

If he was tough on workers and unions in the first sermon, he also came down hard on capital and management in the second. "Treatment of Employees" was solidly based on the text Galatians 5:15: "If ye bite and devour one another, take heed that ye are not consumed one of another" (KJV). He spoke of the mutual

dependence of labor and capital who really have identical inter-
ests. He gave pointed advice to employers: Pay wages as large as
are reasonable and affordable. Pay promptly. He quoted injunc-
tions from Malachi, from Leviticus, and from Colossians about
not oppressing the hireling, not keeping wages overnight, and giving servants what is just and equal. He told them, "Do not say to
your employees: 'Now, if you don't like this place get another,'
when you know they cannot get another." He told employers it
was their duty to see to the welfare of the employee. They could at
least give advice about savings, life insurance, and such matters.
He encouraged capitalists to follow the example of philanthropists
and benefactors who provided public libraries, concert halls, recreation facilities as well as good wages. He charged them to give
time off for sickness and family bereavement. In another sermon
he was ahead of his time in calling for equal pay for women who
do the same job as men. He gave examples in government and
education as well as field and factory.[6]

He illustrated what he termed "philanthropic capitalists" with
brief character sketches of industrialists who took their position as
God's stewards and worked for the benefit of everyone in the company and the larger community as well. Here is a pair of sketches
of such "philanthropic capitalists."

> Peter Cooper was a glue-maker. No one begrudged
> him his millions of dollars, for he built Cooper
> Institute and swung open its doors for every poor
> man's son, and said to the day laborer: "Send your
> boy up to my Institute if you want him to have a
> splendid education." And a young man of this church
> was the other day walking in Greenwood Cemetery,
> and he saw two young men putting flowers on the
> grave of Peter Cooper. My friend supposed the
> young men were relatives of Peter Cooper, and deco-
> rated his grave for that reason. "No," they said, "we
> put these flowers on his grave because it was through
> him we got our education."

---

[6] T. De Witt Talmage, "Hardships of Workingmen," *The Battle for Bread: A Series of
Sermons Related to Labor and Capital* (New York: J. S. Ogilve, 1888), 31, 50–53.

Abraham Van Nest was a harness-maker in New York. Through economy and industry and skill he got a great fortune. He gave away to help others hundreds of thousands of dollars. I shall never forget the scene when I, a green country lad, stopped at his house, and after passing the evening with him he came to the door and came outside and said: "Here, De Witt, is fifty dollars to get books with. Don't say anything about it." And I never did till the good old man was gone.[7]

There was an incident in his early preaching experience when Talmage took a manuscript with him to the platform but lost it in the upholstery of a large divan where he was seated. He was embarrassed by his frantic search on hands and knees desperate to retrieve it before the hymn was finished. Never again! He learned to memorize his sermons and still deliver them as though they were extemporaneous. No doubt using lots of narrative made that easier. In addition, his many dramatic and descriptive illustrations in the historical present tense facilitated memorizing.

He was an exhorter and not an expositor. He studiously avoided logical arguments and did little with such sermonic staples as background studies and word studies. The following excerpt gives an example while justifying this approach to preaching as evangelistically effective.

For instance, here is a man all armed on the doctrine of election; all his troops of argument and prejudice are at that particular gate. You may batter away at that side of the castle for fifty years and you will not take it; but just wheel your troops to the side gate of the heart's affection, and in five minutes you capture him. I never knew a man to be saved through a brilliant argument. You cannot hook men into the kingdom. . . . There is no grace in syllogisms. . . . But there is in every man's heart a bolt that can be easily withdrawn. A little child four years old may touch that bolt and it will spring back and the door will swing open and Christ will come in.[8]

---

[7] Ibid., 14–15.
[8] Alexander Gammie, *Preachers I Have Heard* (London: Pickering & Inglis, n.d.), 72.

The evangelistic objective is strong in his preaching, and he always wanted every sermon to be encouraging. He delighted to close his sermons in heaven. He was clear in everything including the outline of his sermon, almost always topical. Though he grew and matured as a pulpiteer, his first sermon and his last are marked by vivid and imaginative narrative. His first sermon was on the text Proverbs 18:24, "There is a friend that sticketh closer than a brother" (KJV). He described the scene in heaven as Christ set out for his mission to earth. The astonished angels suggested, "Shall ten thousand of us weave our wings together to make a fit chariot for thee to ride upon in thy descent to that fallen world?" Christ waved away their offer. "Shall we bring together all the clouds of heaven and make a fit throne for thee to sit upon?" But this offer too was refused. The Christ could not go in such a way. He commanded them to take away his royal robe and let him go without a single attendant. The angelic host crowded on heaven's vast balcony to watch as he descended. They talked so among themselves at this sight that the shepherds of Bethlehem heard them.[9]

Alexander Maclaren, in a study of Talmage and his preaching noted that most of his texts were taken from the Old Testament. In a sample of nearly five hundred sermons, more than three hundred are Old Testament texts. He drew illustrations from life as he watched it. One describes the process he once witnessed in an ax factory.

> Sweating workers with tongs stirred the blaze. Then they brought out a bar of iron and put it between jaws that bit it in twain. Then they put it on an anvil, and there were great hammers swung by machinery—each one half a ton in weight—that went thump! thump! thump!" He imagined how the iron might protest if it could speak and how the workmen would answer that it was all for a purpose. They would become sharp axes to hew down the forest, build ships and houses and other things for the blessing of mankind. And he applied it to God's molding

[9] Clarence E. Macartney, *Six Kings of the American Pulpit* (Philadelphia: Westminster, 1942). The chapter on Talmage is reprinted as the introduction to T. De Witt Talmage, *500 Selected Sermons* (Grand Rapids: Baker, 1956), 1:3.

and making us into tools for his church, though we might find the process difficult.[10]

He described a picture he saw in a shop window on a trip to Switzerland. He found it commemorated a notable mountain-climbing accident in the area. He told the story of the company of travelers and their guides all roped together when one slipped and pulled each of the others over the precipice. One more muscular climber was able to dig his heels into the ice and hold on, but the rope broke under the weight. Talmage used it to illustrate whole families "bound together by ties of affection, and in many cases walking on slippery places of worldliness and sin." He continued the parallel to say, "There is such a thing as coming to Christ soon enough to save ourselves, but not soon enough to save others."[11]

The following narrative is the climax to a sermon entitled "Anxiety" and has for a text, "Sirs, what must I do to be saved?" (Acts 16:30 KJV). It is the only extended narrative in this sermon and forms a fitting climax to the evangelistic message.

> In the troubled times of Scotland, Sir John Cochrane was condemned to death by the king. The death warrant was on the way. Sir John Cochrane was bidding farewell to his daughter Grizelle at the prison door. He said: "Farewell, my darling child, I must die." His daughter said: "No, father, you shall not die." "But," he said, "the king is against me, and the law is after me, and the death warrant is on its way, and I must die; do not deceive yourself, my dear child." The daughter said: "Father, you shall not die," as she left the prison gate. At night, on the moors of Scotland, a disguised wayfarer stood waiting for the horseman carrying the mail bags containing the death warrant. The disguised wayfarer, as the horse came by, clutched the bridle and shouted to the rider—to the man who carried the mail bags: "Dismount!" He felt for his arms, and was about to shoot, but the wayfarer jerked him from his saddle and he fell flat. The wayfarer picked up the mail bags, put them on his shoulder and vanished in the darkness, and fourteen days were thus gained for the prisoner's

---

[10] *T. De Witt Talmage,* Great Pulpit Masters, vol. 7 (New York: Fleming H. Revell, 1951), 69.
[11] Ibid., 104.

life, during which the father confessor was pleading for the pardon of Sir John Cochrane. The second time the death warrant is on its way. The disguised wayfarer comes along, and asks for a little bread and a little wine, starts on across the moors, and they say: "Poor man, to have to go out such a stormy night; it is dark and you will lose yourself on the moors." "Oh, no," he says, "I will not." He trudged on and stopped amid the brambles and waited for the horseman to come carrying the mail bags containing the death warrant of Sir John Cochrane. The mail carrier spurred on his steed, for he was fearful because of what had occurred on the former journey, when suddenly through the storm and through the darkness there was a flash of firearms and the horse became unmanageable, and as the mail carrier discharged his pistol in response, the horse threw him, and the disguised wayfarer put his foot on the breast of the overthrown rider, and said: "Surrender now!" The mail carrier surrendered his arms, and the disguised wayfarer put upon his shoulders the mail bags, leaped upon the horse, and sped away into the darkness gaining fourteen more days for the poor prisoner, Sir John Cochrane. And before the fourteen days had expired pardon had come from the king. The door of the prison swung open, and Sir John Cochrane was free. One day, when he was standing amid his friends, they congratulating him, the disguised wayfarer appeared at the gate and he said, "Admit him right away." The disguised wayfarer came in and said: "Here are two letters; read them, sir." Sir John Cochrane read them. They were his two death warrants, and he threw them into the fire. Then said Sir John Cochrane: "To whom am I indebted? Who is this poor wayfarer that saved my life? Who is it?" And the wayfarer pulled aside and pulled off the jerkin and the cloak, and the hat, and lo, it was Grizelle, the daughter of Sir John Cochrane. "Gracious heaven!" he cried, "my child, my saviour, my own Grizelle!"[12]

[12] Ibid., 120–21. This same sermon appears also in Clyde Fant and William Pinson, *Twenty Centuries of Great Preaching* (Waco: Word, 1971), 5:306–14, crediting T. De Witt

Following this, as Talmage often did, he made explicit the "more thrilling story" illustrated. A death warrant from the King of heaven and earth, "The soul that sinneth it shall die." But another wayfarer "breasting the storm, gripped by the bridle the oncoming doom and flung it back, and put his wounded and bleeding foot on the overthrown rider." It is not hard to imagine the dramatic delivery in the concluding climax, "Go free! Open the gate! Strike off the chain! Go free! . . . Let all earth and heaven break forth in praise. Victory through our Lord Jesus Christ!"[13]

Talmage was nearly always a textual preacher or a topical preacher with a text attached as a starting point. Sometimes he did build his outline on that text, but more often his structure developed the topic with little true biblical authority. His outlines were always clear and easy to follow. Many preachers still get by with that approach. Talmage is a true master of storytelling in preaching, though not a model of biblical exposition.

Exercise 1. As you read the biographical sketches in these chapters, select at least one or two outstanding preachers for further study. Plan to read one or two biographies of that preacher and ten or more sermons. Beecher or Talmage would be a good selection. Set a goal on the calendar for this exercise.

Exercise 2. You will notice in these two preachers and in others in this study that a preacher may be strong on narrative style and weak in expounding Scripture. Is this a necessary trade-off? Why or why not? Keep this question in mind as you read the concluding chapters.

Exercise 3. The examples of narrative are typical of each preacher. Which one drew more from history and other reading? Which one did more invention of narrative from life observed? Is one method more effective than the other?

Talmage, *500 Selected Sermons* (New York: Christian Herald, 1900), 4:379–91. It has a different title, "Question of Questions," an entirely different introduction and enough difference in the text to indicate it was preached at a different time, probably earlier. The long closing illustration, however, is almost word for word identical in both deliveries.
[13] Ibid.

Chapter 13

LONDON LUMINARIES IN
THE AGE OF SPURGEON

ANYONE WISHING A GLIMPSE OF life in nineteenth-century London may read Charles Dickens. He wrote of rich estates and squalid slums. Inhabitants of both were there in increasing numbers. The ancient town established by the Romans in AD 43 took until 1800 to reach one million inhabitants. In the nineteenth century alone the number soared to more than 6.5 million with all the growing pains one might expect. Churches multiplied too. Where there was a Spurgeon or Parker in the pulpit, those churches attracted large numbers.

London in the nineteenth century was home to G. Campbell Morgan at Westminster Chapel in the center of the city. William Booth founded the Salvation Army among the poor of east London in 1878. Spurgeon ministered to the educated at New Park Street Baptist Church until the old church was rebuilt as a truly new Metropolitan Tabernacle. Joseph Parker attracted but slightly smaller crowds across the river at City Temple. Of these named, only Spurgeon was noted for the power of his narrative in the pulpit. His story is well-known, so we will take a brief survey of Charles H. Spurgeon (1834–1892) as a storyteller. Then we will consider one of his younger contemporaries in London (F. B. Meyer, 1847–1949), and introduce one of Spurgeon's students (F. W. Boreham, 1871–1959).

Charles H. Spurgeon,
Prince of All Preachers

Fifteen-year-old Charles Spurgeon, a few months after his conversion, began teaching a Bible class for younger boys. One day a lad interrupted his lesson. "This is very dull, Teacher. Can't you pitch us a yarn?" Young Spurgeon could and did. Later the Prince of Preachers said he learned to tell stories in that class because he was "obliged to tell them."[1] And so is any preacher "obliged" to tell stories who would maximize power in the pulpit.

While still a teenager with untrained talent for the pulpit, a friend arranged for him to meet Dr. Angus, principal of a theological school, now Regents Park College, Oxford. The meeting was to be in the home of Mr. Macmillan, the publisher. Young Spurgeon arrived on time and was ushered into the drawing room. After waiting two hours, he rang for the maid. He learned that Dr. Angus had waited long in another parlor but left to catch his train back to the city. Spurgeon was disappointed but soon accepted the day's events as part of God's providence. He later said he would have been glad to have theological training but thought God might use him without it.

He was the son of a lay preacher-businessman and the grandson of a Puritan pastor. Charles spent most of his early years with that grandfather. There he delighted to explore the pastor's extensive library. By the time he was six years old, young master Spurgeon was reading the stories in Foxe's *Book of Martyrs* and Bunyan's books. He began at that tender age a lifetime practice of reading *Pilgrim's Progress* twice a year. He read other stories also such as Defoe's *Robinson Crusoe.*

While still a teen, the "boy preacher," as some called him, became pastor of an old church in London called New Park Street Baptist Church. He began with about 80 faithful souls in a decaying auditorium with 1,200 seats. His preaching soon attracted crowds. They had to rent an auditorium with five thousand seats while they built the Metropolitan Tabernacle with six thousand. By age 21 Spurgeon had preached one thousand sermons and was already the most popular preacher of his day. His printed sermons sold 25,000 copies each week.

---

[1] Lewis Drummond, *Spurgeon: Prince of Preachers* (Grand Rapids: Kregel, 1992), 157.

165

Susannah, his faithful wife and suitable helper, tells us that whenever he traveled, "the dear Pastor," as she called him, made frequent
use of a notebook to jot down anything and everything that might
be useful later as a sermon illustration. It would be a mistake to
think that storytelling was the secret of Spurgeon's pulpit power,
but his narrative skill was certainly a major part of his preaching.
He was also endowed by his Maker with a powerful voice, clear
and pleasing. He spent many hours in Bible study and in books and
commentaries. His sermon preparation began with reflection on his
selected text. In fact he had a number of sermons growing and ripen-
ing like so many apples on an apple tree. Then on Saturday evening
he selected one most ripe and ready to share with his congregation.
After Saturday evening dinner with family and friends, he would
excuse himself and retire to his study. There he would make a final
decision on his choice for Sunday morning's sermon and sketch
a few words of outline perhaps on the back of an envelope as he
organized his thoughts. He would preach on Sunday extemporane-
ously. Like several other great preachers, only after preaching did
Spurgeon write out his sermons for publication. Thirty-eight volumes of these were in print during his lifetime. Most of them have
never been out of print in the century since then.

One of his more famous sermons is a meditation on a single sentence in Job 35:10: "But none saith, Where is God my maker, who
giveth songs in the night?" (KJV). It begins with a single paragraph
of introduction placing the text in its context as Elihu's reasonable
but mistaken assumption about the cause of Job's distress. Then the
preacher narrows his focus to the one phrase that provides the title
and theme of the sermon, "Songs in the Night."

The sermon sparkles with allusions to Scripture and Christian
literature such as Bunyan's *Pilgrims Progress*. It includes two
brief narratives from the pastor's experience of the week. One is
from a current event involving the workers in the silk-weaving
industry of London. It would be on the minds of all who read the
London newspapers.

> I am preaching to-night for the poor weavers of
> Spitalfields. Perhaps there are not to be found a class
> of men in London who are suffering a darker night
> than they are; for while many classes have been

befriended and defended, there are few who speak up for them, and (if I am rightly informed) they are generally ground down within an inch of their lives. I suppose their masters intend that their bread shall be sweet, on the principle, that the nearer the ground, the sweeter the grass; for I should think that no people have their grass so near the ground as the weavers of Spitalfields. In an inquiry by the House of Commons last week, it was given in evidence that their average wages amount to seven or eight shillings a week; and that they have to furnish themselves with a room, and work at expensive articles, which my friends and ladies are wearing now, and they buy as cheaply as possible; but perhaps they do not know that they are made with the blood and bones and marrow of the Spitalfield weavers, who, many of them, work for less than man ought to have to subsist upon. Some of them waited upon me the other day; I was exceedingly pleased with one of them. He said, "Well sir, it is very hard, but I hope there is better times coming for us." "Well, my friend," I said, "I'm afraid you cannot hope for much better times, unless the Lord Jesus Christ comes a second time." "That is just what we hope for," said he. "We do not see there is any chance of deliverance, unless the Lord Jesus Christ comes to establish His kingdom upon the earth; and then He will judge the oppressed, and break the oppressors in pieces with an iron rod like a potter's vessel."[2]

The other brief narrative comes from the same sermon. It recounts a pastoral visit he made just the evening before.

Kneeling by the bed of an apparently dying saint, last night, I said, "Well, sister, He has been precious to you; you can rejoice in His covenant mercies, and his past loving-kindnesses." She put out her hand, and said, "Ah! Sir, do not talk about them now; I want the sinner's Savior as much now as ever; it is

---

[2] Charles H. Spurgeon, "Songs in the Night" in Warren W. Wiersbe, compiler, *Treasury of the World's Great Sermons* (Grand Rapids: Kregel, 1977), 550–51.

not a saint's I want; it is still a sinner's Savior that I am in need of, for I am a sinner still." I found that I could not comfort her with the past; so I reminded her of the golden streets, of the gates of pearl, of the walls of jasper, of the harps of gold, of the songs of bliss; and then her eyes glistened; and she said, "Yes, I shall be there soon; I shall meet them by and by;" and then she seemed so glad![3]

Likely the last student Spurgeon personally interviewed for his Preacher's College was a young man named F. W. Boreham. The story of his truly unique narrative sermon method is included in this chapter. But first, just to keep things in chronological order, consider a younger contemporary of Spurgeon in London, F. B. Meyer.

F. B. Meyer, Able Expositor

One Sunday evening after he had preached, a young Frederick Brotherton Meyer was walking home with the pastor with whom he served as associate. "That was quite a good sermon you gave this evening," said Pastor Birrell, "but it was a topical sermon, and if you are going to make topical sermons your model, you will presently come to the end of your topics, and where will you be then?" He advised Meyer to do as he had done for 30 years: "Become an expositor of Scripture. You will always retain your freshness, and will build up a strong and healthy church." Many years later Meyer said that counsel distinctly changed his outlook and his homiletical habit for pulpit and literary work. He said, "I remember the spot where I heard it. . . . It has enabled me to sustain my pastorates with perpetual zest and freshness all my days."[4]

Meyer settled on a pattern of sermon preparation in four broad stages. First, he selected a book of the Bible for close study for two or three months. He read it again and again until its central message became clear. Second, he planned his treatment of the text, dividing the book into sections and subsections. Each contained "a full-orbed thought." Third, he selected from the passage

[3] Ibid., 552.
[4] A. Chester Mann, *F. B. Meyer: Preacher, Teacher, Man of God* (New York: Fleming H. Revell, 1929), 74–75.

what he called the "pivot text." This was a brief and bright verse or part of a verse quotable and easy to remember. He wanted that key text to be terse and crisp enough to stick in memory of all who heard the sermon. The fourth and final step was to weave into the fabric of the message all the main elements of the related context. "Just as all the objects in the field of vision focus in the lens of the eye, and finally, in the minute filament of the optic nerve, so the thoughts, images and suggestions of the context should pass through the chosen text to the heart of those who gather to hear."[5]

F. B. Meyer was born in London in 1847, a younger contemporary of both Spurgeon and Joseph Parker in that city as well as other notables of the English pulpit such as Robert W. Dale and Alexander Maclaren. With his parents he moved to Brighton where his childhood schooling began. He returned to London when he was 15, where that training continued to completion. He would later describe those years of happy, carefree childhood as "a stretch of sunlit years untouched by shadow." He relished the church services with eager worshippers crowded to the balconies and hoped that he too might someday preach to such crowds. When he was 16, he shared his career aspirations with his parents and with his pastor, who all encouraged him to pursue that vision. Dr. Brock, his pastor, required him to preach a sermon before him, and though affirming the young teenager, he recommended that he spend two or three years in the business world first. He spent two years in a London counting house and later said he wished all preachers might have the benefit of such experience. When he was 19, he entered Regent's Park College. He graduated in 1869 and was appointed assistant minister to Charles M. Birrell at Pembroke Baptist Chapel in Liverpool. He began a happy marriage in 1871 that lasted more than 58 years. Mrs. Meyer died just a few weeks before her husband.

His pastorates tended to be brief but bright. In 1872 he moved to a chapel in York. The next year Moody and Sankey found themselves in England without sponsors; the two men who had invited them both died before the evangelists arrived. Soon Meyer invited

---

[5] Ibid., 75–76. The same biographer notes that on the eve of his farewell to the church in Liverpool, the church gave him an offering of 60 guineas "and eight volumes of Kitto's *Biblical Illustrations*." His published sermons give no evidence that Meyer ever used the collection.

the two evangelists to his chapel. He introduced the evangelists to British churches, and this became the real launching of their great tour of England. It made a zealous evangelist out of Meyer as well.

He moved to Victoria Road Baptist Church, Leicester, where he served four years with evangelistic zeal unaccustomed to the staid congregation. It ended one Sunday evening when one of the grave old deacons burst into the chancel of the church where Meyer was zealously conducting an afterservice. "We cannot have this sort of thing here. This is not a Gospel shop." Meyer quietly resigned and planned to leave the city. Fifteen young merchants, however, banded together to guarantee his salary if he would stay and begin preaching in a public hall called Museum Building. The work rapidly grew into a church. In March 1880, three hundred persons assembled to dedicate the selected land to the service of Almighty God. The church known as Melbourne Hall opened in the summer of 1881 and grew to crowds of 1,500 to 2,000.

Much of Meyer's ministry included temperance work, reclamation work, and other social work. He became a politician and borough councilor and headed a movement to close saloons. He was instrumental also in closing nearly five hundred brothels. He regularly met released prisoners and organized efforts to find work for them. One of his hands-on projects for these men was to organize a window-washing service. He printed circulars with his name on them urging the public to give these ex-convicts a chance. When a factory offered to engage them if they could clean the extremely high windows that were never cleaned, Meyer invested in ladders so tall it took four men to carry them through the streets.

In 1904–1905 he was president of the national Federation of Free Churches. He conducted missions in South Africa and the Far East. He also visited the Continent, the USA, and the Near East. He returned to England in 1909. He wrote excellent devotional books, biographical studies, and expositions that were popular and still enjoy wide reception. His name is often linked to Keswick, where he was a most popular speaker.

Meyer's strength in Old Testament exposition owes much to his apprenticeship with a Hebrew scholar. He learned backgrounds in the Hebrew Bible that enriched his Christian preaching throughout his life. An example worthy of closer examination than we will have space to give is the following introduction to his sermon on Isaiah 6:1–8. The title is "God Is Near." Note the impressive amount of detail on temple worship included in this narrative.

One afternoon, about four o'clock, Isaiah, who was then in early middle life, found himself one of a great crowd of worshippers slowly ascending the temple's steps. Together with them he passed the lower platform and still climbed until at last he stood at the summit, at the Beautiful Gate of the temple. Standing there, he little realized that that afternoon was to be the epochal moment of his life; but that afternoon was to introduce an altogether new element into his life work.

Standing there upon that highest step, in the direct line of vision lay, first, the altar upon which the afternoon sacrifice was to be made; beyond it a laver where the priests washed their feet; and beyond that the tall cedar doors that opened upon the Holy Place, which indeed would have unfolded presently, as to Zachariah in after days when he went to offer incense while the people stood without in prayer.

On either side stood probably two hundred and fifty Levites, with the instruments of David in their hands, prepared to sing psalms which were so famous, and about which their Babylonian captors in after days said: "Sing us one of the songs of Zion."

As Isaiah stood there wrapped in thought, those who were nearest him had no idea what was transpiring; but he was swept away from all those sights and sounds, from the sun in mid sky, from the glistening marble of the temple, from the music of the Levite band, from all the crowds that pressed him on every side, and he beheld the sapphire throne of the King Himself. He heard the prayer or chant of the seraphim, and for a moment his whole soul was steeped in the rapture of that vision. But a moment after he was plunged in the profoundest contrition of soul as he contrasted himself with those who served God with sinless lips, and he cried: "Woe is me! for I am undone; because I am a man of unclean lips."

In the same sermon, this personal illustration makes the preacher's point that, for those who, like Isaiah, have eyes to see it, "the whole earth is full of his glory."

> One day in London I was sitting in a dark omnibus. A man came in to examine our tickets, and I thought to myself, You will never be able to tell whether they have been punched aright. As I watched, curious to notice, he touched a little spring on his breast, and in a tiny globe of glass a beautiful glow of electric light shone out. Manifestly the man could see anywhere, because he carried the light with which he saw. So we must understand that when the heart is full of God, you will find God anywhere and everywhere, as the miner carries the candle in his cap through the dark cavity of the earth, and lights his steps.[6]

F. W. Boreham's Unique Narrative Method

F. W. Boreham (1871–1959) was introduced once to a gathering of Presbyterian preachers in Edinburgh, Scotland, as "the man whose name is on all our lips, whose books are on all our shelves, and whose illustrations are in all our sermons."[7]

His was a truly unique way of illuminating a text through the life story of a famous person in history or literature. From his early

> I would, if I could only muster up the courage to say a word to preachers before laying down my pen. Is there any better way of preaching than by storytelling? Indeed, is there any other way of preaching? As soon as the terminology of the pulpit becomes technical and abstract, the tired mind declines to follow. Only so long as a picture is being painted or a story told will the hearers maintain an eager pursuit. And, after all, has not the preacher been called to the service of the Most Sublime Story Teller of all the Ages?
> —Frank W. Boreham

---

[6] *F. B. Meyer*, Great Pulpit Masters, vol. 6 (New York: Fleming H. Revel, 1950), 69–70, 74.
[7] Geoff Pound, "F. W. Boreham: The Public Theologian," Baptist World Alliance, Heritage and Identity Commission. General Council Meeting, July 2004, Seoul, South Korea.

childhood both parents encouraged Frank in reading biography and other literature. This is a trait that not surprisingly appears in the childhood of many of the pulpit masters who came to excel in the use of narrative in their sermons. While a young man in London, Boreham sought every opportunity to hear great pulpit masters like F. B. Meyer, Joseph Parker, and Charles H. Spurgeon. He studied their sermon style and their delivery.

Soon after Boreham became a student in Spurgeon's Pastors College, he took a student pastorate. Before he graduated, he accepted the pastorate of a new congregation halfway around the world in New Zealand. There he perfected his style of writing and preaching. He read biographies and autobiographies of famous people searching for a single text of Scripture that might explain their greatness. Then he preached a sermon on that text using the life of the outstanding character as illustration of the power of that Scripture. He sometimes did the same thing with fictional characters.

Some think Boreham depended too much on storytelling for the content of his sermons. He was not an expositor if an expositor must take an extended Scripture passage and explain it in detail. Instead, he excelled in selecting a key verse and making it come alive through the life of his chosen subject in history or literature. The churches he served grew and thrived on such preaching and his strong evangelistic emphasis. He was already well-known for his books of essays on common things when he began to publish the series of sermons on *Texts That Made History*. Between 1920 and 1928, five of these volumes of sermons appeared. They were poetically entitled *A Bunch of Everlastings*, *A Handful of Stars*, *A Casket of Cameos*, *A Faggot of Torches*, and *A Temple of Topaz*. In the five are 125 sermons, each based on a text that explained the essence of a famous person such as Martin Luther, William Penn, or William Booth. Some of the sermons used a fictional character in literature such as Robinson Crusoe or Uncle Tom to make the text come alive. Boreham's essays are compiled in over 40 volumes. His published books include more than 50 books, many more booklets, and over three thousand editorials and articles for newspapers and Christian journals.

His typical sermon captured attention in the opening words with an episode from the life of his chosen character. This led to the brief text for his sermon, usually a verse that needed application more than explanation. If another illustration was called for, it came most often in a vignette from some other narrative of history or current events. Boreham's storytelling skill was more than an attention getter. Like the parables of Jesus, his narratives were vessels for bringing the water of life to thirsty souls. Boreham explained, "The one passionate desire of my heart has been to lead my hearers to Christ. I have never entered a pulpit without feeling that, if only people could catch a vision of the Saviour, they would have no alternative but to lay their devotion at his feet."[8]

From the famous series of *Texts That Made History* consider one example. Here is the way he began the sermon on "Michael Faraday's Text."

> The lecturer had vanished! A crowded gathering of distinguished scientists had been listening, spellbound to the masterly expositions of Michael Faraday. For an hour he had held his brilliant audience enthralled as he had demonstrated the nature and properties of the magnet. And he had brought his lecture to a close with an experiment so novel, so bewildering and so triumphant that, for some time after he resumed his seat, the house rocked with enthusiastic applause. And then the Prince of Wales—afterwards King Edward the Seventh—rose to propose a motion of congratulation. The resolution, having been duly seconded, was carried with renewed thunders of applause. But the uproar was succeeded by a strange silence. The assembly waited for Faraday's reply; but the lecturer had vanished! What had become of him? Only two or three of his more intimate friends were in the secret. They knew that the great chemist was a great Christian. He was an elder of a little Sandemanian Church—a church that never boasted more than twenty members. The hour at which Faraday concluded his lecture was the hour of the weeknight prayer-meeting. That meeting he never neglected. And, under cover of the cheering and applause, the lecturer had slipped out of the

---

[8] F. W. Boreham, *My Pilgrimage* (Philadelphia: Judson, 1950), 20.

crowded hall and hurried off to the little meeting-house where two or three had met together to renew their fellowship with God.

After a few more lines, the preacher introduced the text in these words:

> In [Faraday] the simplicities were always stron-ger than the sublimities; the child outlived the sage. As he lay dying they tried to interview the professor, but it was the little child in him that answered them. 'What are your speculations?' they inquired.
>
> 'Speculations?' he asked, in wondering surprise. 'Speculations! I have none! I am resting on certain-ties. *I know whom I have believed and am persuaded that He is able to keep that which I have committed unto Him against that day!* And reveling like a little child in those cloudless simplicities, his great soul passed away.[9]

Near the end of his life Boreham wrote these words specifically to preachers:

> I would, if I could only muster up the courage to say a word to preachers before laying down my pen. Is there any better way of preaching than by storytelling? Indeed, is there any other way of preaching? As soon as the terminology of the pulpit becomes technical and abstract, the tired mind declines to follow. Only so long as a picture is being painted or a story told will the hearers maintain an eager pursuit. And, after all, has not the preacher been called to the service of the Most Sublime Story Teller of all the Ages?[10]

---

[9] F. W. Boreham, *A Handful of Stars* (Philadelphia: Judson, 1922), 182–84.

[10] Geoff Pound's blog at www.beststoriesoffwboreham.blogspot.com. This is an excellent and serious resource on all things Boreham.

Exercise 1. Select a biography of Spurgeon to read. An easy and delightful read is Richard Ellsworth Day, *The Shadow of the Broad Brim* (Valley Forge, PA: Judson, 1934). The definitive word to date is Lewis Drummond's *Spurgeon* (Grand Rapids: Kregel, 1992).

Exercise 2. Many nineteenth-century expositors selected a single key verse as a lens to put the larger context in focus. Several are included in these studies including F. B. Meyer. Read two or three of his sermons and make notes on how he used his key text.

Exercise 3. F. W. Boreham is often plagiarized, and his narratives are often borrowed for sermon illustrations. I do not know of a single preacher, however, who has successfully taken him as a model for sermon structure. Read a few of his sermons from the *Texts That Made History* series and see if you can construct one sermon on that pattern.

Chapter 14

BIBLE BIOGRAPHY PREACHERS

EXAMPLES OF EXCELLENT BIOGRAPHICAL PREACHERS
are not hard to find. F. W. Robertson of Brighton preached superb
sermons on Bible biography and did it often. Perhaps half of his
sermons would fit this category. Walter A. Maier, the *Lutheran
Hour* radio preacher, favored this focus for his messages. Both of
these regularly organized their sermons in two parts. For Robertson
it would be two matching or contrasting truths applied to life. For
Maier the first part of the sermon would deal with the text and the
second would apply it to life today. Clovis G. Chappel's favorite
way of telling stories was in sermons on biblical characters. Two
volumes of these were published and are still worth reading. And
Clarence E. Macartney left a rich legacy of instruction in preparing sermons and illustrating them. While not principally a biographical preacher, Harry Emerson Fosdick preached some truly
classic sermons on Bible characters. Terming himself "a modern-
ist," he did not think we should take the Bible literally. Fosdick,
nevertheless, anchored his sermons solidly in a text of Scripture.
His sermon "The Power to See It Through" is built on the only
three references to Demas in the New Testament. "Handling Life's
Second Best" is built on Paul's experience of wanting to go into
Bithynia and accepting God's guidance instead to Troas. These
are usually called "life situation" sermons and they are that, but
they also find their biblical authority in a text about a biblical char-

177

acter. Frank W. Boreham was essentially a biographical preacher, and so was T. De Witt Talmage.[1]

This chapter will focus on two biographical preachers, Alexander Whyte and Dwight L. Moody. But first let me suggest a protocol for preparing a sermon on a Bible character. Start with a text. In this case your biblical authority will be the selected data from the life of the chosen Bible character. It may be a well-known character occupying many chapters of Scripture such as Moses or Paul. You will do well to narrow the focus. Moses at the burning bush is a good study in making excuses when God calls (Exod 3). Paul's experience in finding God's will about going into Macedonia is another case study in following divine leading (Acts 16). Study the character before you decide what truth the passage teaches.

Second, begin to think of a plan for presenting the truth. Give your imagination some room, but keep it under the authority of the Word of God. Your best clue will come when you decide precisely what this text has to say to your congregation this week. Where does the life of this Bible character, or this episode in his or her life, intersect with your life and the lives of those who will give you a hearing?

Third, it is better to state the big idea of the sermon and any parts of that idea in present-tense application form. For example, suppose in reading your Bible you come across the brief mention of Archippus. Paul names him in Colossians 4:17 and in Philemon 2. The tyro might generate a list of notes about Archippus and offer them as the sermon in outline: (1) Archippus was a fellow soldier; (2) Archippus had a ministry; (3) Paul told him to see to it. That is not the best way to organize a biographical sermon. What's wrong? It is all past-tense, historical analysis. It assumes that people will get the point and make application to themselves. That presumes too much. Even if the preacher follows the explication of each sermon division with an application to the listener, there is a better way. One better way would be to introduce the Bible character from the text, note that he was important enough for Paul to name him in his letter to the church and to Philemon. Archippus had a position of trust. Paul considered him a "fellow

---

[1] See Andrew W. Blackwood, "The Ways of Biographical Preachers," chap. 6 in *Biographical Preaching for Today: The Pulpit Use of Bible Cases* (New York: Abingdon, 1954), 111–30.

soldier," though he may not have been as close to Paul as others in that fellowship. The most important thing is that Paul felt that the ministry of Archippus, whatever it was, was in jeopardy. Having introduced the character, let the preacher then state the application in personal form. First, your ministry is a gift of God, or as Paul terms it, "in the Lord." Second, you may succeed or fail in that assignment. Hence the admonition, "See to it!" "Take heed!" And third, your church is admonished to admonish you to complete the work God gives you to do. So Paul tells the church at Colossae to "say to Archippus. . . ." Such a sermon is not locked in past tense all about Archippus; it is in present tense for your hearers today. It becomes a sermon for every believer, for all have a ministry to fulfill.

As you read biographical sermons, you will find that many preachers simply tell the story and apply certain truths along the way. That is one way to do it, but it is the easiest way to do it poorly. Clovis G. Chappel had a gift for making the application clear and powerful, often with a personal illustration. Consider his sermon "A Fine Animal—Esau." The title gives the crucial clue about the spiritual truth to be gleaned from the study of this character. The point is unmistakable in this bit of personal narrative.

> When I was a boy I had a dog to which I was greatly devoted. There were some things that we would enjoy together. If mother gave me a piece of bread I could share it with him, and we could both enjoy it. If we were hunting we both found joy in chasing a rabbit or a squirrel. But there were places where our companionship stopped. When I memorized the Twenty-third Psalm he didn't enter into it with me. When I undertook to pray he stood by with no interest whatsoever. He did not growl nor bark nor bite on such occasions. He simply cared for none of those things. And on such a plane did Esau live his life.[2]

---

[2] Clovis G. Chappel, *More Sermons on Biblical Characters* (1923; repr., Grand Rapids: Baker, 1971), 124.

Fourth, as in preparing any sermon, once the text is interpreted and the general plan of organization is in hand, a preacher needs to give some attention to sermon style. Make it interesting as well as clear and forceful. Blackwood speaks of cultivating "surprise power" in the sermon and gives some excellent examples in sermon plans of past masters as well as some of his own.[3]

Alexander Whyte: The Dean of Biographical Preachers

When Alexander Whyte died in 1921, he was one of the most famous men in Scotland and known around the world. He was known mostly for his preaching, and as a preacher he was best known for sermons on Bible characters. No one yet has matched his excellence in this specialty.

Whyte was a minister of the Free Church of Scotland, a group comprised of those Scottish Presbyterian churches that broke away from the established church in 1843, when Whyte was yet a child of seven. Eventually, Whyte would be honored moderator of that church's general assembly, but let's look a little into his background.

He was born in 1836 of an unwed mother who refused the offer of the birth father to marry her. Though this meant Alec would be raised in poverty in a two-room cottage, she provided him rich Christian nurture. The church of his boyhood met in a fine chapel built by the hands of the members. When the state deposed their pastor, the congregation left their elaborate edifice and went with their pastor into the fields to build a new and better church. Whyte's childhood dream was to be such a preacher. One day he was assigned the care of a neighbor's cows. While he daydreamed about his future plans, the cows invaded a cornfield. The neighbor came running out shouting some stern words of wonder about how the lad would ever earn an honest living. The lad replied, "What would you think if one day I was to wag my head in a pulpit?"[4]

---

[3] Blackwood, *Biographical Preaching for Today*, 140–49.

[4] Warren Wiersbe, *Walking with the Giants: A Minister's Guide to Good Reading and Great Preaching* (Grand Rapids: Baler, 1976), 90. The exchange went like this: the neighbor complained: "I dinna ken fat ye're gaen to dae, or foo in the hale warld ye'll ever earn an honest living." Young Whyte calmly replied: "What wadd ye think if ae day I was to wag my pow in a poopit?" Introduction to *Whyte's Bible Characters*, vol 1, *The Old Testament* (Grand Rapids: Zondervan, 1952), ix.

In his early schooling, he struggled greatly and was severely chastised for failure in memorizing, though he felt he gave it his best. Reading was a passion for him, however. With little formal education, young Alec went to work at an early age, apprenticed to a shoemaker. He subscribed to a magazine on self-education and spent much time with reading, sometimes propping up a borrowed book before him at the workbench and sometimes paying someone to read to him while he made shoes. His mother worried that he would not fulfill the five-year term of his apprenticeship. "Don't cry, Mother, don't be afraid," he told her, "for I will go and serve out my time; but mind you, I'm going to be a minister!"[5]

When he was 18, he took the post of a teacher for two years, a traditional stepping-stone toward university for those who could not afford to go directly. Then he worked his way to an M.A. through "eight winters" at King's College, Aberdeen and New College, Edinburgh. He shared textbooks with classmates and was grateful for other friends who helped him some with expenses. One who helped was the man whose name he shared. His father had left Scotland after Alexander's birth and succeeded in business in America. During some of these university years, Whyte also preached for a Free Church mission station built by the patronage of the Dutchess of Gordon in 1860. The Scottish Church, whether the established church or the free, cherished the custom of singing the psalms in meter, but hymns were beginning to be introduced. Whyte highly valued Charlotte Elliott's new hymn, "Just as I Am," and often used it in sermons until the end of his life.

In 1870 he began his four-decade ministry at Free St. George's Church in Edinburgh, first as colleague to R. S. Candlish and upon his death as sole minister there. From the beginning, his was a strong ministry of pastoral care as well as pulpit work. He was a prodigious worker and wished all lazy ministers could be drummed out of the college and the ministry. His own study method was to devote four to six hours at his desk beginning about eight in the morning. Here his pulpit work took shape. His sermon seedbed was the Bible with special attention to Bible characters. He watered the seed with generous portions of Bishop Butler, William Law, the Shorter Catechism, and *Pilgrim's Progress*. His

---

[5] Wiersbe, *Walking with Giants*, 90–91.

own commentary on the Shorter Catechism was a classic in the religious reading of Scotland.

Whyte read voraciously, especially in the Puritans. He himself has been called "the last of the Puritans." He urged young preachers to find one writer who excited them and helped them, then to buy all that writer's works and master them. Thomas Goodwin stirred that kind of excitement in Whyte. Whyte's book *The Spiritual Life* is a study of that mentor. Whyte was a Calvinist in theology, but he read broadly, especially from diverse devotional writers. In Whyte's mature years he also read princes of the Scottish church such as Samuel Rutherford and mystics such as Brother Lawrence and Santa Theresa.

From 1909 to 1918 Whyte was principal of New College, the theological school for the Free Church in Scotland. His mastery of Bible biography is shown in his extensive writing, especially the multivolume work that is still a standard reference, *Whyte's Bible Characters*.

His sermons were abundantly illustrated from biography, autobiography, and his own experience. An example of this last comes from a sermon he preached on Psalm 103 in a church in one of the poorest districts of Dundee. He was stressing the blessing of pain and anguish of soul in the life of the true penitent. He told of an accident he had in childhood when his arm was crushed in the machinery of a threshing mill.

> In my boyhood in Kirriemuir, I met with a bad accident. This arm [holding up his right arm] was severely injured. It was thought, at first, that I would have to be taken to Dundee infirmary, and lose my arm; but [holding it up again] it's there still. A neighbor woman, a friend of my mother's—Margaret was her name—skilled in dealing with aches and bruises, when she had examined the arm said, "We'll wait and see: we'll not let them take the boy to Dundee yet." The next day, because of the pain I was suffering, my mother was still more anxious about me; but, when Margaret came in, she greatly comforted her by saying, "I like the pain, Janet; I like the pain!"[6]

---

[6] G. F. Barbour, *The Life of Alexander Whyte, D.D.,* 7th ed. (New York: George H. Doran, 1923, 1925), 19–20.

Some of Whyte's finest storytelling sermons you will find in the series on John Bunyan and his *Pilgrim's Progress*. Each address focuses on one character in the allegory. The excerpt below is based on Bunyan himself. It is from the beginning of Whyte's masterful synopsis of Bunyan's autobiography, *Grace Abounding*. Whyte starts with the testimony of Bunyan's conversion to Christ after overhearing three or four village housewives delighting in their own experience of Christ. Whyte does not here explain and apply a single text, but he roots his message much in Pauline theology. After the narrative opening, he builds a contrast between these Bedford women and advice of an old man that was less helpful to Bunyan in his journey to the Celestial City. The sermon (or lecture, some will say) returns in the conclusion to make the theme unmistakable: "Now, young Bunyan's great mistake, which he here writes out for our warning was this, that he took his intricate case to the wrong counselor. He should have sought out some of those ancient women of Bedford into whose sinful hearts the holy law of God was entering deeper and deeper every day, and they would soon have resolved his whole case for him."[7]

For one snippet of a sample from *Whyte's Bible Characters*, consider these opening lines in his sketch of Ham, Noah's second son.

> There was an old vagabond, to vice industrious, among the builders of the ark. He had for long been far too withered for anything to be called work; and he got his weekly wages just for sitting over the pots of pitch and keeping the fires burning beneath them. That old man's heart was as black as his hands. It was of him that God had said that it grieved and humbled Him at His heart that he had ever made man. The black asphalt itself was whiteness itself beside that old reprobate's heart and life. Now Ham, Noah's second son, was never away from that deep hollow out of which the preparing pitch boiled and smoked. All day down among the slime-pits, and all night out among the

---

[7] Alexander Whyte, "Bunyan Himself as Seen in His Grace Abounding," *Bunyan Characters, 4th Series* (Grand Rapids: Baker, 1981), 62–71. Also online, e.g., www.geocities.com/athens/olympus/4199/ancient/.

sultry woods—wherever you heard Ham's loud laugh, be sure that lewd old man was either singing a song there or telling a story. All the time the ark was a-building, and for long before that, Ham had been making himself vile under the old pitch-boiler's instructions and examples. Ham's old instructor and examplar had gone down quick to hell as soon as the ark was finished and shut in. But, by that time, Ham would well walk alone. Dante came upon his old schoolmaster in hell when he was being led through hell on his way to heaven; and so did Ham when he went to his own place.[8]

In his mature years Whyte more and more favored biographical preaching, and he studied the characters more psychologically than historically. Whyte excelled in applying his text as well as illustrating it. One of his contemporaries, Duncan Ross, recalled an occasion when he and Whyte and two other preachers were on what he called "a holiday pilgrimage speaking occasion." The other two spoke first, then Whyte, then Ross concluded with a few words in Gaelic. Forty-seven years later Ross did not recall one word of what the other speakers said, but, said he:

I remember Whyte's address as if I had heard it only yesterday. It was on the words, in Psalm 16, "I have set the Lord always before me;" and after explaining how David's Lord would do so, he became very practical in the application, and called upon the crofters and tradesmen to set the Lord always before them, for, if they did that, they would do their work right well. He called upon the women to set the Lord always before them when doing up the house, cooking the food, rocking the cradle, for, if they did, their hearts would be singing all the while. And then, turning to us ministers, he called upon us to set the Lord always before us while engaged in our studies, for,

---

[8] Alexander Whyte, *Whyte's Bible Characters* (Grand Rapids: Zondervan, 1952), 1:54.

if we did that, then our preaching would be so much the better.[9]

We turn now from the venerable Scotsman to an American evangelist who was much less polished in his use of English but no less captivating in his storytelling.

D. L. Moody: Have Stories, Will Travel

Evangelist D. L. Moody (1837–1899) was a spellbinding story-teller. He was not a homiletician, nor did he have any theological training or, for that matter, much academic training at all. He was a lay preacher from the beginning. When we understand how he became a preacher and an evangelist, we are not surprised that he was almost exclusively a topical preacher. Moody started as a Sunday school teacher for children in the Brooklyn home of his friend D. W. McWilliams. He never expected to go beyond the five- or ten-minute lessons to the children. Then some parents started coming. Eventually he had as many adults as children in his classes. At first his lessons were impromptu. He would call on someone to read a passage of Scripture as he collected his thoughts. Then he commented on the passage before them. Anecdotes were an important part of his teaching from the beginning. When he found himself running dry, he would call for the reading of another passage.

Eventually his classes reached a size that made it necessary for him to do the Scripture readings himself. Meanwhile, Moody discovered a Bible study tool called *Topical Textbook*. Similar to *Nave's Topical Bible*, it arranged Scriptures according to topics. Moody had been a Christian five years before he discovered there was such a thing as a concordance. He found it useful. Eventually Moody accumulated a sizable library, but the *Topical Textbook* and *Cruden's Concordance* plus his Bible became the essence of his theological study and his sermon preparation tool kit. It is no wonder that his method was to select a topic and organize Scriptures related to it. A theme was typically a single word such as *adoption, assurance, grace, hope,* or *love.*

---

[9] Barbour, *Life of Whyte*, 99–100.

If his study method was simple, by the time he became an evangelist, it was not shallow. In the summer he usually started Bible study about daybreak in a quiet house. He made extensive use of small notebooks and large envelopes. The envelopes were his filing system. On them he wrote a text or a topic that might become a sermon. Into them went notes and clippings that seemed to belong with the collection. There might be an envelope on heaven, backsliders, Psalm 23, how to deal with inquirers, or "Let the Wicked Forsake . . ." He also came to favor study of Bible characters, and his preaching reflects that.

He carried a small notebook constantly. If he heard anything impressive, perhaps in another preacher's sermon, he wrote it in his notebook. Many of these notes he later ripped out of the notebook and filed in the topical envelopes. Moody also became an expert at picking the brains of anyone he thought might help him.

One time Moody was walking home in the dark and overheard the conversation of two people behind him. One of them asked, "Did Moody preach tonight?"

"No, he didn't preach, he only talked."

"Did you ever hear him before?"

"Yes."

"How do you like him?"

"Well, we don't like him. He never has a church service, and he doesn't have on any robes. And then his preaching—why, he doesn't preach at all, he just talks."[10]

Moody was delighted with the evaluation—especially that he just talked to them.

Moody's *Bible Characters* were written more as Bible studies to be read than as sermons to be preached, but they are typically D. L. Moody. The little paperback volume in my library was part of the early Moody Press Colportage Library, a series of Christian books designed to provide Christian homes with affordable and helpful literature. Five characters are treated in 11 messages with the first seven on Daniel and characters around him. Then there is

---

[10] W. R. Moody, *Dwight L. Moody*, Heroes of the Faith Series (c. 1900; repr., Westwood, NJ: Barbour, 1985), 395–96. D. L. Moody authorized only one biography. About five years before his death, he commissioned his son W. R. Moody to write it. One chapter is devoted to "Preparing Sermons," and it is no more helpful than one might expect of a lay preacher describing another's preparation for the pulpit.

one study each of Enoch, Lot, Jacob, and John the Baptist. Two brief samples will give a taste for Moody's style in treating Bible characters.

> Daniel was none of your sickly Christians of the [present] nineteenth century: he was none of your weak-backed, none of your weak-kneed Christians: he had moral stamina and courage. I can imagine that aged white-haired Secretary of State sitting at his table going over the accounts of some of the rulers of provinces. Some of the timid, frightened Hebrews come to him, and say:
> "Oh, Daniel, have you heard the latest news?"
> "No. What is it?"
> "What! Have you not been to the king's palace this morning?"
> "No! I have not been to the palace to-day. What is the matter?"
> "Well, there is a conspiracy against you. A lot of those princes have induced King Darius to sign a decree that if any man shall call upon any God in his kingdom within thirty days he shall be thrown to the lions. Their object is to have you cast into the den. Now if you can only get out of the way for a little time—if you will just quit Babylon for thirty days—it will advance both your own and the public interest. You are the chief secretary and treasurer—in fact, you are the principal member of the government: you are an important man, and can do as you please."

In that manner Moody continued for a while longer with Daniel's friends advising him at least to avoid praying as to be seen. Certainly not at an open window as he was accustomed to do facing toward Jerusalem. Then Moody comes closer to home.

> And some of our nineteenth century Christians would have advised after the same fashion:—Cannot you find out some important business to be done down in Egypt, and so take a journey to Memphis?

187

Or can you not think of something that needs looking after in Syria, and so hurry off to Damascus? . . .

How many men there are who are ashamed to be caught upon their knees! Many a man, if found upon his knees by the wife of his bosom, would jump right up and walk around the room as if he had no particular object in view.[11]

The next sample is from his study of Enoch.

One day the cord that bound him to earth and time snapped asunder. God said unto him, "Come up hither," and up he went to walk with Him in glory. God liked his company so well that He called His servant home. Dr. Andrew Bonar has said that Enoch took a long walk one day, and has not got back yet. With one bound he leaped the river of death, and walked the crystal pavement of heaven—in the wilderness yesterday, in the promised land to-day.[12]

Exercise 1. Consider the samples of narrative above for Alexander Whyte and D. L. Moody as typical of the style of each. Can you list four or five noteworthy differences in the style of each?

Exercise 2. Ten biographical preachers are mentioned in this chapter; select one for extended study. From a library or bookstore choose a biography and a volume of sermons for your study. See what you can learn about preaching on Bible characters.

Exercise 3. If you do not already have one, start a file on Bible characters you might use as subject for a sermon. Be aware that any good Bible dictionary or Bible encyclopedia will include an article on almost every character in the Bible.

---

[11] D. L. Moody, *Bible Characters* (Chicago: Moody, n.d.), 47–48.
[12] Ibid., 73.

Chapter 15

THE STORY FOR AMERICA'S
LOST GENERATION

THE 1900 CENSUS IN AMERICA counted 76 million souls. In the next 15 years we would add 15 million by immigration alone. Those already here and assimilated tended to be uncomfortable with the newcomers. They seemed so strange and not like *us*.

They were Russian Jews, Poles and Slavic peoples, plus Greeks and southern Italians. The first half of the twentieth century witnessed a clash of cultures in America. After the 1917 Bolshevik revolution seized power in Russia, many socialists in America joined the Communist Party. Revolution threatened these shores as well. In April 1919 the U.S. Postal Service intercepted more than three dozen mail bombs addressed to prominent U.S. citizens. In the middle of the Roaring Twenties the boom began to fail, and the Great Depression was signaled by the October stock market crash in 1929.

The secular storytellers of the era told us that we were a lost generation. Sinclair Lewis's *Main Street* (1920), F. Scott Fitzgerald's *The Great Gatsby* (1925), and Ernest Hemingway's *The Sun Also Rises* (1926) were strong on diagnosis, but none had a cure for our malaise. These were the years of "the monkey trial" in Tennessee with Clarence Darrow pitted against William Jennings Bryan. It was the age of FDR and the New Deal and

189

another world war. Religion and family became important values in these years. Evangelists like Billy Sunday and J. Wilbur Chapman found welcome ears. Among the American pastors and evangelists in the period from 1900 to 1950 are at least three who are worthy studies for their storytelling skill: Russell H. Conwell (1843–1925), J. Wilbur Chapman (1859–1918), and George W. Truett (1867–1944).

Russell H. Conwell, Master Storyteller

Russell Conwell's sermon on "Heaven's Open Door" is rooted in one clause of Revelation 4:1, "Behold a door was opened in heaven." Before the text or title is introduced, he prepares us with the following personal story.

> In my childhood I once stood in the yard of a country farm-house in the evening, caring for my father's horses while he transacted some business matters in the dwelling. The night was chilly and dark, and threatening clouds hid every star. Some evening gathering of unusual importance made the old homestead strangely full of animation. The curtains of the windows were closely drawn, but shadows of flying forms and happy faces flickered on the shades, while occasionally shouts of laughter and strains of old songs could be heard.
>
> The evident cheer and joy within the house made me doubly lonely. . . . The hour I waited was one of the most wearisome and gloomy of my life. My situation was not made more cheerful by a gruff and coarse man who was waiting around the house like a ghost, and who at last with an oath asked me, from the dark woodshed, why I did not "take those horses out of people's way." I told him I had a father in the house, and I could not go until he came out. At last my childish fears and the bleak wind overcame me, and I cried aloud, and called, "Father! Father! Come, come, I am cold! I am afraid out here!"

Instantly the door opened. A glow of warm light illuminated the whole yard, and my father stood in the door smiling at my timidity. Beyond him I could see the great fireplace piled high with blazing logs. All about the fire a score of youthful faces beamed in its bright rays. Confectionery and fruit stood on the table, and a chorus of sweet voices greeted the luscious feast. When my father had quieted my fears, he returned to the house for a few moments more. While I waited, I saw the door open frequently to let in other guests. Sometimes a child shone in the doorway, sometimes an old man or a lady entered. Once a party of young people came and struggled playfully with each other to be each the first to enter. At last, on suggestion of one of my schoolmates, who lived in the house, my father came and called me in. Oh, that open door! That welcome! That fire! The feast of good things! The games! The fun! Will heaven itself blot out the sweet memory of that glad hour?

The other morning, when I was questioning the Word of God for a message to bring to you, my eyes fell on these words: "A door was opened in heaven." How vividly it brought back that night and its open door![1]

In addition to the sermon's text from John's experience on the Isle of Patmos, the preacher traced other New Testament references where Stephen, Paul, and Peter each saw a door opened in heaven. The sermon ends with two deathbed scenes of the kind that were once commonly used by evangelistic preachers. One was from his army years and the other the pastoral account of the recent death of a child in his presence.

Russell H. Conwell is best known for a motivational lecture called "Acres of Diamonds." He delivered it some six thousand times during more than six decades on the lecture circuit. Along the way he was converted to Christ and became a pastor. In preaching, as in his lectures, he excelled in storytelling. The college he

---

[1] Russell H. Conwell, *Borrowed Axes and Other Sermons* (New York: Kessinger Publications, 1902).

started and presided over eventually grew and merged into what we know today as Gordon-Conwell Theological Seminary.

How did Conwell become so adept at storytelling? If it was a gift, he labored much to perfect it. He was born in Massachusetts in 1843 and entered Yale in 1860. In his second year of college he enlisted in "Lincoln's Army" and right away became a captain of a company of his friends and neighbors that he recruited. A notable temperance orator named John B. Gough encouraged his early efforts at public speaking. He told Conwell to take every opportunity to practice his speaking. Conwell did so at picnics, cattle shows, patriotic rallies, funerals, even a sewing circle, all without pay.

He was still an unbeliever and quite agnostic in those early years, but the Civil War softened his heart. Watching those close to him die gave him pause to think. One death affected him more profoundly than all the others. A youngster named John Q. Ring was too young and too small to enlist, so he went along as Captain Conwell's personal aide. He lived in the tent with him and among other duties took care of an ornamental gold-sheathed sword the men of his company had bought for their captain. Johnny Ring was devoted to his captain, and Conwell came to love him dearly though the youth did annoy the unbelieving captain by devotion to Christ and the daily reading of his mother's Bible. One day a surprise raid of Confederates overran the Union camp. They retreated over a covered bridge and set it on fire to keep the rebels from pursuing. Suddenly Johnny dashed back over the burning bridge and into the captain's tent to retrieve that sword. He managed to get back across the bridge but was too badly burned to survive. The death profoundly shook Conwell and eventually led him to make peace with God.

After the war Conwell became a writer and editor and then entered law, still taking every occasion for public speaking. The lecture circuit as a public institution came into its own in those postwar years. One James Redpath organized the first speaker's bureau and managed a number of notable orators including Ralph Waldo Emerson, Henry W. Longfellow, Henry Ward Beecher, and a young editor and poet in Beecher's church named Theodore Tilton. General Charles H. Taylor suggested to Redpath that young Conwell might be someone who would accept assignments in smaller cities the more famous speakers didn't want. Russell Conwell was delighted in this providence. He began traveling and delivering his increasingly popular speech called "Acres of Diamonds."

While practicing law in Minneapolis, a member of a struggling church in Lexington, Massachusetts sought Conwell's legal advice. The church was down to 18 members, and some of those 18 believed strongly they should sell the deteriorating property and disband. Conwell encouraged them to give one more try. They tore down the decaying church and started over. Conwell came every Sunday to preach for them. Soon he agreed to give up his law practice and come as their pastor. He did not give up his growing lecture circuit, however. The church survived and thrived. Two years later Conwell was called to a Baptist church in Philadelphia. Here he would stay for the rest of his days. He gained fame traveling by train with his popular lecture all over New England and beyond. Yet he managed to build a great church and to establish a college and a hospital and other ministries. He lived until 1925 and died at 82 years of age.

Conwell never wrote his sermons in advance. He knew he was not an expositor or Bible scholar. In the preface to a collection of his sermons, *Borrowed Axes*, published at the very end of his life, he calls himself a "'lay worker' and not a preacher." Two great lessons he brought from his experience on the lecture circuit to his success as a preacher. Arthur Harris, seven years his associate at Philadelphia, records the first one. "You preach-

> "You preachers have too many points in your sermons. Really they are three sermons in one. One point is enough. I make one point only, stick to it, illustrate it in every way possible, so that everyone sees it, and then clinch it and let it go."
> —Russell Conwell

ers," Conwell said, "have too many points in your sermons. Really they are three sermons in one. One point is enough. I make one point only, stick to it, illustrate it in every way possible, so that everyone sees it, and then clinch it and let it go." The other lesson, of course, was his mastery of the art of storytelling.[2]

Another sermon is completely narrative. The title "He Goeth Before You" is taken from Matthew 28:7, "Behold, he goeth before you into Galilee." The sermon begins:

> In Jerusalem, in 1868, a wise old monk told me a most interesting tradition, a combination, no doubt, of fact and fancy, like many others which he related while showing us over those sacred fields. But this one was so new to me, and so permeated with the clearest of gospel truth, that I tell it to you this evening as near as I can as it was told to me.
>
> What follows is a tight plot as the resurrected Christ moved all unseen from Jerusalem to Galilee. He encountered many hurting hearts along the way and stopped to make a difference for each, still unseen. Many of the things he did are a bit puzzling in this first half of the sermon. The next day his disciples started out to meet him in Galilee as instructed. They encountered all the strange things that Jesus had done, not knowing how the unseen Christ had set the stage for them. They fed a widow, healed the sick, and helped a destitute man find work. Peter even took a struggling couple into his fishing business. The story ends with the rendezvous Christ had with the disciples at the Sea of Galilee recorded in John 21.[3]

Conwell's instinct for one-point sermons and narrative was ahead of his times. Beyond this he would not be a great model of homiletics even for textual sermons. He has much to teach this generation of preachers about storytelling, however. It was the great secret of his effectiveness on the lecture circuit and in the pulpit.

---

[2] Arthur Harris, *Personal Glimpses of Russell H. Conwell* (Philadelphia: n.p., c. 1926).
[3] Conwell, *Gleans of Grace* (Philadelphia: Businessmen's Association of Grace Baptist Church, 1887), 17–28.

J. Wilbur Chapman:
Evangelist with Stories

John Wilbur Chapman and F. B. Meyer were contemporaries associated together in Moody's Northfield Bible Conferences. Chapman credited one sentence which Meyer spoke at Northfield with changing the whole tenor of his life and ministry. "If you are not willing to give up everything for Christ," Meyer asked, "are you willing to be made willing?" Chapman said he was "tremendously moved," and added: "The difficulties of years seemed thrust aside. The entire thought was like a new star in the sky of my life, and acting upon Dr. Meyer's suggestion, after having carefully studied the passages in the New Testament which relate to surrender and to consecration, I gave myself anew and unreservedly to Christ. The result has been rich and fully abiding, and I am living, to this hour, in the enjoyment of blessed privileges, and I shall never be able to adequately express my appreciation of what F. B. Meyer meant in blessing to my whole life and ministry."[4]

Chapman was a Presbyterian pastor and evangelist. His preaching sparkled with Bible stories and personal experiences. He was born in Richmond, Indiana, and educated at Oberlin College, at Lake Forest University, and at Lane Seminary in Cincinnati. He was ordained in 1882 at 23 years of age. His wife died four years later, leaving him with a motherless child.

Chapman's early ministerial experience was in pastorates in Ohio, Indiana, New York, and Pennsylvania. He began in the Reformed Church but was a Presbyterian for most of his ministry. Associated with merchant prince John Wanamaker, Chapman led in building the largest Sunday school in America in his day. The greater part of his ministry, however, was in itinerate evangelism. He was an associate of D. L. Moody, and for ten years he succeeded R. A. Torrey and traveled with the same song leader, Charles M. Alexander. Evangelistic tours took Chapman to large cities across the United States and Canada. He also took his evangelistic campaigns to Hawaii, the Fiji islands, Australia, Tasmania, New Zealand, the Philippines, China, Japan, Ceylon, England, Scotland, Ireland, and Wales. Chapman was the first director of

---

[4] A. Chester Mann, *F. B. Meyer: Preacher, Teacher, Man of God* (New York: Revell, 1929), 146–47.

the newly founded Winona Lake Bible Conference. Later he contributed much to the progress of two other summer assemblies— one at Montreat, North Carolina, and the other at Stony Brook, Long Island, New York.

Among his more famous and often-borrowed stories, one turns out to be a myth. It is a very credible-sounding story about Pietro Bandinelli. (The use of specific names, we should note, tends to make an anecdote sound like history.) In the story, Leonardo De Vinci selected Bandinelli as a model for Christ in his masterpiece *The Last Supper*. Then after many years of searching for the perfect model for Judas, the artist found an appropriately hardened and repulsive face. After painting in the features of this last character, the artist discovered it was the same person who many years earlier had posed for the portrait of Christ. Art historians have pointed out many errors in the story. The masterpiece was not on canvas but oil and tempera on plaster. There were not many years involved in the painting; Leonardo took two years (1495–97 AD). Anyone looking at the masterpiece can see that the model for Jesus and for Judas could not be the same person; their heads are very differently shaped. Furthermore, Judas is not portrayed with a hardened, repulsive face. I cannot say that Chapman invented this story and offered it as history, but though often repeated since Chapman told it, it has not been traced to any source earlier than Chapman himself.

Significantly, Chapman composed the hymn "One Day," which is still used where hymns are still sung. It is a narrative. It traces the life of Christ from his virgin birth and sinless life in the first stanza, through the suffering of the cross in second and the vigil at the garden tomb in the third. The fourth stanza records the resurrection, and the fifth looks forward to the return in glory. Even the chorus is a narrative summary of this gospel story:

> Living, he loved me! Dying, he saved me!
> Buried, He carried my sins far away!
> Rising, He justified freely, forever!
> One day he's coming—O glorious day!

Here is a narrative illustration from Chapman's sermon on "The Precious Blood of Christ" (1 Pet 1:19).

My friend, Dr. George F. Pentecost, was determined to climb Pike's Peak alone. His friends said to
him, "You cannot do it without a guide who knows
the way." But Dr. Pentecost said, "I know that I can
climb it alone." So he started off. They told him that
at a certain curve in the mountain there was a hut,
open to any traveler, if by any chance he should miss
his way going up. He was getting along very well,
when suddenly a snowstorm overtook him. Without
warning the blinding snow covered him and he began
to drift. He staggered and fell, and then there came
to him the warnings of his friends. He had practically given himself up to die, when he realized, as
he lay upon the ground, that his hands were touching
some dry twigs. It came to him that if he could start
a fire he might still escape. He felt in his pocket for
matches, and found one. But the wind was blowing
a perfect gale. I heard Dr. Pentecost say that he took
that single match and, shielding it in his hands from
the snow, started to strike it, but he was afraid and
he put it back into his pocket again. Finally, in his
desperation, he got up closer under the shadow of a
rock and struck the match, shielding the little flame
as best he could, and touching it to the dry twigs.
The fire was started and his life was saved. There
was just that one little thing between him and death.
What a blessing that he did not treat it carelessly.
Tonight I am standing here to say that there is just
one thing, between you and judgment, and that one
thing is the precious blood of Christ. I beg you not to
treat it carelessly.[5]

Ralph G. Turnbull described Chapman as a preacher with no
tricks of speech and no notable rhetorical skill. He was "a pastor
doing the work of an evangelist." He preached unlike most evangelists of the day, "standing almost without gesture or motion,

---

[5] Copied by Stephen Ross for WholesomeWords.org from *Evangelistic Sermons* by
J. Wilbur Chapman (New York: Fleming H. Revell Company, 1922). www.wholesome-
words.org/etexts/chapman/jwcblood.html.

with a quiet, pleasing voice, a sympathetic manner, and a direct appeal." His themes focused on the redemptive work of Christ, but he reached the churched as well as the unchurched. Indeed, Turnbull's judgment is that his chief work lay in reactivation of church people who had a nominal faith but who needed to make a decisive personal commitment.[6]

In 1904, the evangelist launched the first of many citywide campaigns organized with simultaneous meetings in large churches across the city. In Pittsburg 17 evangelists and a large staff held meetings in nine districts and recorded seven thousand professions of faith. The next year there was a similar effort in Syracuse, New York. In 1907 Chapman led six weeks of meetings in Philadelphia, dividing the city into 42 districts with three weeks of meetings in half the city followed by three more weeks of meetings in the other half. Charles M. Alexander joined the team at this time and paired with Chapman for the central meetings. In the second phase the Chapman and Alexander team led in Russell Conwell's Baptist Temple. The most successful campaign was Boston in 1909. It was organized beyond belief, and the newspapers loved it. In addition to the Chapman and Alexander central crusade in Tremont Temple, 30 other evangelists and singers conducted a total of 990 services. Each Sunday afternoon there were special services for men only. There were days for "old folks," mothers, young people, and parents. There were special meetings promoted for drunkards, actors, university students, office workers, shop girls, and for prostitutes. Although the whole city was not awakened, the effort was still considered the most successful campaign of his career. Such citywide campaigns soon lost their appeal, and Chapman went back to preaching more traditional revivals.

Chapman's sermons were organized in the fashion common among evangelists and pastors of the day. He selected a topic or theme and then matched it with a brief text, usually a single verse or even a part of a verse. Typical is this opening: "I am preaching tonight on what I believe to be the most important subject in the Bible. . . . My text is found in the First Epistle of Peter 1:9—'The Precious Blood of Christ.'" The development is wholly topical

---

[6] Ralph G. Turnbull, *A History of Preaching* (Grand Rapids: Baker, 1974), 3:174.

with no further reference to his announced text. He did use several other Scriptures, however, in reference to the Old Testament sacrificial system, including Leviticus 17:11: "The life of the flesh is in the blood." New Testament cross-references included Galatians 3:13 and John 10:18.

Chapman preached as an evangelist in a time when most evangelists used deathbed stories. Such twanging on heartstrings would not be effective sermon illustrations today. They may still have emotional appeal, but a negative reaction would likely be great in most gatherings. Here is one of Chapman's closing stories in an evangelistic appeal typical of the genre.

> I had read the funeral service in a beautiful home, when the undertaker came to the door and said: "Will all the friends kindly retire. The members of the family are coming in." The daughter of the home came in leading her father. The mother was lying in the coffin. The old man bent forward and said to the wife who had journeyed with him all the years: "Good-bye. I will soon see you." The daughter said it after him, and two or three of the boys said it. The eldest boy was a drunkard. He stood inside the door with the hot tears running down his cheeks. I walked over to him and said: "Tom, come and say goodbye to your mother." Partly from weakness, and partly because he was under the influence of drink, he staggered forward. But I never heard a boy cry like that. Such sobs as came from his heart! Over and over he kept saying: "Mother, Mother!" His sister stepped forward and said: "Tom, don't take on so. Mother has gone to Heaven, and you will soon see her." He threw one arm around my shoulder and the other around hers, and cried out: "Oh, my God! I am not going. I am not going."[7]

---

[7] J. Wilbur Chapman, *Evangelistic Sermons* (New York: Revell, 1922). Selection copied from www.WholesomeWords.org. The sermon is "Prepare to Meet God" from Amos 4:12. It does not develop the text or context but talks about God as all powerful and everywhere. He sees all, and the only way to be prepared is to believe on the Lord Jesus Christ. The story quoted above is the third of three narratives which conclude the sermon. All describe dying men hopeless without Christ.

Chapman, after serving several churches as pastor, had an effective evangelistic ministry in the decades that closed the nineteenth century and opened the twentieth. If we do not judge him by twenty-first century tastes and trends, we can appreciate his power in the pulpit and learn from his ability to hold great congregations with a simple message that featured gripping stories.

George W. Truett, Soul-Winning Pastor

Where I attended seminary, the custom in first-year preaching classes was to invest one class period listening to a taped sermon of George W. Truett. The sermon that day began with slow and deliberate cadence and words crisply spoken: "We are to think today on the greatest saying of our Lord concerning The Conquest of Fear." After two sentences about the pervasiveness of human fear, Truett quoted his text of two brief verses: "Fear not; I am the first and the last, and the Living One; and I was dead, and behold, I am alive for evermore, and I have the keys of death and Hades" (Rev 1:17–18 ASV).

That class was a memorable experience and a most profitable investment of time for a preaching class. Truett's outline here, as in all his sermons, was simple and clear. First, Jesus bids us to be unafraid of life. He reminds us that He is "the first and the last, and the Living One." Again, He bids us to be unafraid of death. He reminds us, "I was dead, and behold, I am alive for evermore." His third and final division was "He also bids us to be unafraid of eternity. I have the keys of death and of Hades."[8]

Truett is widely regarded as one of the greatest preachers ever, though he was not an expositor if exposition means a detailed analysis of an extended passage of Scripture. He preferred the brief and memorable text. It is safe to say that he treated his text true to context. Storytelling power was one of his greatest strengths, and personal experiences were his staple. We will consider one extended example, but first let's put his life in context.

Truett was born two years after Appomattox in the Blue Ridge Mountains of rural Clay County, where western North Carolina

---

[8] The sermon is printed with very slight revisions of the tape. The revisions do not always improve the sermon as delivered. George W. Truett, *Follow Thou Me* (Nashville: Broadman, 1932), 103.

dips a toe into the hills of Tennessee and Georgia. His mother was a devout believer. In later years he often memorialized her in his sermons. His father was not a Christian until midlife. He nevertheless insisted the family attend church faithfully, and he strongly encouraged the reading of Christian classics by supplying the home with the writings of Bunyan, Baxter, Pendleton, and others. Several denominational papers were regularly read in the home also. Young George read everything available; he was a speed reader and blessed with a retentive memory. George was the seventh child. An older brother, George Spurgeon Truett had scarlet fever at age 12, which left him deaf. His father taught him to read lips, and all the siblings learned to use their lips in clear enunciation, never mumbling. This would be a backdoor blessing in George's life.

He grew up aspiring to be an attorney. He completed high school at Haynesville Academy in 1885, at age 18. At age 19, he took the responsibility of a one-room school just a few miles across the Georgia line. About 50 pupils ranging in age from seven to 20 learned all subjects from him. That same year, 1886, in a series of evangelistic meetings, he became a Christian and a member of a Baptist church in Clay County. About the same time he decided to start his own private school in Hiawassee, Georgia. He launched it in January 1887 charging one dollar per month for all grades. It grew rapidly to three hundred enrolled and several faculty members.

He passed up an opportunity for a scholarship to Mercer in favor of following his family to Whitewright, Texas, in 1889. He was still determined to be an attorney, but the members of the church in Whitewright needed a pastor. Though he had often filled in, it was never from the pulpit. That sacred place, he strongly believed, was only for those ordained of God. One night to his great surprise and over his great objections, the church voted to ordain him. It was a great struggle, but he accepted it as the call of God on his life.

In those years Baylor University was in grave financial peril. President B. H. Carroll enlisted young Truett to come as a fundraiser to save the college, which he did. Then he enrolled as a freshman. When he graduated four years later, he planned to go on to seminary. Again, he was pressed into other service. First Baptist Church of Dallas had no pastor or other staff. A committee of the church contacted him repeatedly about coming to serve them. He finally agreed to be elected and began in 1897 in the pulpit that would be his home for the rest of his days. During his 44-year pastorate, the church grew from seven hundred members to more than seven thousand.

Early in his ministry at Dallas, a tragic incident almost took him out of the ministry. He and two friends were on a bird hunt when Truett shifted his shotgun from one arm to the other and accidentally discharged the birdshot into the leg of his dear friend J. C. Arnold, chief of police for Dallas and a former Texas Ranger. It was not considered a life-threatening wound, but Truett sensed with great foreboding that this would not end well. His friend went to the hospital for treatment but soon died of a heart attack. Truett told his wife he would never preach again. For some weeks he did not preach but grieved the loss of his friend. He did return to the pulpit, however, and to his supportive and beloved people, he returned as a brokenhearted pastor.

He was a faithful pastor and evangelist, visiting in the homes and taking a personal interest in the spiritual condition of the citizens of a growing Dallas. More than all else, though, it was as a preacher that Truett made his mark, and as a preacher he will be remembered. He stood erect in the pulpit, six feet tall and for many years two hundred pounds. He had a remarkable preaching voice. One day a certain prominent stage actor distinguished for excellent enunciation and pure tones was passing along on a Dallas street. He heard a remarkable voice and followed the sound into the First Baptist Church, where Truett was preaching. Soon he forgot about the voice in attention to the message. He returned often to hear Truett and was soundly converted.

If Truett's preaching was his greatest ministry, one of the most distinguishing features of his sermons was storytelling. His characteristic sermon illustration was a story from his personal experience in ministry. One typical story is this one recalling the first soul he won to Jesus.

I was a lad, barely grown, a young teacher, in the Blue Ridge Mountains. One morning, as we were

202

ready for prayers in the chapel, there hobbled down the aisle to the front seat a lad, sixteen years of age; a strange, eager, lonely-looking lad. I read the Scriptures and prayed, and then [the superintendent] sent the teachers to their classes. But my crippled lad stayed. I supposed that he was a beggar, and I thought, "Surely he deserves alms; his condition betokens the need." So I sent to him at recess and said, "My lad, what do you want?" And he looked at me eagerly and said: "I want to go to school. Oh sir, I want to be somebody in the world. I will always be a cripple; the doctors told me that. But," he said, "I want to be somebody."

He had won me. He told me of his poverty, and so he was given free tuition and books. How bright his mind! How eager to know he was! One day I called him into my office and said, "My boy, I want you to tell me more about yourself." And he told me that, some months before, his father had been killed in the great mill in an adjoining county, where he worked, and the few dollars he had saved up were soon gone. And then the people seemed to forget his mother's poverty and her need, and she said: "We will go to the next county, where they don't know us. Perhaps we can do better where we are not known." He said, "I want to help mother and be somebody in the world, and so I asked you to let me come to your school."

It was time, after a moment, for the great bell to ring for books. I laid my hand on the head of that little fellow and I said to him: "Jim, I am for you, my boy. You are my sort of boy. I believe in you thoroughly, and I want you to know that I love you." And when I said that last word, the little pinched face looked up into mine—almost a lightening flash—and he said: "I didn't know any body loved me but mother and the two little girls. Mr. Truett, if you love me, I will be a man yet by the help of God." And when, a few Friday nights after, I was leading the boys in their prayer meeting, as was my custom, I heard Jim's crutches rattle over there in the corner. I looked. He sat in a chair by himself to keep the boys off his worn and wasted limb, and getting up, sobbing and laughing at the same time, he looked across at me and said: "Teacher, I found the Savior, and that time you told me that you loved me started me toward him."[9]

Harry A. Ironside, Itinerate Expositor

My introduction to H. A. Ironside came in my seventeenth summer. Working in Texas and Arkansas, away from family and friends, I spent considerable time reading. Exploring a Christian bookstore one afternoon, I selected Ironside's *Expositions in Joshua* and drove out to the city park. I settled down in the pine thicket with my back against a tree and read until the summer sunset afforded no more light to read. I left that pine thicket a fan of Ironside for life. Though I outgrew his dispensationalist teaching and never really embraced his Arminian explanation of election, Ironside became a model to me in explaining, applying, and especially in illustrating the Scriptures.

Henry Allan "Harry" Ironside was born in 1878 in Toronto, Canada. Before he was two years old his father died. The young mother and children moved to Los Angeles when he was eight. By that age he was already memorizing Scripture and reading the Bible faithfully. By the time he was 14, he had read through the Bible 14 times. He began preaching, joined the Salvation Army, and began training to become an officer. He was a captain by 18 but soon became dissatisfied with the group's official position on sanctification. He resigned and joined the Plymouth Brethren, the church of his parents during his early childhood. This was also the church of expositors such as J. N. Darby, William Kelly, and C. H. Macintosh. The influence of their tradition of verse-by-verse, chapter-by-chapter preaching through whole books of the Bible is plain in Ironside's homiletic.

---

[9] Powhattan W. James, *George W. Truett: A Biography* (New York: Macmillan, 1945), 32–33. Spelling modernized.

Ironside traveled the U.S. and Canada in Bible Conference preaching and teaching for more than three decades. For a dozen of those years, he also devoted two months each summer to mission work among the Indians of the American Southwest. Though his own formal education ended with the eighth grade, he held many meetings under the direction of the Moody Bible Institute and was a frequent visiting professor in the early years of Dallas Theological Seminary. His only pastorate was nearly two decades at Moody Memorial Church in Chicago. He was often away from that pulpit on preaching tours until he resigned in 1948 to continue traveling the U.S., Canada, the British Isles, and elsewhere. He was on a preaching tour in New Zealand when he died in 1951.

Ironside was a worthy model for brightening discourse with stories—especially personal stories. Here is a slightly abbreviated version of the introduction to his exposition of Ephesians 2:1–7.

> While holding meetings in southern California I took the inter-urban car one Saturday to go from Los Angeles to a well-known beach resort. We had hardly left the city when a rather peculiar-looking lady came and sat down beside me. She was attired in a strange garb that made her look as though she was dressed up in red bandanna handkerchiefs pieced together. She wore a shawl on her head with a lot of spangles over her forehead, she said to me, "How do you do, gentleman? You like to have your fortune told?" I said, "Are you able to tell my fortune?" She held out a winsome little palm and said, "Cross my palm with a silver quarter, and I will give you your past, present, and future." "You are very sure you can do that if I give you a quarter?" I said. "You see, I am Scotch, and should hate to part with a quarter and not get proper exchange for it." She looked bewildered for a moment, but then said very insistently, "Yes, gentleman, I can give you your past, present, and future. I never fail; I have wonderful second sight. Cross my palm with a quarter. Please, gentleman. I will tell you all." I said, "It is really not necessary, because I have had my fortune told already, and I have a little

Book in my pocket that gives me my past, present and future." "You have it in a book?" she said. "Yes, and it is absolutely infallible. Let me read it to you," I said, and I pulled out my New Testament. She looked startled when she saw it, but I turned to this second chapter of the Epistle to the Ephesians and said, "Here is my past, 'And you . . . who were dead in trespasses and sins: wherein in time past ye walked according to the course of this world, according to the prince of the power of the air, the spirit that now worketh in the children of disobedience: among whom also we all had our conversation in times past in the lusts of our flesh, fulfilling the desires of the flesh and of the mind, and were by nature the children of wrath, even as others.'" "Oh, yes," she said; "it is plenty; I do not care to hear more." "But," I said as I held her gently by the arm, "I want to give you my present also, 'But God, who is rich in mercy, for his great love where-with he loved us, even when we were dead in sins, hath quickened us together with Christ, (by grace ye are saved;) and hath raised us up together, and made us sit together in heavenly places in Christ Jesus.'" "That is plenty, gentleman," she said; "I do not wish to hear any more." "Oh, but," I replied, "there is more yet, and you must get it; and you are not going to pay me a quarter for it either. I am giving it to you for nothing. It is my past, my present, and my future. Here is the future, 'That in the ages to come He might show the exceeding riches of his grace in His kindness toward us through Christ Jesus.'" She was on her feet, and I could not hold on any tighter lest I should be charged with assault and battery, and she fled down the aisle, saying, "I took the wrong man! I took the wrong man!"[10]

With the text now introduced, Ironside explained and applied it to the believer's past, present, and future. When Haddon W. Robinson was a teenager, he heard Harry Ironside preach. In his

---

[10] H. A. Ironside, *In the Heavenlies* (New York: Loizeaux Brothers, 1937), 96–98.

journal Robinson noted: "He preached for an hour and it seemed like twenty minutes; others preach for twenty minutes and it seems like an hour. I wonder what the difference is?"[11] Surely, a big part of that difference was Ironside's storytelling skill. Lengthy narrative illustrations are common in Ironside's expositions. One sermon he preached more often than any other was "Charge That to My Account." It begins with a three-verse text from Philemon, followed by three long paragraphs of background to that text. Together these comprise approximately one-fourth of the sermon. Then there is a long narrative illustration from the life of a contemporary. This makes up over one-fourth. The second half of the sermon is divided between an imaginative narrative of what might have happened as Philemon first read Paul's letter on behalf of Onesimus (28%) and application of the message in terms of Christ's vicarious substitution (21%).[12]

Most of Ironside's expositions are homilies that are not clearly outlined. Most of his narratives, explanations, and illustrations of the text are not lengthy. More often the illustrations are snapshots from the ongoing pilgrimage of Christian life. Some of his stories, like Beecher's, do not relate a single specific event but describe a scene that commonly happens. For example, in an address on the "The Sphere of Christian Privilege," Ironside shed light on the phrase "in the heavenlies" this way:

> Sometimes when we have a good meeting and the people think they have been helped, some well-meaning brother closes in prayer and says, "Lord, we thank Thee that we have been sitting together in the heavenly places in Christ Jesus this morning." I say to myself, "The dear brother hasn't got it yet. He thinks because there is a glow in his heart, because he feels happy, that means he is sitting in heavenly places in Christ." But I am sitting in heavenly places in Christ just as truly when I am oppressed with the trials of the way as I am when I am flourishing and have everything that heart could desire. It is a

---

[11] Scott M. Gibson, introduction to *Making a Difference in Preaching,* by Haddon W. Robinson (Grand Rapids: Baker, 1999), 11.

[12] The sermon is in E. Schuyler English, *H. A. Ironside: Ordained of the Lord* (Grand Rapids: Zondervan, 1946), 27. Calculations are mine.

question of fact: Christ is there in the heavenlies, and God sees me in Him. I am blessed in Him and all the treasures of heaven are at my disposal.[13]

Crowds gathered to hear Ironside expound the Scriptures. His published expositions are still in print and very much in demand.

Exercise 1. Examine the story by Russell H. Conwell that begins "In my childhood." Use it to review the five stages of the plot presented earlier. Note the clear progression from opening situation, through the stress, the searching, to the solution and the new situation.

Exercise 2. What makes this Conwell story so effective? What makes the listener today identify with the boy of a century and a half ago? What emotions do you share? What vivid mental images does the narrative evoke? How does descriptive language make the story better? How many of your five senses are stimulated by details in the narrative?

Exercise 3. Truett and Ironside made large use of stories from their own lives and ministries. What are some advantages and disadvantages of a preacher talking about himself in a sermon?

---

[13] Ibid., 23.

SUGGESTED READING

Instead of a list of works consulted or works cited in the writing of this book, this essay instead of a bibliography is a selection of those works I judge to be most helpful to one interested in further study of storytelling in preaching. For convenience it is arranged topically and generally in order of publication under each heading.

The Neglected Story Sermon

For most of the 1960s and 1970s the most widely used homiletical textbook was H. Grady Davis, *Design for Preaching* (Philadelphia: Fortress, 1958). Davis included "a story told" as one of five "organic forms" a sermon may take, but no one, it seemed, was shaping sermons as narrative. Now another text has replaced Davis as the most-used homiletical textbook. It is Haddon W. Robinson, *Biblical Preaching: The Development and Delivery of Expository Messages*, 2nd edition (Grand Rapids: Baker, 1980, 2001). Robinson continues "a story told" as one of the five basic shapes sermons take, and telling stories is now more important in preaching.

The Rediscovery of Story in Preaching

Fred Craddock's *As One without Authority: Essays on Inductive Preaching* (Enid, OK: Phillips University Press, 1971) sounded an early warning that today's preachers must turn to inductive patterns including storytelling to gain a hearing. Then Charles L. Rice's article "The Preacher as Storyteller" in *Union Seminary Quarterly Review* 31 (Spring 76): 182–97, was something of a call to order. Another early voice for narrative was Fredrick Buechner, *Telling the Truth: The Gospel as Tragedy, Comedy and Fairy Tale* (New York: Harper & Row, 1977).

1980: The Year of the Narrative

As if homileticians suddenly rediscovered story, 1980 became the year of the story sermon. Charles Rice and his distinguished former professor of preaching at Union Theological Seminary, Edmund A. Steimle, and another of Steimle's former students, Morris J. Niedenthal, collaborated to produce *Preaching the Story* (Philadelphia: Fortress, 1980). That same year Fred Craddock was featured at the 1980 Furman Pastors' School, Atlanta, with his lectures on "Preaching as Storytelling." Also in 1980 Tom Long submitted his Ph.D. dissertation at Princeton on "Narrative Structure as Applied to Biblical Preaching" and began to write and teach the same. Richard A. Jensen was among the first in modern times to advocate an approach to preaching that makes the entire sermon a story. He was speaker for the national Lutheran Vespers radio broadcast and in demand for clinics and seminars for preachers. In Jensen's 1980 book, *Telling the Story: Variety and Imagination in Preaching* (Minneapolis: Augsburg, 1980), he treated three sermon forms. The first he called "didactic." These were traditional sermons like 90 percent of the preaching he had heard and done. He considered the form diagnostic preaching with no power to cure. The second form he considered his default style and called "proclamatory" preaching. It marked him as a disciple of Bultmann and the "New Hermeneutic." The third form was story preaching. Jensen agreed with Amos Wilder that a narrative text should be preached in narrative. In addition, Eugene Lowry's *The Homiletical Plot* (Atlanta: John Knox, 1980) also debuted that year.

Throughout the 1980s a steady stream of monograph sequels followed: Lowry stressed the sermon as an event in time in *Doing Time in the Pulpit: The Relationship between Narrative and Preaching* (Nashville: Abingdon, 1985). Then came his *How to Preach a Parable: Designs for Narrative Sermons* (Nashville: Abingdon, 1989). He described and illustrated four designs for narrative sermons. Richard Eslinger, a student of David Buttrick, wrote *A New Hearing: Living Options in Homiletical Method* (Nashville: Abingdon, 1987). This book gave the reader a useful introduction to the homiletical thought of Charles Rice, Henry Mitchell, Eugene Lowry, Fred Craddock, and David Buttrick. These resources often served as textbooks for new seminary courses being developed on narrative preaching.

Some of these first writers are still misunderstood, as explained in the introduction. They did not use the term *narrative* to reference a sermon text from the narrative genre of Scripture. Nor did they uniformly describe a storytelling style of preaching. Instead Lowry notably used the designation to describe a sermon structured in such a way as to lead the hearers through a sequence of stages similar to one navigated by someone who follows the plot of a story. That emphasis continued in the last decade of the twentieth century even as homiliticians began to give more attention to storytelling per se. By the end of the twentieth century, Robert Fulford's Yale Lectures proclaimed *The Triumph of Narrative: Storytelling in the Age of Mass Culture* (Toronto, ON: Anansi, 1999).

Eugene Lowry's chapter "The Narrative Quality of Experience as a Bridge to Preaching," in *Journey toward Narrative Preaching*, edited by Wayne Bradley Robinson (New York: Pilgrim, 1990), is a narrative summary of how Lowry learned his innovative style of narrative preaching. A naturally gifted pianist, disciplined and seriously trained, with a flair for jazz, Lowry gradually made the connection between his music's movements and his homiletical style. Jazz musicians take a piece of music and "get sideways" in the opening. The improvisation moves from this complication through reversal to harmonic resolution, or as the musicians call it, the "return home." Storytellers call this resolution of the plot, "denoument." Lowry does not just tell stories in his preaching; his sermon structure tracks that journey.

Articles in Journals, Magazines, and Anthologies

Articles provide much of the cutting-edge literature on narrative in preaching. Here are some of the most important in order of publication.

Charles Rice, "The Preacher as Storyteller," *Union Seminary Quarterly Review* 31 (Spring 1976): 132–97. Rice set storytelling in cultural and theological context and showed implications for preaching.

David Reynolds, "From Doctrine to Narrative: The Rise of Pulpit Storytelling in America," *American Quarterly* 32, no. 5 (Winter 1980): 479–98.

George M. Bass, "The Evolution of the Story Sermon," *Word and World* 2 (Spring 1982): 183–88.

Methodist bishop and former chaplain of Duke University William H. Willimon has written helpfully in this area beginning with "Stories and Sermons," *The Christian Ministry* 14 (November 1983): 5–7. See also Steven Shuster, "Story Preaching: The Literary Artist's Gift to Preachers," *Journal of Communication and Religion* 12, no. 1 (March 1989): 22–27.

John S. McClure launched a trial balloon in the rarified air of narrative chatter hopeful of moving toward consensus on terminology: "Narrative and Preaching: Sorting It All Out," *Journal for Preachers* 15, no. 1 (Advent 1991). He noted the word *narrative* is used in reference to biblical materials, in the management of sermon ideas, in illustrations that seek to relate the preacher's ideas to common experience, and in describing a congregation's worldview. He proposed a new set of subcategories in an attempt to clarify terms. So far his plan has not been widely adopted.

Select Chapters on Narrative

There are some important chapters on narrative in more general books on homiletics. One of the best and most basic is chap. 11, "The Narrative Approach," in Donald L. Hamilton, *Homiletical Handbook* (Nashville: Broadman, 1992). Two are in James Earl Massey, *Designing the Sermon: Order and Movement in Preaching* (Nashville: Abingdon, 1980), These are chap. 2, "Designing the Narrative/Story Sermon," and chap. 7, "Three Illustrated Designs." There is one chapter on "Storytelling," chap. 5, in Jedd Medefind and Erik Lokkesmoe, *The Revolutionary Communicator: Seven Principles Jesus Lived to Impact, Connect and Lead* (Orlando, FL: Relevant Media Group, 2004). Charles L. Campbell, "A Not-So-Distant Mirror: Nineteenth Century Popular Fiction and Pulpit Storytelling," *Theology Today* (January 1995) tracks the history of a century of epochal innovations in preaching with stories. And Alton H. McEachern, who has also written dramatic monologue sermons and how to do them, wrote the chapter on "Narrative Preaching" in *Preaching in Today's World*, compiled by James E. Barry (Nashville: Broadman, 1985), 151–57. A good summary of narrative trends since the mid 1970s is Thomas G. Long, "What Happened to Narrative Preaching," *Journal for Preachers* 28, no. 4 (Pentecost 2005): 9–15. Long is one who has been in the mainstream of the movement. Frederick Buechner's chap. 11, "The Truth of Stories," is worth reading for his treatment of the parable of the prodigal son, in *The Clown in the Belfry: Writing on Faith and Fiction* (New York: Harper, 1992). Martin Thielsen, "From Precept to Parable: A Case Study for Story Preaching," *Preaching* 10, no. 3 (May–June 1995): 43–49. Also the theme of *Preaching* magazine's 13, no. 5 (March–April 1998) was "Why Story." Several articles and interviews of interest are there.

Books and Articles That Meld Homiletics and Storytelling

Such books are still too few. Calvin Miller was strongly influenced by an outstanding expositor (Ray Stedman) and an outstanding storyteller (Ray Bradbury). This dual influence shows in his prolific writing. See Miller, *Marketplace Preaching* (Grand Rapids: Baker, 1996), and Miller's *Spirit, Word, and Story: A Philosophy of Preaching* (Waco, TX: Word, 1989), which devotes four chapters to "story." Most recently comes what may well prove to be his *magnum opus* of more than forty books so far: Calvin Miller, *Preaching: The Art of Narrative Exposition* (Grand Rapids: Baker, 2006).

The rest of this section is listed in order of publication. Bruce C. Salmon, *Storytelling in Preaching: A Guide to the Theory and Practice* (Nashville: Broadman & Holman, 1988) was a well-written book now out of print, but the author tells me he has boxes of remainders in storage. It includes a helpful annotated bibliography but nothing since 1988, of course.

Richard A. Jensen, *Thinking in Story: Preaching in a Post-Literate Age* (Lima, OH: CSS, 1994).

Jack Maquire, *The Power of Personal Storytelling: Spinning Tales to Connect with Others* (New York: Penguin/Putnam, 1998).

David L. Larsen, *Telling the Old, Old Story: The Art of Narrative Preaching* (Wheaton: Crossway, 2001).

Mark Miller, *Experiential Storytelling: (Re)Discovering Narrative to Communicate God's Message* (Grand Rapids: Zondervan, 2004).

The Ethical Issue of Persuasion in Preaching

Storytelling has always had its critics, and one of the major objections to pulpit stories is the ethical issue of persuasion in preaching. Articles on these issues are Raymond W. McLaughlin, "The Ethics of Persuasive Preaching," *Journal of the Evangelical Theological Society* 15, no. 2 (Winter 1972): 93–106; and Duane Litfin's "The Perils of Persuasive Preaching," *Christianity Today* (February 4, 1977). Robert McAfee Brown's article, "The Power of Story: The Nathan Syndrome," is included as a chapter in *Persuade Us to Rejoice: The Liberating Power of Fiction* (Louisville: Westminster/John Knox, 1992).

The Wider World of Storytelling

All this is the homiletics experience of narrative. The broader world of storytelling has never known the neglect that pulpit storytelling suffered. Storytelling in general has enjoyed good health throughout human history. Nevertheless, the art has been enjoying a new vitality in Western civilization for the past two decades. What explains this grand renaissance? Storytelling as an academic discipline has moved from an interest practically limited to elementary school teachers and librarians to command the attention of every age group, every culture, and every social class. In business and government, in education and entertainment, in philosophy and family life, in medicine and science as well as religion, storytelling is *in*. Witness the ten-megaton explosion of literature on storytelling. Some significant books from the secular world of storytelling can help the preacher. Here are some books worth reading in order of publication. First an old one often reprinted is Ruth Sawyer, *The Way of the Storyteller* (New York: Viking, 1942). Note also Jack Maquire, *The Power of Personal Storytelling: Spinning Tales to Connect with Others* (New York: Putnam, 1998). Part 3 has seven chapters on getting story ideas. They are worth seeing. Doug Lipman, *Improving Your Storytelling: Beyond the Basics for All Who Tell Stories in Work or Play* (Little Rock: August House, 1999) offers a load of helpful guidance including a chapter on "learning the story" instead of memorizing it. One of the best books of all on storytelling was written mainly for business and industrial leaders. It is the often-quoted Annette Simmons, *The Story Factor: Inspiration, Influence, and Persuasion through the Art of Storytelling* (New York: Basic Books, 2001). This is an excellent primer. Simmons is much in demand for seminars training managers and executives to tell stories. Preachers also will find her book practical and exceedingly informative. Another for business speakers and all about storytelling is Doug Stevenson, *Never Be Boring Again: Make Your Business Presentations Capture Attention, Inspire Actions, and Produce Results* (Colorado Springs: Cornelia, 2003). Basic and helpful in its special niche is Nancy Mellon, *Storytelling with Children* (Gloucestershire, UK: Hawthorn, 2000).

The Study of Plots

For the study of plots, don't miss Christopher Booker, *The Seven Basic Plots: Why We Tell Stories* (London: Continuum, 2004). This 705-page tome of a British writer and story editor analyzes hundreds of well-known stories and convincingly demonstrates that every one of them may be categorized into one of seven basic plot plans. And each plot proceeds in five stages. Next is a 12-volume set most preachers will not need in their personal library. It is nevertheless a useful reference volume for the study of plots. It is probably in your public library: Frank N. Magill, ed., *Masterplots: 2,010 Plot Stories and Essay Reviews from the World's Fine Literature,* vols. 1–12 (Pasadena: Salem, 1976). Each of the 2,010 entries begins with summary reference data identifying the type of work—whether novel, autobiography, or other type. This summary will include the author, type of plot, when published, and more. Second is a list of principal characters, and third, a brief critique, usually one paragraph. Then the heart of the entry is a plot summary of two or three pages without dialogue. Finally two or three more pages in each article offer "Further Critical Evaluation of the Work."

First-Person Narrative Preaching

First-person narrative preaching was formerly called the dramatic monologue and is a special sermon form. See J. Kent Edwards, *Effective First-Person Biblical Preaching: The Steps from Text to Narrative Sermon* (Grand Rapids: Zondervan, 2005), for guidance on how the preacher can enter into the biblical story through one of the characters in the story. And Haddon W. Robinson, *It's All in How You Tell It: The Preparation and Delivery of First-Person Expository Messages* (Grand Rapids: Baker, 2003) is a small book well named and a worthy manual for all willing to add an occasional monologue sermon to their regular fare. An article of note on this skill is Jeffrey Arthurs, "Performing the Story: How to Preach First-Person Narrative Sermons," *Preaching* 12 (March–April 1997).

Online Resources

The Internet is changing the way we read and do research in the twenty-first century. If you do a Google search of the Internet for "storytelling," instantly you will get more than 19 million hits. Among those responses are many Web sites catering to a new generation of storytellers: The Center for Story and Symbol, The International Storytelling Center (sponsors of an annual National Storytelling Festival attended by thousands), Christian Storytelling.com, and Storyteller.net, just to name a few. One of the longest running ministries for ministers in this field is Robert Bela Wilhelm's Storyfest Productions. Wilhelm sponsors clinics and festivals of sacred storytelling all over the world. His Web site is bobwilhelm@mac.com. Storytelling festivals are multiplying. A number of them cater to preachers.

Narrative Preachers and Their Sermons

There is no better way to learn the art of preaching than through the study of preachers and their sermons in their historical context. The old, classic history is the two-volume work by E. C. Dargan, *A History of Preaching*, vols. 1–2 (Grand Rapids: Baker, 1968), with a third volume meant to update the work: Ralph G. Turnbull, *A History of Preaching*, vol. 3 (Baker, 1974.) More recent is David L. Larsen's excellent work, *The Company of the Preachers: A History of Biblical Preaching from the Old Testament to the Modern Era* (Grand Rapids: Kregel, 1998). And the magnum opus of O. C. Edwards Jr., *A History of Preaching* (Nashville: Abingdon, 2004), vol. 1 in print and vol. 2 included in digital format on one CD-Rom. Useful for brief articles on more than two thousand church leaders, mostly preachers, is Elgin S. Moyer's *The Wycliff Biographical Dictionary of the Church*, revised and enlarged by Earle Cairns (Chicago: Moody, 1982). Warren W. Wiersbe has written a lot on the study of great preachers and edited and updated a lot more. His *Treasury of the World's Great Sermons* (Grand Rapids: Kregel, 1977) was issued originally in ten pocket-sized volumes. Wiersbe's reissue is in one large volume. Wiersbe's *Listening to the Giants: A Guide to Good Reading and Great Preaching* (Grand Rapids: Baker, 1980) includes a number of studies he wrote earlier as articles for *Moody Monthly*. Wiersbe and Lloyd M. Perry, *The Wycliffe Handbook of Preaching and Preachers* (Chicago: Moody, 1984), is another useful reference volume. This work begins with a significant summary of the history of preaching and includes seven hundred or more "Capsule Biographies of Preachers," most in three lines or less.

Name Index

Arthurs, J. 214

Barbour, G. F. 182, 185
Barclay, W. 128
Barry, J. E. 211
Bass, G. M. 144, 211
Beecher, H. W. 152, 153, 156
Beveridge, W. I. 137
Blackwood, A. W. 178, 180
Booker, C. 35, 40, 41, 42, 44, 213
Boreham, F. W. 58, 164, 168, 172, 173, 174, 175, 176, 178
Broadus, J. A. 70, 80, 81
Brown, R. M. 212
Buechner, F. 14, 86, 209, 211
Burnett, H. 37
Burnett, W. 37

Campbell, C. L. 85, 211
Chapman, J. W. 190, 195, 196, 197, 198, 199, 200
Chappel, C. G. 177, 179
Choate, J. M. 41
Colson, C. W. 34
Conwell, R. H. 156, 190, 191, 192, 193, 194, 208
Craddock, F. 2, 13, 24, 28, 84, 209, 210

Dargan, E. C. 131, 214
Davis, H. G. 2, 28, 29, 76, 88, 127, 209
Drummond, L. 165, 176
Dunamel, P. A. 28, 29

Edwards, J. K. 213, 214
Escott, C. 67
Eslinger, R. 95, 210

Fant, C. 155, 162, 163
Feehan, J. A. 17
Fry, C. L. 137
Fulford, R. 210

Gammie, A. 159
Gibson, S. M. 207
Gladwell, M. 24

Hamilton, D. L. 211
Harris, A. 193, 194
Henson, G. 51

Holland, H. S. 98, 103
Holland, N. N. 15, 16, 59, 60
Hughes, R. E. 28, 29

Ironside, H. A. 95, 204, 205, 206, 207, 208

James, P. W. 204
James, S. 17
Jensen, R. A. 209, 210, 212
Jeremiah, D. 121
Jones, L. 4

Kennedy, D. J. 124

Larsen, D. L. 212, 214
Lewis, R. and G. Lewis 74
Lipman, D. 213
Litfin, D. 212
Lokkesmoe, E. 211
Long, T. 209, 211
Lowry, E. L. 2, 3, 87, 88, 89, 210

MacArthur, J. 20, 60
Macartney, C. E. 88, 89, 144, 160, 177
MacDonald, M. 142
MacEwen, W. 67
Macpherson, I. 17, 18, 132, 146
Magill, F. N. 213
Mann, A. C. 168, 195
Maquire, J. 212, 213
Massey, J. E. 211
de Maupassant, G. 118, 119
McClure, J. S. 211
McConkey, J. H. 48, 49, 51
McEachern, A. H. 138, 211
McKeever, J. xiv, 15
McLaughlin, R. W. 212
Medefind, J. 211
Mellon, N. 113, 115, 213
Merritt, G. 67
Miller, C. 29, 51, 79, 128, 129, 212
Miller, D. G. 79
Miller, M. 212
Mitchell, H. H. 94, 95, 210
Moody, D. L. 169, 178, 185, 186, 187, 188
Moody, W. R. 186
Moyer, E. S. 214

Niedenthal, M. J. 209

Oden, T. C. 123
Osbeck, K. W. 121

Pennell, T. C. 12, 136
Phelps, D. M. 58, 59
Pinson, W. 155, 162, 163
Pound, G. 172, 175

Reynolds, D. 211
Rice, C. L. 209, 210, 211
Robinson, H. W. 2, 76, 138, 206, 207, 209, 213
Robinson, T. W. 138
Robinson, W. B. 210
Ross, S. 184, 197

Salmon, B. C. 212
Sawyer, R. 213
Shaddix, J. 3
Shuster, S. 16, 59, 60, 211
Simmons, A. 17, 19, 52, 53, 213

Spurgeon, C. H. 164, 165, 167, 173
Stanley, A. 4
Steimle, E. A. 209
Stevenson, D. 213
Swaine, D. V. 26
Swindoll, C. R. 34, 83

Talmage, T. 151, 155, 156, 158, 161, 163, 178
Thielsen, M. 211
Truett, G. W. 200, 208
Tucker, A. B. 118, 151
Turnbull, R. G. 197, 198, 214

Vines, J. 3

Whyte, A. 178, 180, 184, 188
Wiersbe, W. 167, 180, 181, 214
Willimon, W. H. 211
Willson, P. J. 6, 85, 86
Woychuk, N. A. 56, 143–144

Young, Ed Jr. 151

Subject Index

aesthetic value 17–18
alternating the story 86
apostles 92–94
application 28, 86, 87
attention 11–12
authority 13

Bible lesson model 82
biographical sermons 177–88
Black preaching 94–95

cartoon 119–20
character 23, 24, 25, 28
children's sermon 104–16
comedy 41
conversion 45–47
creativity 94–98

delaying the story 87
delivery, sermon 111, 140–48
denouement 23
detail, integrity of 28
disequilibrium 3–4
drama 36

emotion 60
evangelistic preaching 160, 195–204
explanation 16–17
expository preaching 168–72, 204–08

family stories 138–39
fiction and reality 133–34
first-person narrative sermon 137–38
flashback 28
functional elements 80

genre 79

hymns 120–21

illustration 17
induction 77
introduction 76

Jesus as storyteller 4–6, 74–76
just-suppose stories 130–31

leitourgia 128

listener-identity value   18–20
logic   60, 75

maskil   91
models for organizing narrative sermons,
    seven   82–89
motivational speaker   190–94

narrative preaching
    definition of   1–4
Narrative Worksheet   25
new situation   31, 33
news stories   124–25
notebook habit   120, 186

objections to storytelling in
    sermons   20–21
observation skills   136–37
one-point sermon   4–5

parables   4–5
passages, precept   128
preparation of inductive sermons   76–82
personal stories   48–53
persuasion   12–16, 58–72
pilgrimage   47–53
planning, long-range   81
plot   23, 25, 28, 30–33, 35–44
    comedy and tragedy   41–42
    overcoming the monster   36–39
    quest   39
    rags to riches   38–39
    rebirth   42–44
    voyage and return   40–41
plot movements   32
Plot Movement Worksheet   33
poetry   120–21
point of view   26, 30
points   16, 29, 81
portability   11–12
prooftext   79–80
psychology of storytelling   59–60

quotations   120
removability   28

resolution   32
retelling-the-story model   85–86
running the story   88

Scholasticism   59
search   31, 32, 33
searching   31
series of sermons   107–11
sermon, jewel   81
sermon, one-point   81
sermon, story   28, 59
setting   25, 26, 28, 30
significance, unifying   28
sin-as-entertainment syndrome   51
situation   31, 32, 33
situation, new   31, 32
solution   31, 32, 33
story, elements of   6–7
story preaching   2
story sermon   2, 144, 209, 211–12
story writing   132
stress   31, 32, 33, 41
style   142–45
summarization   118–19
suspending the story   87

tension   5
testimony   45–57, 58–72, 124
testimony sermon   61–68
text   77–79
therapeutic stories   112–16
third-person   27–28
tragedy   41–42

unifying significance   25
unity   28

view, point of   27, 81
vision story   53–57

word studies   128–30
WWJD (What Would Jesus Do?)   84–85

Scripture Index

Genesis
1:2   157

Exodus
3   178
34   27
34:10   27

Leviticus
17:11   199

Numbers
8:1–3   79
12:2   13
14:20–25   80

Deuteronomy
4:9   106
26:1–11   85

Judges
13–16   42

1 Samuel
16:7   109
16:10–13   109
16:19–23   109
17:34–35   109
18:6–11   109

2 Samuel
12:7   13

Ezra
7:28   28

Nehemiah
4:6,14   28
9:5–37   92

Job
35:10   166

Psalms
16   184
23   108, 186
51   23
78   91
78:1–4, 6–7   91
103   129, 182
105   91
15:40,41   92
106   91
16:7,13   92
120–134   130
130:6   130

Proverbs
18:24   160

Isaiah
6:1–8   171
6:9–10   30
53:6   108
55:10–11   70, 90, 105
66:1–2   93

Jeremiah
23:29   70
37:17   53

Ezekiel
33:31–32   18

Amos
1–2   123
4:12   199

Matthew
5:12   75
5:14   75
5:18   75
5:23–24   75
5:25–26   75
13:14–15   30
14:13–21   95
15:2   139
18:20   111
19   65
19:6   65
28:7   194

Luke
2:52   107
10:29   16
10:36–37   83
13:4   75
15   3, 16, 48, 79
15:1–7   108

John
4:27–29   61
6:35   108
8:12   108
8:58   108
9:1–33   69
10:8   103
10:18   199
10:27–28   108
14:1–8   108
15:1–8   108
20:8   99
21   194
21:17   110

Acts
1:8   68
7   92
7:49–50   93
7:51–53   93
9:1–19   47
13:16   94
13:26–41   94
16   178
16:30   161
18:24,28   61
19:8   68
22:1–22   47
26:4–23   47

1 Corinthians
2:1,3–5   60
2:4   68
7   65
7:10   65
10:13   86
15:26   37

2 Corinthians
5:11   68
9:12   128
12:1–10   48

Galatians
5   153
5:15   157

Ephesians
2:1–7   205

3:14   57
6:13–17   110

Philippians
3:21   111
4:11   109
4:19   123

Colossians
4:17   178

2 Timothy
4:1–2   107

Philemon
2   178
18–19   95

James
1:9–11   122
3   118
5:13–16   51

1 Peter
1:9   198
1:19   196
2:21   84
5:8   36

1 John
1:8–10   86
3:14–18   57
4:8   130

Revelation
1:17–18   200
4:1   190
22:17   110